SAN FRAN
HOMICIDE IN
5-HENRY-7

MY INSIDE STORY OF THE NIGHT STALKER CASE, CITY HALL MURDERS, ZEBRA KILLINGS, CHINATOWN GANG WARS, AND A CITY UNDER SIEGE

FRANK FALZON
WITH DUFFY JENNINGS

Charleston, SC
www.PalmettoPublishing.com

San Francisco Homicide Inspector 5-Henry-7
Copyright © 2022 by Frank Falzon with Duffy Jennings

First Edition

Paperback: 979-8-88590-738-5
Hardcover: 979-8-88590-739-2
eBook: 979-8-88590-740-8

For my wife, Donna, our four children, and nine grandchildren.

With their love and support, all things are possible.

A POLICEMAN

A policeman is a composite of what all men are, the mingling of a saint and sinner, dust and deity.

Gulled statistics wave the fan over the stinkers, underscore instances of dishonesty and brutality because they are "news." What that really means is that they are exceptional, they are unusual, they are not commonplace. Buried under the froth is the fact: Less than one-half of one percent of policemen misfit the uniform. That's a better average than you'd find among clergymen.

What is a policeman? He, of all men, is once the most needed and the most wanted. He's a strangely nameless creature who is "sir" to his face and "pig," or worse, to his back.

He must be such a diplomat that he can settle differences between individuals so that each will think he won. But … If the policeman is neat, he's conceited; if he's careless, he's a bum. If he's pleasant, he's a flirt; if not, he's a grouch.

He must make instant decisions which would require months for a lawyer to make.

But … if he hurries, he's careless; if he's deliberate, he's lazy. He must be first to an accident and infallible with a diagnosis. He must be able to: start breathing, stop bleeding, tie splints and, above all, be sure the victim goes home without a limp. Or expect to be sued.

The police officer must know every gun, draw on the run, and hit where it doesn't hurt. He must be able to whip two men twice his size and half his age without damaging his uniform and without being brutal. If you hit him, he's a coward. If he hits you, he's a bully. The policeman must know everything—and not tell. He must know where all the sin is and not partake.

The policeman must, from a single human hair, be able to describe the crime, the weapon, the criminal—and tell you where the criminal is hiding.

But if he catches the criminal, he's lucky; if he doesn't, he's a dunce. If he gets promoted, he has political pull; if he doesn't, he's a dullard. The policeman must chase a bum lead to a dead-end, stake out ten nights to tag one witness who saw it happen but refuses to remember.

He runs files and writes reports until his eyes ache, to build a case against some felon who will get "dealed out" by a shameless shamus, or an honorable who isn't honorable. The policeman must be a minister, a social worker, a diplomat, a tough guy, and a gentleman.

And, of course, he'll have to be a genius because he will have to feed a family on a policeman's salary.

—Paul Harvey, American radio broadcaster

TABLE OF CONTENTS

FOREWORD

As the children of a San Francisco police homicide inspector in the violent 1970s, my siblings and I weren't troubled about the dangers Dad faced at work so much as we were by the phone calls at home. Those phone calls caused much anxiety in the house. Dad would get home after a long, hard day and then, sometimes even before he could put away his gun, badge, and handcuffs, the telephone would ring. We'd flinch at the jangling noise and stare nervously at one another, silently accepting the inevitable. There was only one telephone in the house back then, so whoever was closest would answer it. You'd say "hello" and you would hear those words: "This is the Operations Center calling for Inspector Frank Falzon." Your heart would drop. It was Dad's week on call, and there'd been another murder in the city. He had just walked in the front door and now he had to go right back out. No dinner. No sleep. No idea when he'd be back.

That happened again and again. It was especially terrifying for us younger kids who didn't quite understand the nature of the job or the true meaning of murder and death. My older brother Dan, however, was always captivated by Dad's work and probably wished he were jumping into the car and heading to the crime scene with him. But Dad almost never talked about his work at home. Family was always his priority, and he did his best to leave his job at the office, as it were. Our mom, Donna, despite her own concerns, was the anchor who always kept things on an even keel, kept us focused on our own day-to-day lives of school, homework, sports.

We all dreaded those instant turnarounds as much as Dad did, yet we knew he totally loved his job. He rarely complained about work, but he couldn't hide the stress of it, the demands he put on himself. We could see the tension in his face, the preoccupation with a case. Dad was so driven he could squeeze a week's worth of work into twenty-four hours. And for some reason even he still doesn't understand, he caught more big murder cases than anyone in the homicide detail. He was always in the newspapers or on the TV news. In the era of *Bullitt, Dirty Harry, The Laughing Policeman,* and other popular San Francisco-based cop movies, he became a celebrity in his own right. To me and my siblings, Dad was larger than life.

Along with the phone calls, I remember those early days when we lived in the Outer Sunset District near Ocean Beach. It was a weekday morning ritual for Dad to hose off the fog-shrouded, unmarked police sedan before I jumped in with Dan and my sister Debbie. (Our little sister Kerri was still too young for elementary school.) Then we'd swing by the Clearys' house to pick up Dad's partner, Jack, and three of his four boys. They dropped us off at school and went downtown to work. It was no different than all the other dads who drove their kids to school, except for one thing—ours were a real-life version of *Streets of San Francisco,* a popular TV show of the time with Jack in the Karl Malden role as the veteran detective mentoring Dad in the Michael Douglas part as the young, up-and-coming homicide cop. Jack, ten years older than Dad, was a wise and experienced first partner to show him the ropes. Dad had other partners over the years—Herman Clark, Dave Toschi, Carl Klotz—all skilled detectives, but none closer than Jack during those early years in the city. Later, in the 1980s and after they had both retired, Dad and Carl forged a similar lasting relationship, remaining friends and golf buddies until Carl died in 2013. Meanwhile, Dad and Jack Cleary, now ninety, and our families, remain close friends today.

The storied tradition of police work as generational is true for both the Falzons and the Clearys. Dan and I both joined the San Francisco Police Department, he in 1983, me in 1994, as did all of Jack's sons: John, Michael, Tom, and Kevin. Dad's cousin, Gary Fox, was also a

San Francisco cop, as is his son, Jason. Gary's other son, Matt, is with the Daly City Police Department. My brother later moved on to the FBI and eventually retired from the bureau. He now conducts and oversees internal investigations for Kaiser Permanente. I am still with the SFPD as an acting captain in the Administration Bureau.

I wasn't planning on following my father and brother into law enforcement. I had a well-paying job in the heavy equipment industry, but I soured on the monotony of corporate life and eventually took the police exam. I didn't even tell Dad before I took the test. I wanted to show him I could do it on my own. I am both privileged and proud to wear my father's original star number, 507. Dad was there to pin it on me when I graduated from the police academy. For Dan's part, he always admired Dad's dedication to public service and his dogged pursuit of the killers. Dan knew his calling at a young age, and we all knew he was destined for the SFPD early on. Dan would say, and I concur, that while the stories shared here are specific to our dad and his colleagues, they also represent the greater body of work, past and present, by so many dedicated men and women who chose law enforcement for nothing more than the personal satisfaction of helping to ensure justice for the victims, often at great personal and professional sacrifice. There is no greater calling, in our view, than public service.

It's a much different department today than during our father's time in terms of organizational structure, workload, employee benefits, technology, and many other changes over the years. At the same time, those changes formalize the work more and tend to diminish the mystique of it. The SFPD homicide detail in Frank Falzon's era was made up of fourteen to sixteen inspectors working out of a functional but drab office on the fourth floor of the Hall of Justice. The nondescript, gray, eight-story building at 850 Bryant Street served as the city's police and county sheriff's headquarters and housed the county jail, criminal courts, district attorney, public defender, coroner, city morgue, and other administrative offices.

Most inspectors in what was then an all-male detail were native born San Franciscans or grew up in the city. They were graduates of the city's top public and private high schools; several had some college, and many were military veterans. They were mostly in their forties, married with children, and had more than fifteen years in the department, at least ten in the Bureau of Inspectors. Many of them knew each other from their old neighborhoods or schools. For the most part, they had grown up in stable blue-collar families, learning the values of discipline, responsibility, and right from wrong. Most were good athletes and had competed with or against one another in high school and on city recreational teams. They didn't always get along with one another, but overall, given the intense workload and the relentless pressure for results from superiors, politicians, and the public, it was a close-knit unit.

Homicide inspectors—ranked as sergeants on today's force—were viewed as elites among their peers. It was the pinnacle of police work. They tended to be mature, physically fit, tough, proud, determined, smart, and resourceful. They worked in two-man teams, rotating seven-day weeks, on call 24/7. Not all cities do it that way, but the thinking was always that two heads were better than one, bringing different but compatible skills and expertise to each murder case. The detail was responsible for handling, on average, one hundred to one hundred and twenty homicides a year, or about fifteen per team. (Dad investigated some three hundred cases during his twenty-two years in homicide.) In addition to homicides, they investigated suicides, questionable fatal accidents, and other suspicious deaths to rule out homicide. They also responded to all officer-involved shootings, fatal or not, and frequent requests for assistance from out-of-town departments. Dad and Jack even went to Italy once to help with the investigation of mass murderer Juan Corona, who used special pens from Italy to log his victims' names in a ledger. Once they arrived at a murder scene, homicide inspectors assumed absolute command of the investigation. For all this, they earned roughly \$30,000 annually, plus \$4,000 to \$5,000 in overtime. None of them, especially Dad, will tell you they were in it for the money.

As Jim Bloom, a former aide to Mayor Dianne Feinstein, put it recently, "Frank Falzon is an icon. He is to San Francisco what Eddie Egan and Frank Serpico were to New York." Both were legendary cops featured in popular Hollywood movies. Egan was fictionalized as narcotics detective "Popeye" Doyle in the 1971 film *The French Connection*, winner of five Academy Awards, including Best Picture and Best Actor Oscar for Gene Hackman as Egan. The 1973 film *Serpico* won a Golden Globe for Al Pacino in the title role.

Dad has been depicted in movies, plays, and video games, and has been featured internationally in dozens of documentaries, radio and TV interviews, magazine articles, and books. Now, for the first time, he is telling his personal story in a book that takes readers behind the scenes of the investigative process, sharing the complex challenges and the gratifying rewards of pursuing killers during a singularly bloody era, and how his work impacted him, his family, the police department, and the City of San Francisco.

When we first heard that Dad was finally going to write a book about his career, something we and many others had cajoled him to do for years, we were thrilled but admittedly skeptical. "It's about time," everyone said. Still, I knew it would be a ton of work, and with Dad nearing eighty I wondered if he had it in him. Not the stories—he always had the stories. Long after he retired, he regularly regaled the family, old partners, friends, fraternal clubs, civic groups, reunions, and just about anyone who would listen with his stories. the Night Stalker, the City Hall murders of Mayor Moscone and Harvey Milk (by my dad's old childhood friend, former fellow cop and softball teammate Dan White), the Zebra serial murders, his off-duty, street corner shootout with an armed robber—all those and more poured out of him time and again. Along with them came the anecdotes of morbid humor, the gags, the pranks that are so common to locker rooms, dormitories, barracks—anywhere first responders collect to blow off steam and cope with the heartbreak of the human tragedies they see every day. He even made up a set of cue cards for one of his frequent talks that he called "A Funny Thing Happened on the Way to a Murder."

It turned out he was simply waiting to find a co-author he could trust to innately understand him and capture his stories with the writing skills he lacked. When he reconnected in 2021 with Duffy Jennings, an author and crime reporter from his same era who had covered many of Dad's cases for the *San Francisco Chronicle*, a true partnership was born. Our family is truly grateful for that stroke of serendipity. Even though Dad was showing his age, he has always been determined to be successful, to catch killers, to help the victims' families. The same was true for his post-retirement job at a title company, his home building projects, and anything else he put his mind to. This book is ample proof that I shouldn't have doubted his resolve.

—Dave Falzon, SFPD, Star 507

CHAPTER 1
A SATANIC KILLER-RAPIST STRIKES

The thing about a murder scene is, you never know what you're walking into.

Over all my years as a San Francisco police homicide inspector during the ultra-violent seventies and eighties—the "golden age of serial murder," as renowned crime historian Harold Schechter put it—there were times I thought I'd seen everything. But the crime scene I walked into on Sunday, August 18, 1985, topped them all.

I was wrapping up a quiet week on call with my partner, Inspector Carl Klotz. We hadn't caught a new case all week and were spending Sunday morning catching up on paperwork in the homicide detail office at San Francisco's Hall of Justice, the city's police headquarters. We looked forward to our weekend solitude when we were on call. The nice thing about working on weekends is that we had the office to ourselves. We had time to discuss cases in relative quiet and to organize files for the week ahead without the constant din of weekdays. Come Monday, the office would be abuzz with other inspectors talking among themselves, trying to be heard over the clamor, making phone calls. District attorneys, inspectors from other details, lab guys, street cops, reporters, and others dropped in to talk about the latest cases. It could be hard to concentrate.

Carl and I lived near one another across the Bay in Marin County, so we had driven in together that morning, as we often did. We crossed the Golden Gate Bridge, breezing into the city without the usual week-day rush hour traffic. The fog that typically cloaks the bridge and the western edge of the city on summer mornings was just burning off, leaving behind a few clouds and patches of blue sky. It was still cool, in the low sixties, but promising to warm up by the afternoon. We stopped for donuts on Van Ness Avenue, got to the office, put on a fresh pot of coffee in the kitchen, and got to work.

Somewhere around ten-thirty, I said to Carl, "Let's take a break and get out of here for a while. I need to swing by Goodman's to pick up a new faucet for that in-law unit I'm remodeling."

We drove out to Goodman Lumber, a San Francisco institution for do-it-yourselfers needing wood, hardware, tools, and building supplies. It was on Bayshore Avenue in the southeast part of town, near Candlestick Park. We were browsing around the store when my pager vibrated on my hip. It was the SFPD Operations Center trying to reach us. Seldom, when my beeper went off, was it good news. Almost always it brought word of a new murder.

We walked quickly out to the radio car and got in. I usually drove because I get queasy riding in the passenger seat. I've always had an inner ear disorder that causes sporadic attacks of vertigo. I started the engine and waited for the radio to power up, then grabbed the microphone from its holder on the dash and pressed the button.

"5-Henry-7 to headquarters," I said, using my individual radio call sign. The number five designated the Inspectors Bureau, Henry was phonetic for the H in Homicide, and I was inspector number seven in the detail. Carl was number four.

"Yes, 5-Henry-7?"

"You paged us, headquarters. What's up?"

"We have patrol officers from Taraval Station on the scene of a one-eighty-seven at a private residence at 1620 Eucalyptus Drive," replied the dispatcher, using the penal code section for murder. "The coroner has been notified."

"5-Henry-7 and 5-Henry-4 responding to 1620 Eucalyptus," I confirmed. "Please roll the crime lab and the photo unit. Let 'em know we're on our way." I replaced the mike and shifted the lever of the old four-door, unmarked blue Ford Fairlane into gear.

Headquarters replied, "Ten-four, 5-Henry-7."

"So much for our quiet week," I said to Carl as we pulled out of Goodman's parking lot.

It was a fifteen-minute trip across town. Eucalyptus Drive is in the southwest corner of the city, just a block from Lake Merced and close to the San Francisco Zoo and the Harding Park Golf Club.

I knew the Lakeshore neighborhood well. It's a well-manicured, upper-middle-class residential section not far from Ocean Beach and the Outer Sunset District, where I had lived with my family for many years. My kids had gone to school and played in the area. My wife and I went out to dinner in the Sunset on weekends. The Sunset and Lakeshore were respectable neighborhoods, not used to violence. A murder in a private home in a quiet area like this was rare. I was thinking it could be a domestic dispute or some other kind of family argument gone terribly wrong.

Two black-and-whites sat in front of the house as we pulled up. The house was a tidy gray-and-white, two-story, stucco-and-wood building, with flowers and shrubs in planters flanking both sides of the driveway. A stairwell on the right side of the house led up to the front door. The living area was on a single floor over the garage. I noticed Captain Mike Lennon, the commanding officer of Taraval Station, talking to a reporter in the driveway. On the outside, everything appeared serene. As I said, you never know what you're walking into. As homicides go, this one shattered the norm.

We found the uniformed officers who were first on the scene, Patrolmen Hermann Chu and Mario Ceballos. I always tried to get my information from the patrol officers as opposed to the command officers. The patrol cops' eyes and ears are almost always more accurate and keener on details because they are responsible for making the initial police report.

"The victims are an elderly Asian couple who live alone in the house," Officer Chu said. He identified them as Peter Pan, sixty-six, an accountant at San Francisco General Hospital, and his wife, Barbara, sixty-two, a bank secretary. "They were both shot in the head. The husband is deceased. Mrs. Pan was also beaten and may have been sexually assaulted." She still had a pulse, Officer Chu said, so an ambulance had transported her to the emergency room at San Francisco General Hospital before Carl and I arrived.

The Pans' son, David, told the officers that his sister had been at the house for dinner the night before and nothing was amiss when she left around 8:30 p.m., said Patrolman Ceballos. "One of the neighbors told us they heard what sounded like a baby crying, or whimpering, for about twenty minutes between 10:30 and 11:30 p.m." He said another neighbor noticed a light on in the house at 10:00 p.m. That was odd, the neighbor said, because by that hour the house was usually dark.

David Pan and his fiancée told the officers they had come by at ten o'clock that morning to have breakfast with his parents, as they often did on Sunday. They had found the house ransacked. In the bedroom, David found his father lying in his bed, not moving, a pool of blood on the pillow beneath his head. His mother was unconscious on the floor. He lifted her back onto her bed and called the police.

Inspector Larry Dubour from our crime lab had arrived at the scene shortly before Carl and me. "Looks like the intruder pried open a ground-level side window with a tire iron to gain entry," he told us, pointing out the jimmied window and the heavy metal bar bearing the name "Toyota" stuck into the ground beneath it. There were athletic shoe prints in the dirt as well. Inside the house, Carl and I were struck immediately by the disarray in the kitchen and living room, typical of a residential burglary. Furniture was out of place, contents of drawers and shelves were strewn across the floor, food containers in the kitchen were upturned.

I went into the master bedroom to look at the male victim before the coroner's assistants finished preparing the body for the trip downtown to the morgue for the autopsy. Mr. Pan was lying on his side, in his nightclothes, with a single bullet wound in his temple. The killer had also rummaged through drawers and closets in the bedroom. As I stood beside Mr. Pan's bed, Coroner Boyd Stephens walked in. He had come to supervise the identification and removal of Mr. Pan. I always appreciated when Dr. Stephens came to a crime scene in person. A skilled physician, he was often able to note some facts about a victim's wounds or other circumstances that we may not have seen right away.

Inspector Dubour surmised that both victims had been asleep when the intruder crept in. It appeared he shot Peter Pan in the head with a small caliber weapon as soon as he entered their bedroom, Larry said. Shell casings found in the bedroom indicated the gun was a .25-caliber automatic. Larry surmised that the intruder then violently raped Mrs. Pan and viciously struck her in the head with the gun multiple times, judging by her wounds and the blood spatter on the walls and ceiling.

Finally, he shot her in the head and left her for dead. But he took his time leaving the house.

In the kitchen, the killer had helped himself to leftover food from the Pans' refrigerator, drank from a quart of milk, then vomited on the kitchen floor. In the living room, he had scratched "JACK THE KNIFE" in big block letters using some type of sharp tool. Below that he etched a two-foot-wide pentagram, a five-pointed star, inside a circle. It's a symbol commonly identified with Satanism, or devil worship. There was no mistaking a glistening white substance puddled on the carpet in front of the etched wall: fresh semen.

"It was a heinous crime," Dubour still remembers. "The guy was so nonchalant after what he did, to hang around and have a snack with some milk. He was an animal. Worse than an animal. The house was in a nice area, neat and clean, just like my parents' house not far from there. I thought *these could be my parents*. We dusted for prints but weren't able to lift any. Just to be thorough, I took the milk carton and some other items to a private lab, but all they could get were glove smudges." It would be years before semen DNA could be developed for scientific proof in criminal cases.

We did not tell reporters about the vomitus or the semen. The media later reported the wording scratched on the wall both as "Jack the Ripper" and "Jack the Knife." Lennon or one of the patrol officers may have mentioned that to a reporter before my partner and I arrived, but it was never verified by us. We did mention the pentagram to the press, but we always kept certain details of a crime scene from the media to have leverage against a suspect during questioning. If he said something about a crime that we had withheld from the public, it could prove that he had been there. Once my partner and I arrived at a crime scene, we took complete charge of the investigation. We decided what information could be made public and what was to remain undisclosed.

I'd seen Satanic symbols and other strange calling cards at murder scenes before, but never quite like this. It was out of character for the neighborhood. Any neighborhood, for that matter. This guy breaks in, attacks two people sleeping in their beds, eats their food and regurgitates it, carves his hideous message into the wall, and then likely stands there praying to Satan while he pleasures himself. It had to be someone strung out, or mentally disturbed, or in an altered state. We were completely baffled about why he chose the Pans' house.

At that point, we had no indication that the so-called Night Stalker, a serial killer who had been terrorizing Southern California for several months, had come to San Francisco. Also dubbed the Valley Intruder or Walk-in Killer by the Los Angeles media, this sadistic psychopath had invaded more than two dozen homes in Southern California, killing, raping, torturing, disfiguring, beating, and burglarizing his victims.

Oddly enough, that very Sunday morning, the *San Francisco Examiner & Chronicle* sitting on the desk in our office carried an article on page B-1 from the *Los Angeles Herald Examiner* about the Night Stalker's reign of terror. Millions of people in the greater Los Angeles region were gripped by fear over where he would strike next.

At the time, Carl and I made no connection between the Los Angeles crimes and our case. We would soon learn, however, that this monster was in our city and we needed to stop him, fast.

CHAPTER 2
MANHUNT TURNS TO L.A. SERIAL KILLER

Carl had become one of my trusted and best friends. We first met as classmates at the police academy. Our friendship grew over the years. After three years as partners, we knew each other's expressions, habits and foibles, tastes in food, drinks, and movies, and sense of humor. It was a *Starsky and Hutch* kind of relationship, but an older version, and without the cool red Gran Torino. Unlike me, Carl smoked, heavily, and I rode the hell out of him about it for years. At the golf course he'd light up a cigarette on the first tee, smoke it down as he played the hole, then light up again on the next tee and repeat it for the entire round. But he was always careful to hold it out his side of the cart, or the car, to keep smoke out of my face.

Both of us were always working on our diets. I'd needle him at a restaurant because he'd ask for extra gravy or extra mayo, but he'd say to the waitress, "Just a little extra, on the side." He wanted everything on the side, but it was still extra something. Carl gave off a rough exterior, but he was really a teddy bear, very conscientious and sincere. He was the foil for a lot of practical jokes in the office because he would take the bait time and again.

We spent an hour or so at the Pan crime scene before going back to the Hall of Justice. We knew it would take every bit of our skills and re-sources to track down the killer. All we had to go on were the tire iron, footprints in the dirt outside the jimmied window, and the bullet shell casings. We had no fingerprints, no witnesses, and no apparent motive beyond the satanic pentagram. We put out a teletype, a statewide all-points bulletin, with a description of the crime scene, the method of entry, and the items taken. We updated it, following confirmation by the autopsy, with the caliber of the gun used. You're always hoping that other agencies might notice similarities to cases in their own jurisdic-tion and give us a heads up about it.

Monday morning, Carl and I were back in the office having our first cup of coffee and planning our next steps in the Pan investigation. The two shell casings found in the Pans' bedroom and other forensics were a good place to start. We walked over to the crime lab, just down the hall from our office. We asked firearms expert Rich Grzybowski to prioritize the Pan murder. The casings, we learned, bore an unusual reddish pink sealer around the primer and shared a peculiar firing pin pattern. Carl and I planned on working late that night interviewing the Pans' neighbors, zeroing in on the time between 10:00 p.m. and 11:00 p.m. when reports of someone whimpering or crying had been heard. We asked the other inspectors in the homicide detail if anyone knew of or might be working on similar cases.

Later that afternoon, we reached out to our parole agent friends, asking about recent parolees with the same MO of burglary and as-sault. Also on our "to-do" list was contacting pawn shops to be on the lookout for pieces of stolen jewelry that the Pans' son had described to us. The to-do list is one of my favorite investigative tools. With so many things happening—phones ringing, interruptions from bosses, D.A.'s, colleagues, and reporters—it is tough to remember everything you want to accomplish. So, I tried to write it down when the thought was fresh in my head. I would set up a to-do list of everything either of us could think of for a thorough investigation. We would then work together or go separately and complete the tasks on our list. Once an item was done, we'd sign it off with the date and time.

I called my former partner, Jack Cleary, now in the district attorney's investigation unit. I asked Jack if he could send his investigator, Audrey Moy, to the hospital to see whether Mrs. Pan could tell us anything about what had happened. I respected Audrey as an investigator, and I felt Mrs. Pan might feel more comfortable confiding in another Asian woman. But Audrey was unable to get a statement. Barbara Pan was still in critical condition after surgery to remove a bullet from her head and to treat her other injuries. The recovered slug was a .25-caliber round, "severely mutilated," as ballistics would later tell us. Even if Mrs. Pan were able to talk to investigator Moy, she likely would have said little. The Chinese culture then viewed rape as shameful and something to be kept quiet. Victims seldom reported it, and to acknowledge it risked social stigmatization.

Meanwhile, Larry Dubour, our crime lab tech, was already back at the crime scene carefully going over every detail when he got word to call the coroner, Boyd Stephens, who was conducting his autopsy of Mr. Pan. Dr. Stephens told Larry that an X-ray of Mr. Pan's head revealed no bullet. The shot in his temple had been "through-and-through," Stephens said, meaning the bullet must still be somewhere in the bedroom. "When I heard that, I went right to the bloody pillow," Dubour recalls. "I had to tear it open and dig down through the feathers, but I found it."

That same Monday morning, three hundred seventy miles south of us in the Los Angeles suburb of Glendale, police detective Jon Perkins was agitated. First, there had been little progress in solving the double murder of Max and Lela Kneiding in their home on Stanley Avenue a month before. When I interviewed Perkins for this book, he told me, "I was on vacation when it happened, but our homicide on-call team was already out on a murder, so they asked me to come back in." Perkins is a thirty-five-year veteran of the Glendale Police Department who retired in 2009. He's now head of a private investigation business specializing in stalkers of celebrities. "Some officers first on the scene thought it might be a murder-suicide, but it was obvious to me that it wasn't. It was a vicious murder. Two people dead in their own home, back door open with a broken windowpane. It was July, very hot. The Kneidings had their fan going and the blood had been sprayed around the room. Both had been hacked with a machete and shot in the head. She had her throat slashed. It was grisly. And LAPD had a murder the same morning with the same MO."

In that other July 20 attack, someone broke into the home of Chainarong and Somkid Khovananth in Sun Valley, fifteen miles away from Glendale. It was just before 6:00 a.m., only hours after the Kneiding assault. The intruder killed the husband instantly with a .25-caliber gunshot to the head. He then beat, raped, and sodomized the wife. He tied up the couple's eight-year-old son, then forced the mother around the house to point out any valuable items. During the assault, he demanded that she "swear to Satan" that she was not hiding any money from him.

The other thing nagging at Perkins that morning was that a multi-agency task force investigating more than a dozen cases similar to the Glendale attack had yet to put out a statewide teletype, even though there had been at least ten murders over several months matching the same pattern, including the Kneidings and the Sun Valley murder. "I was bothered by that," Perkins said. "I had just come from a task force meeting. This Walk-In Killer hadn't struck for a couple of weeks. I wasn't sure if he was dead, in custody, or had left the area. But the empty suits at the meeting said, 'We'll just have to wait until the next murder.'" His reference to empty suits was the two detectives in charge of the task force, Gil Carrillo and Frank Salerno of the Los Angeles County Sheriff's Office homicide bureau.

"That's when I raised the issue about them not sending a tele-type out to all agencies," Perkins continued. "I told them I wasn't comfortable with that. Later that same morning I got a call from a patrol officer, one of my former trainees, who said he'd been listening to the radio and heard part of a story about a late-night walk-in murder over the weekend. Not in the L.A. area, but he couldn't say where. He was wondering if our intruder was back.

"I checked with the L.A. Sheriff's Office and LAPD. As the officer who called me said, no such case had occurred in L.A. County. Then I just started calling all city and county law enforcement agencies located next to major freeways or highways throughout California. I started with San Diego PD and San Diego County Sheriff's Department and worked my way up north until I called San Francisco and got hold of Carl Klotz. He didn't know me, and I still recall the reluctance in Carl's voice after I introduced myself and explained the reason for the call. I talked about the characteristics of our case—point of forced entry, executes the male, rapes and sodomizes the female, the distinctive shoe prints, the .25-caliber automatic, the casings with the pink primer. When I mentioned the primer, Carl suddenly got excited. He sounded like a little kid."

Perkins did some great police work on his own, no question about it. No case of this magnitude gets solved without the kind of effort Jon Perkins was giving his homicide case. Thanks to him, bingo, Carl and I now had a strong match with the L.A. cases. Rich Grzybowski got on a plane the next day and hand-carried the bullets and casings from the Pan case down to L.A. for a ballistics comparison with the bullets and shell casings in the Valley Intruder attacks.

And then we got another break we weren't expecting.

As I was going through reports of recent burglaries in the city, I was startled by one in the exclusive Marina district two nights before the Pans were attacked that had similarities to the Pan case. I was just as surprised to see that my son Dan and his partner, Marty Kilgariff, were the reporting officers. Dan, my first born, was twenty-four at the time. He had joined the department two years earlier and was working as a patrolman out of Northern Station on Ellis Street. He and Marty had responded to the burglary at the home of a San Francisco dentist named Jack Saroyan at 3637 Baker Street. It was a three-story house in an affluent neighborhood a half-block from the Marina Yacht Harbor and the Palace of Fine Arts, a popular tourist spot where the Pan-Pacific Exposition had been held in 1915. The house had been built in 1928 and today would be valued at $3.5 million. According to the report, the Saroyans went out to dinner at 7:20 p.m. Their twenty-two-year-old niece, Rosemary Ovian, was staying at the house with a friend.

The effort by the burglar to gain entry into the three-story residence showed his tenacity. Sometime after 10:00 p.m., the man first went to the backyard of a house two doors away. He crept down a long driveway on the side of the house and into the backyard. The house was under renovation, and there were old kitchen cabinets and heavy scaffolding strewn about the yard. He lugged a cabinet and a seven-foot plank over the fence, through the yard adjacent to the Saroyan house, over another fence, and into the Saroyans' yard. Using the cabinet front and the plank, he fashioned a crude ladder and scaled up to a partially open second-story window. Using a tire iron for leverage—a Toyota tire iron, in fact—he pried open the window and clambered into the kitchen.

"This wasn't his first burglary," Larry Dubour of the crime lab said when I talked to him about it later. "He was a full-time burglar, and he was a stealthy sonofabitch" to have hauled the wood and scaled the plank. Larry said the prowler was wearing gloves throughout the burglary. "But he must have taken them off for some reason when he came through the window because we did lift one good print off the inside of the glass where he grabbed it when he climbed in." The intruder then ransacked the house, taking cash, jewelry, furs, cameras, a Hitachi VCR, and a Toshiba portable stereo. The niece and her friend both slept through the entire episode in a basement bedroom, and the prowler never found them, probably because he was interrupted.

"The guy was probably still inside the home when he heard the garage door opening," Dubour conjectured. "The master bedroom curtains had been parted in a way that indicated someone stood there looking out the window." It was 11:40 p.m., and the Saroyans were arriving home from dinner. When they got inside, they found their home ransacked. The intruder was gone. "The front door was ajar," said Dubour, indicating the burglar probably went out that way while the Saroyans were parking their car in the garage. If Larry's right, that was a helluva close call for all of them. Almost certainly it saved the girls downstairs because the burglar didn't have time to go through the entire house.

Dan and Marty wrote in their report that they had interviewed Dr. and Mrs. Saroyan and gotten descriptions of the stolen items. Among the jewels taken were a fourteen-carat gold bracelet and a cultured pearl necklace intertwined with fourteen-carat gold strands with a gold clasp. What the dentist told them next about the missing jewelry was every cop's dream and every thief's nightmare: On each piece, he had engraved "B1676712"—his California driver's license number.

L.A. Serial Killer

'Night Stalker' Slaying Starts Manhunt in S.F.

By Birney Jarvis

Warning residents to lock their doors and windows, San Francisco police launched a widespread manhunt yesterday for the "Night Stalker" killer who has frightened Los Angeles.

The suspect, who has been linked to seven killings since March in the San Fernando and San Gabriel valleys of Los Angeles County, was positively linked yesterday to the murder of San Francisco accountant Peter Pan in his two-story home near Lake Merced on Saturday night.

Pan, 66, was shot in the head while asleep in his bed. His wife, Barbara, 64, was critically wounded during the attack and remains in a coma at San Francisco General Hospital after undergoing surgery for a bullet wound to the head.

Police said the killer entered the Pan home through an open window, a hallmark of the "Night Stalker's" five-month reign of terror in the Los Angeles area.

San Francisco Captain of Inspectors Diarmuid Philpott said that after analyzing the "physical evidence" of the attack on Pan and his wife, investigators have linked the case "to the suspect in two cases in the Los Angeles area attributed to a serial killer."

CHAPTER 3
TRACKING THE NIGHT STALKER

The day after seeing the burglary report by my son and his partner, we got Rich's ballistics report on the Pan slugs and casings compared with .25-caliber bullets recovered from two of the Southern California shootings that had occurred on August 6 and 8. "All examined bullets and casings were fired from the <u>same</u> .25 ACP semi-automatic pistol," he noted, underlining the word *same*. "Also, all Los Angeles spent casings are of the same Western manufacture and all have the unusual pink sealer of the primer cap." He added that a shoe print from the Pan house and one of the L.A. break-ins shared "class characteristics." We would later determine they were a relatively rare model made by the Avia shoe company.

Now Carl and I were pumped. We had no idea that our guy was working Southern California. And, until our case, they had no idea that he was in San Francisco. We didn't know how big this thing was about to become. We flew to L.A. and spent a couple of days working with LAPD and the Los Angeles Sheriff's Office. Each had set up a task force and had teams of officers running down the leads on all their cases. I was impressed with both departments, but one thing was obvious—they weren't working together, sharing information. Carl and I were like sponges, soaking up whatever we could learn. They laid out their cases and the MO at each crime scene but weren't volunteering anything that we could bring back to San Francisco. A lot of cops and agencies are competitive like this. They don't want anyone else to get credit for something they are doing. I copied documents and helped myself to informational flyers, slipping them into my folder. I wasn't asking, and no one said I couldn't.

Two guys in L.A. who *were* especially helpful were LAPD homicide detectives Leroy Orozco and Paul Tippin. During our conversations with them, they told us about an encounter that an LAPD motorcycle cop had with a man he stopped for a traffic violation back in June. As the officer began to question the driver, the driver bolted away on foot and escaped into the surrounding neighborhood, leaving the car behind. It had been stolen. Inside the vehicle police found a black address book containing an appointment card of a local dentist with the patient's name, "Rick." What the motorcycle cop didn't know was that there had been an attempted kidnapping of a young boy in the same neighborhood at the time he stopped the car. Orozco and Tippin believed Rick could have been the Night Stalker and that he had tried to grab a kid off the street. Rick, thinking the officer pulled him over for the kidnapping attempt, ran. Police later staked out the dentist's office on the day of Rick's next appointment, but he failed to show. The single most important piece of information we returned to San Francisco with was knowing that our suspect had a first name: Rick.

On Wednesday, August 21, the head of our homicide detail, Lieutenant George Kowalski, sent a memo to Captain Diarmuid Philpott, Acting Deputy Chief of Investigations, outlining what we had determined were "striking similarities" between the Pan case and fourteen homicides in the Los Angeles area. He listed thirteen factors: a .25-caliber automatic, shell casings, jewelry taken, gloves worn, lug wrenches used, middle-class or upper-middle-class neighborhoods, male victims shot immediately, female victims raped and sodomized, pentagram drawn on a wall or door, Avia sport shoe prints, residence ransacked, crimes committed late evening or early morning, and (some) victims were Asian.

The suspect, added Kowalski, was described as a white male,

between six foot and six foot two inches in height, with a "very thin build, brown curly wavy hair, reddish tinge, visibly rotten teeth." He frequently wore a black Member's Only waist-length jacket and a black AC-DC ball cap.

Two days after Lieutenant Kowalski's memo detailing all the similarities between our Peter Pan murder and the L.A. murders, San Francisco Police Chief Con Murphy wrote to then-Mayor Dianne Feinstein at our request, asking the city to offer a $10,000 reward for information leading to the capture of the man suspected in the Pan attack. He attached an artist's sketch of the assailant, along with our informational bulletin. She agreed and scheduled a news conference for later that day. It didn't go quite the way we had expected. I have always liked Feinstein, and I gave her a lot of credit for the way she pulled the city together after the City Hall assassinations in 1978. But now, as she stood before reporters on Friday, August 24, she not only announced the reward, but revealed that ballistics evidence had conclusively linked the Pan murder with at least two of the L.A. victims.

Carl and I and the other police officials listening to the news conference were stunned that she would disclose key evidence that we worried might compromise the case against the killer. "It was a buffoon statement," one unnamed officer told *Chronicle* reporter Bob Popp, who covered the announcement. Another officer said it was "premature" and would give the killer, who we knew was likely monitoring news coverage of his killings, an advantage. "There goes the gun into the Bay," said a third officer, asking for anonymity. Of course, Mayor Feinstein made a big mistake by revealing these previously confidential facts. On the other hand, Chief Murphy hadn't specifically told her not to talk about those things.

The evidence, Feinstein said, showed that the serial killer is "somewhere in the Bay Area." Police officials warned San Franciscans to keep their doors and windows locked and sent extra police patrols into neighborhoods between 10:00 p.m. and 6:00 a.m., when the assailant most often struck. Police also set up a "Night Stalker" hotline, which drew more than one hundred calls in the first two days from people believing, according to news reports, they had seen the killer "walking, riding buses, and driving cars."

Some detectives thought the Night Stalker, after learning of Feinstein's comments, drove out to the Golden Gate Bridge and tossed the gun into the Bay, along with the Avia sports shoes. I doubted it because I believe that even as she was answering reporters' questions, he was already on the freeway heading south again. Either way, the gun and shoes used in the Pan case were never recovered.

Feinstein's surprise announcement also stirred tension between us and the Los Angeles County Sheriff's Office. A sheriff's spokesman said the department had been in contact with Feinstein "regarding her disclosure of confidential information concerning the valley intruder investigation." Upstaged by the San Francisco news conference, Los Angeles County Sheriff Sherman Block called his own press conference that night, at the unusual hour of 10:00 p.m., to announce that fourteen killings had been positively linked to the killer. He also complained that the news media had disseminated sensitive information that "significantly jeopardized" the investigation.

The night after the two press conferences, someone stole an orange 1976 Toyota station wagon from a restaurant parking lot in Los Angeles. Hours later and some fifty miles south of the restaurant, the Night Stalker struck again at an apartment in Mission Viejo. Shortly before 3:00 a.m. on Sunday, August 25, he crept into an apartment through a living room window left open in the 99-degree heat and shot twenty-nine-year-old Billy Carns three times in the head. He then trussed Carns' girlfriend, Inez, with Billy's neckties, raped her, beat her, and forced her to pray to Satan before he ransacked the house and fled. She was able to free herself and call for help. Carns wasn't expected to live, but he survived the shooting, only to suffer from lifelong mental disability.

On Monday, August 26, the California Highway Patrol issued an alert for the killer to forty-three of its district offices along three main freeways that connect L.A. with the Bay Area. "The CHP is making an all-out effort to apprehend this individual, especially now that it appears he is quite mobile," said officer Kevin Kelly. Five hundred CHP officers stationed in the alert zone had been "briefed extensively" on the killer and his methods, Kelly said.

That same day, Lieutenant Kowalski hosted a closed-door meeting at the Hall of Justice for twenty-four officers and officials from several Bay Area law enforcement agencies, including county sheriffs, local police, and the U.S. Park Police, to brief them on the latest developments in the search for the Night Stalker. "We are going to be prepared in case he comes back," said Kowalski. After the meeting, Carl and I flew to L.A. again to compare case notes and help coordinate the statewide manhunt.

Even as we were headed back to Los Angeles, a woman in Lompoc, three hundred miles south of San Francisco and one hundred fifty miles north of L.A., contacted local police sergeant Harry Heidt. "I might have information on this Night Stalker murderer," the woman, Lori Ochoa, told him. "My brother, Earl, knows a Mexican guy who looks like the composite drawing of the Night Stalker we saw on the TV news." She told Heidt that the man lived in Los Angeles but traveled back and forth to San Francisco. "His name is Rick," she said. "He was in the Bay Area around the sixteenth or seventeenth. He knows Earl's mother-in-law."

Following up on this tip, Sergeant Heidt talked to Ochoa's brother, Earl Gregg, and learned he had visited his mother-in-law, Donna Myers, in El Sobrante, an East Bay community twenty miles northeast of San Francisco, some five days earlier. She had showed Gregg a gold bracelet she had bought from a friend of Rick's for twenty dollars. "There's a number engraved on the inside band," Gregg said. "What number?" asked Heidt.

"B1676712," Gregg replied.

CHAPTER 4
"RICHARD RAMIREZ!"

After talking with Earl Gregg, Lompoc Police Sergeant Harry Heidt ran the engraved number from the bracelet through the Department of Motor Vehicles and found it was a driver's license number issued to Jack M. Saroyan of San Francisco. He called Saroyan's office at 450 Sutter Street and learned about the burglary at his home two weeks earlier. Next, Heidt contacted our burglary detail in San Francisco to share what he'd learned from Gregg, without naming him. "I had a contact who felt the person responsible for their burglary may be involved in the walk-in murders in the San Francisco and Los Angeles areas," he put in his report.

The inspector in our burglary detail took down the information but didn't think to call homicide right away because they had no reason at that point to connect the Saroyan burglary with a homicide. Finally, after a couple of days, I heard about the Lompoc call. It was Thursday, August 30. I was in the office by 7:30 a.m. and called Sergeant Heidt first thing. I was really pumped about tying my son's report to the recovered Saroyan bracelet. I told Heidt it was imperative that I speak to his informant.

"I gave all the information to your burglary unit," he said, "and they made it clear that in San Francisco, burglars stick to their own area. They discounted the information regarding your stalker case."

"I don't really care what the hell our burglary unit said," I replied. "I need to talk to your informant."

"I want you to know, Inspector, that I'm not giving up my informant," Heidt shot back tersely.

"I understand," I told him, my voice starting to rise. I was standing up at my desk, my loud response drawing stares from the other guys in homicide. "I'm going to make myself very clear. If somebody is murdered this weekend, and I can prove that you withheld vital information that could have prevented that murder, I'm going to come to Lompoc myself and put you in handcuffs! Do I make myself clear, Sergeant?"

"Okay, Inspector, calm down," Heidt said, lowering his own voice. "I'll make a phone call. If my informant wants to talk to you, he will call you." We both hung up. Carl and the other guys in the office tried to get me to rein in my emotions. Carl wasn't convinced we were onto something. "I don't know if there's a link, Frank," he said. "You're getting all worked up for no reason."

Just then, my phone rang. It was Earl Gregg calling from Lompoc, almost as if he had been sitting right next to sergeant Heidt during our previous call.

"Listen, Earl," I said, "I want to know about this bracelet. Where did you get it?"

"I got it from my mother-in-law. She lives up there. Her name's Donna Myers."

"And where did she get it?"

"She told me she got it from her boyfriend, who got it from a friend of his named Rick. She paid him twenty dollars for it."

"Okay, I'm going to need Donna's address and phone number."

Gregg supplied his mother-in-law's address on 22nd Street in San Pablo, across the Bay from San Francisco, and a phone number. I told him not to contact her, that we were going to be paying her an unexpected visit. I hung up the phone and looked at Carl.

"Let's go!" I said. He still wasn't all that excited about it, but he got up to put on his coat. I looked over at Inspector Mike Mullane. "We're onto something big here, Mike," I said to him. "This thing might blow up today. Do you want to go with us?"

The three of us headed down to the garage. On the way to our car, I took a detour to the cafeteria. I needed a sugar fix. I bought a powdered donut and gulped the whole thing down on the way to the car. The other guys saw me brushing white dust off my jacket and gave me a bunch of crap for not getting donuts for them. We all laughed and drove out across the Bay Bridge for San Pablo. In the car I'm thinking *this is it*. Every bone in my body knew this was the break to end California's stalker killer nightmare.

When we go into another jurisdiction on a case, it's common courtesy to stop by the local police headquarters to let them know we will be working in their area. The San Pablo chief was very cordial toward us and offered his cooperation. Since we didn't know the area, we asked if he had an officer who could accompany us to Donna Myers' residence. "I'll give you one of my best men," he said, and assigned the detective on duty, George Spencer, to go with us. I got into a San Pablo police car with Spencer; Carl and Mike followed behind in our car.

Sitting in Donna Myers' living room a few minutes later, I'm firing questions at her one after another. Every answer is music to my ears, and now my beloved partner is fast becoming a believer and kicking me in the shin under the coffee table every time she says something that tells us we're on the right track.

"Where did you get the bracelet?" I ask.

"From my boyfriend, Armando Rodriguez," she says. "He got it from his best friend, Rick." Carl kicks me in the shin.

"What does Rick look like?"

"He's tall, skinny, Mexican, with dark curly hair and real bad teeth."

Another kick in the shin.

"How does he dress?"

"He wears an AC/DC baseball cap and a black Members Only jacket."

Another kick. Now I turn to Carl with a look that says *okay, I get it, you're excited, but enough already.*

Donna added that Armando and Rick had been childhood friends growing up in El Paso. She believed they both belonged to a cult that worshipped Satan.

Donna gives us Armando's address and phone number. He lives in El Sobrante, ten minutes away. Mullane agrees to stay with her to make sure she doesn't call Armando to warn him before we get there. Carl and I get into the San Pablo car, and Detective Spencer drives us to Armando's house. The property is encircled by a fence and has a tall steel-gated entry with a long driveway leading up to the house.

Across the street we notice there's an El Sobrante fire station. We go to the firehouse and ask to use their telephone. When Armando answers, I say, "Armando, this is Inspector Falzon from the San Francisco Police homicide detail. I need you to come outside so we can talk to you." He refuses. I tell him I have some very important information for him, and that I need him to come down to the gate because he will need to hear it from me in person. I emphasized the words *homicide detail,* hoping he might think a family member was killed. He hangs up. We go back across the street and are in front of the gate when I see him walking down the driveway with two snarling Doberman Pinschers on leashes.

"Look, Armando," I say. "What I have to tell you is so important, I'm not going to talk to you with two growling dogs staring me down. Come out from behind the gate and we can talk." I turn and start walking away. Just as I reach the car, I turn back around, and there's Armando standing behind me. The dogs are behind the gate. With a sigh of relief, I say, "We need your help."

"What the fuck do you want with me?" he says in a menacing voice.

"We believe your friend Rick is the Night Stalker, and he's terrorizing the entire state," I say. "We believe he's one of the most prolific serial killers in the history of California. You can help us solve this case."

"Fuck you, motherfucker!" Armando shoots back. "My friend Rick is not your killer. When he's in San Francisco, there are murders in L.A., I know that, and when he's in L.A., there are murders in San Francisco! So, fuck you. You're not getting anything from me!"

"Okay, Armando, you're coming to San Francisco with us," I tell him. "You're under arrest for possession of stolen property."

"Fuck you. I'm not going anywhere with you."

Carl opens the back door of the San Pablo police car. I pat down Armando for weapons. He's clean. I place him into the back seat, and Carl gets in on the other side next to him, behind Detective Spencer, who's now sitting in the driver's seat. I open the front passenger door and, as I get in, I notice five or six El Sobrante firemen out in front of the fire house, directly across the street, watching us.

I lean over the back seat and plead with Armando. "We really need your help, Armando. Please, all we need is Rick's last name."

"Who the fuck do you think you are, putting your motherfucking hands on me?" he shouts.

All I can think about is all the murders in L.A. and the Pans, and I think this is the link to break our case. We have the co-conspirator. We have a Satan worshipper in our back seat. He knows Rick from El Paso, Texas. They were friends as kids. I notice that unintentionally, I guess for emphasis in response to my adrenaline rush, I have closed my right hand into a fist. Armando notices my fist resting on top of the seat in front of him and he comes up with both of his hands clenched.

"Man, you think you're fucking tough?" he says. "You wanna fight me, motherfucker?"

I remember my training—you don't take the first punch; you don't take the first bullet. I fire my fist into the back seat. It catches Armando below his left eye. Armando falls over onto Carl, who immediately pushes him back upright. A small amount of blood trickles from the cut under Armando's eye. Armando dabs at the cut, looks at his fingers, and sees the blood. He's furious. He calls me every name in the book.

"Look what you did to me, you motherfucker! You really think you're a tough son of a bitch, don't you? Is that as hard as you can hit?"

To this day, I don't know if I would have hit him again or not. My emotions were raw. Job or no job, if I could help it, no one was going to die this weekend. In twenty-two years of questioning suspects, I had never used my hands. Now I was about to nail him again.

"No, I'm not a tough guy," I said, "but I am going to show you how hard I can hit, pretty boy! I'm going to split you from the top of your head down to your ass!" With my right fist clenched, my arm coils back into position. Lifting myself up in the seat, I start to move toward Armando as if I'm about to deliver a powerful blow. I'll never know if I was bluffing or not, but the punch doesn't happen because Armando falls back in the seat, arms crossed defensively in front of his face, and screams:

"DON'T HIT ME! RAMIREZ! RICHARD RAMIREZ! THAT'S HIS NAME. RICHARD RAMIREZ!"

I slumped back down in my seat and exhaled audibly. I was emotionally drained. I looked over at Detective Spencer. "Please, George, drive us to the Hall of Justice in San Francisco," I said.

We finally had the name. Convinced we had broken the case, my mind was in a whirlwind, thinking of all the work that was about to occur to assure a conviction of Richard Ramirez.

We got back to the homicide detail a little before 11:00 a.m. and immediately began to trace anyone named Richard Ramirez in the state's Criminal Identification and Information database. There were six, but none of the six had a San Francisco arrest record. We notified the investigative bureau at the CII that all six were in the statewide database. Armando positively identified the one who was his friend, Richard Ramirez.

Over the next few hours, we notified the LAPD that we had learned "Rick" was Richard Ramirez. We sent the same information to the Los Angeles Sheriff's Office and the Orange County Sheriff's Office. We had a search warrant drawn up on Armando's house and later recovered numerous items of jewelry from the Pan murder and the L.A. cases. That solved both the Pan murder and the Saroyan burglary.

Richard Ramirez, the Night Stalker
Murderpedia.org

Our chief of police, Con Murphy, was pleased with our work. He asked Carl and me to be in his office at 7:30 p.m. for a conference call between LAPD Chief Daryl Gates and his homicide team, Detectives Orozco and Tippin, along with LASO Sheriff Sherman Block and his team, Detectives Salerno and Carrillo. The three chiefs were all on the line with the detectives standing by in the room.

When the call began, Sheriff Block immediately asked that San Francisco "stand down" on any public announcement about Ramirez until his men had the time to work up their cases. Chief Murphy covered up the phone and repeated to us what Block had said. I looked at the chief and said, "We'd be crazy to

Richard Ramirez's best friend,
Armando Rodriguez

stand down." He looked puzzled. I continued. "Think about it, Chief. Everybody in the Hall of Justice knows our murder case is made, we're holding a murder warrant in our hands. We stand down, and someone dies this weekend—how is that going to play out in the press?"

Chief Murphy nodded affirmatively, removed his hand from the phone, and conveyed our refusal to stand down. Chief Gates chimed in. "I agree with Con," he said. "Tonight at 10:00 p.m., we'll all do a televised news conference identifying Richard Ramirez as the Night Stalker." At ten o'clock, we held our press conference in the large conference room on the fifth floor at the Hall of Justice. It was packed with reporters as we made our announcement. The next morning, Friday, August 30, Ramirez's mug was on the front page of every major newspaper in the state.

Ramirez, meanwhile, had taken a bus to Tucson to visit his brother. He returned to Los Angeles early on Saturday morning, August 31. Police who were staking out the bus terminal should he attempt to escape on an outbound bus didn't see Ramirez arrive on the inbound bus. He went into a convenience store, where he saw his face on the front pages of newspapers, and fled the store when people recognized him and started chasing him. He ran across the Santa Ana freeway and attempted a carjacking with a woman occupant, but bystanders chased him away. He jumped over several fences and attempted two more carjackings, but a group of residents yelling "El Matador!" (the killer) eventually tackled him and beat him until police arrived and took him into custody.

Salerno and Carrillo called and asked if we would please come to L.A. and serve our San Francisco murder warrant so they could hold Ramirez in custody until they could work up their cases. On Sunday morning, Carl and I were back on a plane to Los Angeles and went directly to the county jail. Ramirez was now being held on our murder warrant.

After nearly three years of legal jousting, motions, discovery, and other procedural delays, the trial of Richard Ramirez began in July 1988 and lasted some fourteen months. In court Ramirez raised his hand to show a pentagram drawn on the palm and yelled, "Hail, Satan!" Armando Rodriguez was given immunity from prosecution and testified at the trial. He later thanked me for turning his life around. He told me he felt we treated him fairly, that immunity had given him a second chance at a law-abiding life, and that he would try make the most of it. He had signed up for college classes to become a physical therapist.

After a year-long trial, Ramirez was convicted in September 1989 of thirteen murders, five attempted murders, eleven sexual assaults, and fourteen burglaries, all committed in the Los Angeles area. He was sentenced to die in San Quentin State Prison's gas chamber.

On his way to San Quentin later that year, Ramirez was brought to the Hall of Justice in San Francisco, where Mike Mullane and I had him booked for the Pan and Saroyan cases so we would have backup charges that would keep him behind bars just in case any of the L.A. verdicts were overturned on appeal for some reason. But he never went to trial on our cases because of his multiple L.A. convictions and death sentences.

While he was in our custody and being booked for the San Francisco charges, Mike Mullane and I stood by during the process. Ramirez was chatting away, saying he had turned down *60 Minutes* and other major media for interviews, and that he didn't mind going to the gas chamber. "I'm not afraid to die," he said. Then, as he was being taken back to the holding cell to wait until the officers escorting him could complete the transfer to San Quentin, Ramirez stopped, turned around, looked at me with a big grin, and held up his hand to show me the pentagram on his palm.

"Hey, Falzon," he smirked, "I bet you'd love to know about the two old ladies, wouldn't you?"

I was dumbfounded. I didn't know that he knew my name. And in that moment, I didn't understand him. "What the hell are you talking about?" I asked.

"You know, the two sisters on Telegraph Hill. Yeah, that was me."

Suddenly, it hits me. He's talking about the home invasion and frenzied stabbing deaths of two sisters, Mary Caldwell, seventy, and Christina Caldwell, fifty-eight, in their Telegraph Hill apartment in February of 1985, six months before the attack on Peter and Barbara Pan.

"I did a really good job on that one, huh?" Ramirez said, laughing as the guards led him away.

Eventually, Ramirez was also linked through DNA to the killing of nine-year-old May Leung in the Tenderloin District in 1984. The little girl's partially nude body had been found hanging from a pipe in the basement of her apartment building.

We suspected Ramirez was responsible for other murders, break-ins, and burglaries. We learned that when he was in San Francisco, he often stayed in a Tenderloin hotel, the Bristol, where he had carved a pentagram on the wall over his bed. He had faith Satan would protect him when he was in his favorite room at the Bristol, number 305.

Following the success of the Night Stalker investigation, San Francisco Police Chief Con Murphy retired on December 31, 1985. He came to our office to thank me and Carl, saying the successful end of the Night Stalker case had helped to offset heat he had taken for a couple of scandals, including a police academy graduation party that had involved a prostitute. "Now I'm going out on a high note," he said

Inspectors Mike Mullane, Larry Dubour, Carl Klotz, and I were awarded Meritorious Conduct medals for our work on the Night Stalker case. I had received meritorious awards in the past, but this one was especially gratifying, given the work involved and that we had taken down a vicious serial killer and serial rapist who would likely have kept up his attacks until he was stopped.

Richard Ramirez was never executed. He died of cancer on June 7, 2013, at the age of fifty-three after more than twenty-three years on Death Row. He never expressed any remorse for his crimes.

Celebrating our breaking of the Night Stalker case with my partners,
L-R Mike and Elaine Mullane, Me and Donna, Kristine and Carl Klotz

CHAPTER 5

SONNY

I didn't always want to be a homicide cop. Growing up in the 1940s, all I ever wanted was to be a Seal. Not the Navy kind—they wouldn't be formed for twenty years—but the baseball kind. For as long as I can remember, it was my dream to play for my hometown team, the San Francisco Seals of the Pacific Coast League. The Giants wouldn't arrive in the city until 1958. The Seals was our big-league team.

San Francisco's homegrown ballplayer Lefty O'Doul, a two-time batting champion during his eleven-year Major League career, managed the Seals. The ball club had up-and-down seasons during World War II and later in the 1940s, largely because so many young men had gone to fight overseas. But they did win the pennant in 1947 with a record of 105 wins and 81 losses. I was five then, and I was already a huge fan. Several of those players were among my early baseball heroes. But none of them was a bigger hero to me than my dad, who introduced me to the American pastime.

Frank Tabone Falzon was born in 1905 in the Republic of Malta, a small island nation fifty miles off the southern tip of Italy. The youngest of twelve kids, he learned carpentry at a young age and excelled at soccer. In his early teens, he came to the U.S. through Canada, escorted by two of his older brothers, Charlie and Lawrence.

After staying for a short time in Detroit, where many Maltese immigrants had settled, Frank moved to San Francisco and went to work for Bethlehem Steel. He settled in the Bayview District in the southeast corner of the city, close to the Hunters Point shipyard. The Bayview then was an industrial, blue-collar section known as Butchertown. It was a central community for many Maltese immigrants, where they had their own Catholic church, St. Paul of the Shipwreck. It was there that Frank met Katherine Bridget Fox, a first-generation San Franciscan and herself one of ten kids—six boys and four girls. Frank and Katie soon married and moved into a Victorian rental home on Oakdale Avenue, just off Silver Avenue, where they started their family.

My sister, Patricia Ann, came first, followed by Jean Mary. I was born four years after Jean in 1942. The last child was Richard John, two years after me. Dickie, as we called him, weighed just two pounds, fifteen ounces at birth and was not expected to live. Dickie remained in the hospital in an incubator for several weeks before being allowed to come home.

Because I was born on February 22, George Washington's birthday, the nurses at St. Luke's Hospital suggested to my dad that George would be the perfect name for the new baby boy. "No way," he said. My dad insisted his son was going to be named Frank Joseph Falzon. Catholic faith in those days dictated a boy's middle name be for a saint. Dad chose Joseph, the patron saint of workers and the father of Jesus. Since I wasn't a junior but had the same first name as my father, he called me Sonny from day one and it stuck. All my aunts, uncles, and cousins called me Sonny.

By the time I was four, maybe five, I had a ball and bat in my hand. As far as my dad was concerned, his son was going to play the all-American sport. Not soccer, as he did; that was the European sport. He wanted me to play baseball from the moment I could walk. He wanted me to win, and so did I. He would say, "Sonny, whatever you do in life, give it one hundred percent. If you can't give one hundred percent, don't do it at all!" I idolized my dad, and all the kids on my block looked up to him. One day he gathered a bunch of us together and said we were going to race to the end of the block. "Since Sonny is the youngest and the smallest, we're going to let him get a little head start," Dad told everyone. I was placed a couple of feet in front of the others. I wanted to win that race so bad. When Dad said "Go!" I took off as fast as my little legs could carry me. As I neared the finish at the end of the block, I looked over my shoulder. I couldn't believe I was winning. My dad, with both arms stretched out, was holding all the other kids back so they could not pass. He wanted his Sonny to win.

When we went to Seals games, we stopped to see the harbor seal that was kept in a water tank beneath the grandstand as a living mascot. Inside the 18,000-seat ballpark, Dad and I always sat behind the Seals dugout. It was important, he said, to support the home team. I learned to dislike the rival Oakland Oaks, whose star player, Sam Chapman, always seemed to get the key hit to beat my Seals. Dad and I would get popcorn or peanuts, a beer for him and a soda for me. "I'm going to catch a foul ball for you," he often promised, although he didn't bring a mitt. "But how will you catch it, Dad?" I asked. "In my beer cup!" he said, triumphantly. He never did snag a foul, but he always believed he would.

My favorite Seals players were Dario Lodigiani and Joe "The Ox" Brovia. Lodigiani was a San Francisco-born all-star infielder who started with the Oaks, went to the majors with the Philadelphia Athletics and Chicago White Sox, then returned to play for the Oaks, and finally to the Seals from 1949 to 1951. Brovia was a power-hitting outfielder from Davenport, California, just north of Santa Cruz. He played 1,800 games in the minors, including parts of five seasons for the Seals. In 1955, he had the classic "cup of coffee" (baseball jargon for a short stint in the Major Leagues)—twenty-one games with the Cincinnati Reds. Those players were among my early heroes, but again, no one was ever more of a hero to me than my father. Dad was gregarious, affable, and handsome, and he made me so proud. When he walked into a room, it seemed to me that everyone gravitated to him, and the room was suddenly much brighter.

On Friday nights when we didn't go to ball games, Dad and I usually did something else special together. Sometimes we went to the Bayview Theatre or Avenue Theatre to see a movie. One movie I will always remember was the 1949 film noir *White Heat*, starring James Cagney as Cody Jarrett, the psychotic leader of a criminal gang. I loved Cagney's swagger and style. Dad thought Cagney was the greatest actor of that era. If it weren't the Seals game or the movies, Dad would take me to the Rolph Playground baseball field off Army Street, now known as Cesar Chavez Street. I remember a vendor there with a red and yellow popcorn machine. Dad would buy us each a bag, and we'd sit in the stands watching a semipro baseball game. All that mattered to me was that I was with my most favorite person in the world, my dad.

Every Wednesday, my mom's sisters, Margaret, Rose, and Anna, would come over to our house to play cards, talk, and smoke cigarettes for hours on end while me and my cousins played in the backyard. We had chickens, rabbits, a duck, and a pigeon coop that was part of an old barn I called my playhouse. One day I overheard my aunt Margaret say that she could tell one's fortune by reading the palm of their hand. When my dad came home for lunch that particular Wednesday, she looked at his palm and proclaimed, "Oh my, Frank. Your lifeline is amazingly long. You're going to live forever!" When I heard that I was the happiest a little kid could be.

Not long after that, Dad got sick, and he spent days at home in bed. I didn't know what was wrong, but it lasted for months. He grew weaker by the day. Early in April 1951, about a year from when he first became ill, some men came in an ambulance. I watched as they carried my dad on a gurney down the stairs. Mom and I were in the hallway below the staircase, and the more she cried, the more I cried. I was crying hysterically, my head buried in Mom's apron. I couldn't bear the thought that Dad was leaving the house. The men put him in the vehicle and drove away. I had no idea then that I would never see him again. I had just turned nine. My heart was broken. I yearned for our special times together, just the two of us enjoying life. Mom sensed my deep sorrow.

"Dad has to go to the hospital for a while," Mom told me. "He's very sick." She was quite protective of me, especially knowing how close Dad and I were. So protective, in fact, that after Dad went to the hospital, I was sent to stay with my Aunt Margaret, Uncle Ed, and their four children for a few days. I did not know it then, but my dad had already passed away when he was taken away from the house, not by an ambulance but by a coroner's wagon.

One morning a few days after I got to their house, my aunt, uncle, and their three girls got dressed up. They said they had somewhere special to go. I was told my cousin Buddy was staying home to take me to a Seals game. Much later in life, I would piece together what had really happened. It was never a subject I could dwell upon; the hurt was just too deep. As a young kid, I believed what I was told. While I was at the Seals game with Cousin Buddy, it turned out, my father was being buried. Pat, Jean, and Dickie were there at the services to support Mom. Looking back on it, Pat and Jean were old enough to know the truth about Dad, and Dickie was too young to understand. My mother, her heart broken over the death of the man she loved, couldn't handle seeing her Sonny crying uncontrollably again over the loss of the father he adored, so she made sure I wasn't around for the funeral arrangements or the service.

After I returned home from Aunt Margaret's, every day I would ask Mom, "When is Dad coming home from the hospital?" One day when just she and I were sitting in the kitchen, I asked again. "Sonny, I have something to tell you," she said, her eyes welling with tears. "Your dad won't be coming home. He died, and now he's with God." My heart fell. I was overwhelmed. My dad was gone forever. No further explanation was given, nor did I ever ask. I didn't cry this time; I knew Mom was suffering inside as much or more than me. I learned much later that he had melanoma, a type of cancer that little was known about back then. Later, as I grew up, Mom always warned me to be careful about moles that changed in size. From that day forward I carried a chip on my shoulder and anger in my heart. How could a just and fair God take our father from us? Losing Dad changed all our lives. "You're the man of the house now," my mother told me. Those words scared me, but they resonated with me, too, even at such a young age. I vowed to do anything I could to honor my father's memory. I promised to take care of my mother and our family. But it wasn't easy growing up so fast.

My dad, Frank Tabone Falzon

Mom and Dad

Falzon Family: L-R, Uncle Lawrence, Katie (Mom), my sisters
Patricia and Jean, my brother Dickie standing, Sonny kneeling

CHAPTER 6
RACKET SQUAD

With Dad gone, we were strapped for money. Whatever money we had went to his doctor bills. My dad's brother, Lawrence, had flown out from Detroit to pay for the cost of the funeral and burial. Mom soon went to work at the Schlage Lock Company, leaving my oldest sister Pat to look after us younger kids. But even with Mom working, we were having trouble making the rent. Her brother, Ben Fox, and his wife, Louise, offered to share their home with us.

They had eight children—my cousin Gary and his seven sisters. They would have another boy, Jim, later. Gary was two years younger than me and quite athletic. Gary was a good ballplayer and he became one of my closest and dearest cousins. The Foxes lived in a two-bed-room, one-bathroom home at 20th Avenue and Vicente Street in the Sunset District. It was directly across from Larsen Park, where a Vought F-8 Crusader fighter jet, donated by the Navy, stood in the middle of the playground area. Gary, my brother Dickie, and I spent many hours playing at "Jet Plane Park." Generations of San Francisco kids remember going to Larsen Park to play on the old aircraft. Several doors down the street lived the McCoy brothers, Frank and Mike, who became close playground friends back then. Like me, both Cousin Gary and Frank McCoy joined the San Francisco Police Department. Frank McCoy worked at Northern Police Station and became a homicide inspector.

We sat near one another in that detail for years. As a patrolman, Gary was the manager of the Mission Station softball team, and they were always a formidable opponent against his cousin Frank's team from the Bureau of Inspectors. Eventually, Gary was promoted to the Inspectors Bureau and became part of our department-wide all-star softball team representing San Francisco against other jurisdictions. The two cousins were together again on the ballfield.

To accommodate his expanded family, Uncle Benny built two rooms in his garage area with a half bath. My cousin Gary was given the second upstairs bedroom. Mom and my sister Pat slept in the smaller of the two downstairs rooms next to the half bath. My sister Jean, brother Dickie, and I stayed in the big room that was lined with bunk beds. It sounds crazy, but I loved the arrangement. I loved my cousins, and it was like being at camp every night. What Uncle Ben and Aunt Louise did for us was over-the-top generous. These were two amazing, loving people. The next two years were the best. Many nights when Uncle Benny came home from work, he'd toss me a quarter and tell me to run down to the corner store to buy the afternoon edition of the *San Francisco Call Bulletin*. The paper cost twenty cents. "If you get back within three minutes," he'd say, "you can keep the nickel change." I took off, flew down the block, bought the paper, and dashed home. Sometimes I made it in three minutes, sometimes not. Either way, Uncle Benny always let me keep the nickel. I used the money to buy Topps baseball trading cards that came in a small package with a flat piece of bubble gum inside. Me and the other kids played a game flipping the cards against a wall. Whoever was closest got to keep the other's card. I had quite a collection back in the day.

Mom worked hard, earned promotions, and she finally saved enough money for us to move back close to our old neighborhood. We rented the upstairs flat of a converted old horse barn on Goettingen Street off Wayland Avenue in the Portola District. She saved enough to buy us a television, a luxury in the 1950s. I became addicted to shows featuring "good guys" against "bad guys," like *Superman, Hopalong Cassidy, The Lone Ranger,* and *The Cisco Kid.* I loved the law-and-order shows. The hero always wore the white hat. My all-time favorite show was *Racket Squad,* starring Reed Hadley as Captain John Braddock, a fictional detective who saved unsuspecting citizens from con men and bunko artists. One episode I still remember was called "Sting of Fate." A man and woman teamed up to fake injuries in hotels to extort money. First, they tore a piece of the carpet, then the woman pretended to catch the heel of her shoe on the ripped hole, supposedly twisting her ankle. Her male accomplice then used hornets he kept in a bottle to sting the woman's ankle to simulate the swelling of a real sprain. The hotel management panicked and was about to pay off the couple to avoid legal trouble, but a hotel employee helped Braddock expose the scam. At the beginning of each show, Braddock, who both hosted and starred, looked at the camera and said something like, "What you are about to see is based on actual cases from police files on confidence men who scheme to separate you from your money. Don't be a sucker!" And then at the end, he'd say, "We'll be closing this case, or I should say, the courts will decide the fate of the accused. Remember, there are people who can slap you on the back with one hand and pick your pocket with the other. It could happen to YOU!" *Racket Squad* and the other TV shows helped to set the foundation for my later decision to join the San Francisco Police Department.

Not far from where we lived was Portola Park playground, which had two baseball fields, a big gymnasium, tennis courts, and a large open grass play area. Portola Park became my second home all through my years at St. Elizabeth's School, where I went for grammar school, as well as during my time at St. Ignatius High School. Portola Park was known as a baseball factory for high school varsity and college players. Grove Mohr, a former baseball coach at St. Ignatius High School, was the park director. He loved to win and recruited top players from around the city to play for Portola Park's teams. In the eighth grade, I formed my own team from players I knew at St. Elizabeth School and others I'd befriended at Portola Park. That team won its division and played for the city championship at Seals Stadium. Following the game, I was named MVP and was asked to appear on the TV show *Dugout Dope* with the Seals' announcer Don Klein, the longtime sports director at radio station KCBS. *Dugout Dope* served as the pregame show for the Seals game on Saturday afternoons. Klein's other guest that day was the Seals' best hitter, outfielder Bob DiPietro. A San Francisco native, he made it to the Boston Red Sox for just four games at the end of the 1951 season. He made it a memorable cup of coffee by throwing out Mickey Mantle at home plate in Yankee Stadium! DiPietro gave me some quick batting tips during the show. It was quite a thrill for me as a kid to be on TV and get batting instructions from a professional.

Our downstairs neighbors in the flats on Goettingen were Mike and Dolores Maloney. Mike was a dead ringer for the actor James Arness, star of the TV show *Gunsmoke*. Mike became a big brother or surrogate father to me. We built and flew model airplanes and went fishing off the piers on the waterfront. One day while fishing, I slipped and fell fifteen feet into the Bay. I sunk deep into the water and kicked my way back to the surface to hear Mike hollering, "Can you swim?" I went down again, thrashed my way back up, and hollered back, "No, I can't!" With that, Mike jumped in, grabbed me, and we both held onto the slimy moss-covered piling and began yelling for help.

We had been fishing next to a docked Chinese junk. Several men of its crew, who spoke no English, helped us out of the water using ropes and a ladder. They took us aboard their boat, filled two tubs with warm water for Mike and me to sit in, fully clothed, and gave us hot tea. Mike had saved my life and was my new hero.

At St. Ignatius High School I played varsity baseball and football and freshman basketball for the Wildcats. Baseball was always my first love. I was on the 1958 city championship varsity baseball team as a sophomore. Early in my junior year, again on the varsity squad, I was told I would play first base, but one day during practice coach Jim Keating put me in right field. I was pissed. As I trotted out to my position, I flipped him off. To my great embarrassment, he saw me and kicked me off the team right then and there. I was humiliated beyond measure at being such a smartass. I sat out that baseball season watching my team win another city championship. Coach Keating had taught me to eat crow, and I did. I apologized and played winter ball for Keating, giving up varsity football in my senior year that fall to get ready for baseball in the spring.

Our varsity football team under coach Pat Malley won the 1958 city championship against Polytechnic High School, coached by the legendary Milt Axt. Axt had been a baseball and football standout for Santa Clara University before becoming a renowned high school coach in San Francisco. We matched up well with Poly's formidable squad that included future Forty Niners star running back Gary Lewis and future Forty Niners head coach George Seifert. A crowd of 26,000 filled Kezar Stadium on Thanksgiving for the big game. We dominated Poly in that Turkey Day contest.

As a senior I was back on the baseball team playing first base and batting cleanup. We battled rival Sacred Heart down to the wire. Altogether we played three games against Sacred Heart. In the first game, at one of the Big Rec diamonds in Golden Gate Park, we lost a heartbreaker, six to five. In the second game, a pitchers' duel, I got the hit that beat the Irish two to one on the Hennessey diamond at Funston Playground. But we lost the championship at Candlestick Park, which had just opened after the Giants played their first two seasons at Seals Stadium while Candlestick was under construction. I remember striking out twice against the Sacred Heart ace, future Baltimore Orioles' left-hander Frank Bertaina.

One day during my sophomore year, I talked two of my St. Ignatius High School baseball buddies, Billy Ayoob and John Giovanola, into driving over to meet my cousins, Lorie and Kathy Fox. Kathy was playing out in front of her house with three friends, Janelle, Dori, and a freckle-faced girl named Donna Coudures. Donna was a year younger than me but was also a sophomore. She went to Mercy High School, a Catholic all-girls college prep school across town on 19th Avenue. I thought she was very cute. That night I called to ask her out for Friday night, but she said she already had a date. I thought she was playing hard to get, so on Friday I went to her house and rang the doorbell. Donna opened the door, saw me, and said, "I told you I had a date tonight. What are you doing here?" I left with my tail between my legs, but on the way down her front stairs I tried to save face by calling out, "You had your chance!" I was being a smartass again. Not long after that I saw her at a St. Ignatius basketball game. She came over and sat with me. We haven't been apart since. We dated steadily through our junior and senior years. A few years later, John Giovanola married my cousin Kathy. To this day the four of us remain close friends.

Barely a month after our May graduation, on June 26, 1960, Donna and I were married at the Church of the Epiphany, followed by a reception in her uncle Frankie's rumpus room. The Reverend Richard Fry, the parochial vicar, performed the marriage ceremony and came to the reception. Because I was eighteen and Donna was seventeen, Father Fry quipped, "I give this marriage six months." As I write this, we're going on sixty-two years married.

Based on my baseball skills, I qualified for a partial scholarship to Santa Clara University and a full scholarship at Gonzaga University. On my mother's limited income, we couldn't afford the additional costs for me to go away to school, so the universities were out for me. My school team days were over after St. Ignatius. But I continued to play baseball on weekends and later started a softball league in the police department.

Mike Maloney, my old neighbor who fished me out of the Bay, was by then a foreman at Schmidt Lithograph Company. I had worked for a printing business and an insurance company in the summers during high school. Mike was able to get me a full-time job as an apprentice lithographer. Donna went to work for the telephone company at Second and Berry Streets as a toll rater. We moved into her grandmother's basement on Guttenberg Street. There was a room lined with knotty pine paneling, a small kitchen, and a bathroom. We paid no rent, only the electric and water bills. Our first child, Daniel, was born the following year. He was just a few weeks old when I dressed him in his first baseball outfit. Father, mother, and son together in our little basement apartment—I couldn't have been happier.

Not long after that we had saved enough to make a down payment on our first home on Arguello Boulevard in the Linda Mar section of Pacifica, a coastal town just south of the city. Since I was only nineteen, Mike and his wife, Dolores, co-signed the loan for us. Our daughter, Debbie, was born in August 1962 and our second son, David, came along in February 1964. Our fourth and last child, Kerri, would join us in 1971.

I worked at Schmidt Lithograph for three years, but my days as a lithographer grew limited because I was allergic to the coal oil and methyl ethyl ketone solvent used to clean up the big presses I worked on. The chemicals even got into my gloves, leaving a painful rash on my hands and arms. I could have transferred to another part of the company, but I wasn't sure I wanted to continue that line of work.

I kept thinking more and more about a career in law enforcement.

Me and Donna, 1970

Our young family in 1971, L-R, Dan, 10,
Debbie, 9, Dave, 7, Kerri, 10 months

CHAPTER 7
MY BEAT ON THE STREETS OF SAN FRANCISCO

I was making good money working in the lithography business, and with Donna's paychecks from the phone company we were able to put the down payment on the Pacifica house. But with my allergies to the chemicals, a new mortgage, two kids and a third on the way, I knew I had to make a change. I was looking for something more long term and secure. I started by taking the Daly City Police Department written entry examination, but I flunked, missing too many multiple-choice questions.

I determined I would not fail again. I read a book on how to study for civil service exams and memorized practically every word. Then I took twenty-one different tests covering nearly every police and fire department from San Francisco south to Mountain View. I passed every one, but the San Francisco Police Department was always my first choice. I not only passed the written exam but the background check, the physical agility requirements, the oral interview, and the lie detector—or so I thought. I was a bit nervous before the polygraph, although I had nothing to hide. Afterward, the guy who administered it said to me, "You did fine on almost every question, but I did get a reaction to the question about smoking marijuana." I was floored.

"What?" I exclaimed. "That can't be! I've never even smoked

cigarettes. I took a puff once and I knew immediately that it wasn't for me." He never said another word. I think he was just testing me to see how I'd react. It was 1964, and smoking grass was replacing the can of beer for a lot of young people.

I left Schmidt Lithograph prematurely, but I quickly found work at HS Crocker Printing while I waited for an opening on the San Francisco Police Department list. Typically, out of one thousand applicants only thirty are accepted. I was notified that a spot was open in the police academy class in the fall of 1964. Civil service rules at the time required city employees to live in the city. To comply, we moved from the Pacifica house, but we kept it as a rental, did a cash out refinance, and bought a house in the outer Sunset District at 47th Avenue and Ulloa Street. It was perfect for us, near Parkside Square, a small park with a ballfield.

On September 16, 1964, I reported for my first day of training. I was twenty-two and very excited to be with the other twenty-five recruits in the class, all of us smartly dressed in our pressed khaki pants, blue shirts, and black neckties. That first day we were issued stars and batons. My star number was 507. When I pinned that shiny silver, seven-pointed star to my shirt, I was so proud. I had tremendous respect for cops. I truly believed they were there to protect us from the bad guys. I knew a couple of the men in my academy class already and quickly made friends with the others. One of them, Bill Arrietta, came up to me, patted me on the chest, and said, "Hey, Falzon, congratulations! Be on your best behavior. Our next speaker is going to be the chief himself."

Chief Tom Cahill was a tough Irishman and popular with the rank-and-file. We were seated alphabetically, which put me in the second row, first seat, directly in front of the speaker. I had gone to high school with the chief's son, also named Tom, so I thought he might recognize or remember me. At one point during his welcome talk, Chief Cahill warned us: "Remember, the three things that will get you fired immediately are booze, broads, and bad debt." As he talked, I had the sense that he was looking directly at me. His speech was pretty much fire and brimstone. "If you're right, I'll stand behind you one hundred percent, but God help you if you're wrong!" *He must remember me from St. Ignatius,* I kept thinking. *Why else does he keep staring at me?* When he finished, we were all dismissed except for me. The chief pointed at me. "Officer, I want to see you after class."

When the room had cleared, I walked right up to him and saluted. "Yes, Chief?"

"Officer," he said brusquely, "one thing you need to learn is you should never ever embarrass the badge! Do you understand me?"

"Yes, sir!" I replied with another salute. "I will never embarrass the badge."

"Then why the hell are you wearing your Dubble Bubble on your star?"

I looked down. When Bill Arrietta patted my chest, he had stuck a thick, gooey wad of pink bubble gum on my badge. I apologized to Chief Cahill and tried to remove the gum, but it was like a cheesy pizza, all stringy and sticky. Mortified, I quickly turned and slunk out of the room. Bill was in the hallway laughing his ass off. So began my police career—and the years of pranks that went with it.

After more than three months at the academy, we graduated and were given our first station assignments. I reported to Potrero Station for my first tour of watch on December 31, 1964. New Year's Eve, of all days to start. Rookies were paired with veterans, and although I didn't realize it at first, my partner, Jim, was a drinker. We rolled out onto the streets of the Bayview District in the late afternoon and went straight to a bar on San Bruno Avenue. No sooner were we in the door than the drinks began lining up on the bar. I refused and everyone made

Police Academy graduation, December 1964
Left, Chief Tom Cahill, Right, Rookie Officer Frank Falzon

fun of me. The teasing continued, but I had been warned that I was on probation for a year. "Slip up and you're fired." I refused to drink. Eventually we left. Jim took us to two more bars further out on San Bruno Avenue and the same thing happened. In the third bar, a band was playing, people were dancing, attractive cocktail waitresses kept bringing us drinks, and I kept refusing. One lady asked Jim, "Who's your cute partner?" She removed my uniform hat and danced away with it. My partner was getting smashed by then. All I could think about was getting my hat back and getting out of there. "Look," Jim said to me, "you can't trust a cop who won't drink. We're not leaving until you have a drink." I ordered a bourbon and 7-Up and took a few sips just to appease him. "Now I trust you," he said. I got my hat back, we left, but it dawned on me there was no way he could drive. Jim had been throwing them down one after another for hours. I was able to convince him that I should drive.

I got behind the wheel and realized I was still so green I didn't even know how to operate the two-way radio or answer the calls from the dispatcher. Sure, we'd had training sessions in the radio cars to learn defensive driving techniques and the general operation of the radio and all the call signs and codes. But this was different. It was happening in real time, and I was just hoping we wouldn't get an assignment. It was getting near the end of our shift, and I was looking forward to returning to the station when the radio speaker jolted me. "Headquarters to Potrero Four. Report of a 459 at 720 Argonaut Street. Please respond." *Shit, a burglary! Not now! Hell, I don't even know where Argonaut is.* I looked over and saw my partner slumped against the passenger window, fast asleep. "Ten-four, headquarters," I replied to the dispatcher, using one of the few status codes I could recall. I looked around the squad car for the Thomas Bros. San Francisco Street Guide, a map book we'd been given at the academy. *I grew up in this district. Why don't I know where Argonaut is?* It turned out to be a newly built subdivision down by the Sunnydale projects.

We pulled up to a townhouse a few minutes later. I'd collected my thoughts by then and I was thinking, *Okay, Falzon, you can handle this.* When I opened the door, Jim stirred. "What the hell are you doing?" he demanded. I told him about the radio call and that I was going to handle it. "Bullshit!" he growled. "You don't know what the hell you're doing, rookie!" Jim refused to stay in the car. He opened the passenger door and fell onto the sidewalk. I quickly came around and helped him to his feet. A woman standing on her doorstep asked if my partner was all right. "He's not feeling well," I said. We went into the house, Jim slumped into a living room chair, and the woman took me out to the backyard. "Some of the neighborhood kids took the chain off my son's bike," she said, pointing to the bike. *Really?* I was thinking. *That's just petty theft.* But for her sake I acted like it was a bank job and prayed, *Please don't call the department about my drunk partner.* I jotted down some info about the chain to appease her, telling her we'd do everything we could to find her son's bike chain. Then I helped Jim back to the car. Back at the station, the sergeant blew a gasket.

"Who the fuck was out with Jim tonight?" he shouted. Everyone knew but me, apparently, that Jim was a drunk and was typically given a desk assignment for his shifts. Under no circumstances was he allowed out on the street.

"I was," I said, nervous about what I might have done wrong.

"You're new, right?"

"Yes, Sergeant. It's my first night."

He looked around the station and called out again.

"Who the hell was dumb enough to put a rookie out on the street with Jim, for Chrissakes?" The sergeant was angry. He looked at Jim. "Get your ass upstairs and out of uniform!" he barked. "If I see you still in the station in five minutes, I'm booking you." I couldn't wait to change into my street clothes and head home. I feared I would be fired when the woman called to report me for being with a drunk. But she didn't call. What a first night on the street. Definitely not what I expected.

Four months later, Jim was drinking late one night after work. Another cop took him home. He lived with his mother. The cop rang the bell and waited, but no one came to the door, so he left Jim there outside on the stoop. Not long after the cop left, Jim choked to death on his own vomit right there on his mom's front steps. I was upset to hear this about my first patrol partner, even as briefly as I knew him. Back then, drinking had long been part of the culture on the force. Lots of cops drank to cope with the stress of the job. Some who drank did it on the job, like Jim; most others waited until they were off duty. It was understandable, I suppose, but Jim's death only reinforced my own decision not to drink. It was one reason that I later started a police softball league, hoping to get my buddies to play ball after work instead of going to a bar.

I wasn't happy at Potrero Station. I would later adjust, but my first choice was to work at Northern Station. A family friend who was a police veteran told me that all the best cops and the most action were at Northern. After a few months, I put in a scratch—what we call a transfer request. I'd been at Potrero a year when Herman George, a Black officer at Northern Station, was transferred to Potrero, and I was able to swap spots with him. Sadly, Patrolman George was gunned down about a year later as he sat typing a report inside the SFPD's Hunters Point substation. On November 13, 1967, three gunmen had burst into the satellite office and shot Herman six times. He died of his wounds a month later. Another Black officer wounded in the attack survived. The case was never solved, although investigators later developed evidence the attack was carried out by members of the Black Panthers as a vendetta against "Black pigs."

George's murder hit me hard for two reasons: one, he was a fellow officer, and two, I remember thinking then how lucky I was. Without the transfer to Potrero Station, it could have been me assigned to that substation instead of him. In retrospect, of course, that wouldn't matter if indeed Black officers were targeted. Any time a cop is killed it is a sobering experience for other cops. The reality of death is there constantly, but you can't let it absorb you. It's always in the back of your mind that today may be my last day on the job.

I reported to Northern Station on Ellis Street at Van Ness Avenue in January 1966. It was the best assignment I could have hoped for. Whether in a radio car or walking the beat, it was never dull. There was always something happening. I couldn't wait to get to work every day. Everyone I worked with was a cop's cop, hardworking and dedicated. I loved it. At Northern Station I was paired up with Eddie Erdelatz Jr., who'd graduated from the academy in the class before mine. Eddie was a lot like me. He was my age, dedicated, hard-working, and had a great sense of humor. His father was Edward J. Erdelatz, the former

All-American football player at St. Mary's in Moraga, California, who coached at St. Mary's, the University of San Francisco, the U.S. Naval Academy, and the 49ers. He was also the first head coach for the Oakland Raiders during the 1960-61 season.

Eddie and I were working the Northern 2 car, which covered a thirty-five-square-block area of the city from Octavia Street to Steiner Street and Fulton Street to Geary Boulevard. When we weren't in the radio car, we were on foot patrol, in uniform, much of that on the seven blocks of Fillmore Street. We carried dimes in our pockets for a pay phone in case we got into trouble and weren't near a police department call box. There were no walkie-talkies or cell phones yet. The only way to communicate with headquarters when we were walking the beat was by call box or pay phone.

I looked forward to working with Eddie every day. Going into a high-crime area like the Fillmore, I knew my partner was fearless, always had my back, and would bring humor and joy to a tough job. Eddie was the best partner I could ever have hoped to work with. Lucky me.

At that time, the Fillmore was a hotbed of illegal activity: prostitution, drugs, gambling, after-hours coffee houses where you could get a shot of booze in your cup of joe. The more serious crimes—burglaries, robberies, and murders—were an everyday threat. Much of this illegal action took place in the seedy Fillmore area hotels: the New Yorker, the Booker T. Washington, the Eddy, and the Manor Plaza. At the corner of Fillmore and Eddy Streets was a place called the Louisiana Fish Fry. I figured at one time it had been a soda fountain because it had a long counter, numerous stools, and large windows that overlooked Eddy Street. In my time, working girls would sit on the stools and wait for customers to come in or call out from their car, and off they'd go into one of the hotels or vacated buildings that had a strategically placed mattress for short-term use.

One night in March 1966, Eddie and I had just finished dinner when we came upon a large group of women in front of the Booker

T. Washington Hotel involved in what I can best describe as a rau-
cous cat fight. Two gals from out of town had squared off against
some local women in a dispute over territory. They were all screaming and grappling with one another. One of the out-of-towners was
named Maristone Chapel. She was a big Black woman who looked
like Shaquille O'Neal in drag. With her was another woman, Joyce
Randall. When we approached them, they became belligerent and began screaming obscenities at us. We decided to arrest them for disturb-
ing the peace.

Eddie grabbed Chapel by the arm. She slapped his hand away,
screaming, "Keep your white motherfucking hands off me!" He grabbed
her again and she said, "Didn't you hear me? I said keep your white
motherfucking hands off me!" Then she picked up Eddie by the lapels
of his double-breasted uniform coat and slammed him into a chain
link fence. Another woman, a local gal named Jean Walker, joined in.
Together they managed to yank Eddie's nightstick away and started beating him with it on his arms and shoulders while he tried to shield his
head from the blows. I'm not believing what I'm seeing. Eddie is six feet,
a hundred and eighty pounds. I tried to intervene to help him. First, I
turned to Joyce Randall and grabbed her arm. "You stay here!" I ordered.
Then I turned back to Eddie and Chapel. "You heard my friend," Joyce
said. "Keep your motherfucking hands off me!" She raised her right hand
and dug her long, sharp fingernails into my windpipe and clawed down-
ward. There was now blood, my blood, on my light blue uniform shirt.
I grabbed Joyce and pushed her face down onto the hood of a nearby
parked car and got one handcuff on her.

Just then, a small, bespectacled Black guy came out of the nearby
First Baptist Church. He sees a white cop manhandling a Black woman, so he decides to come to her aid. I felt my nightstick being removed
from its special pocket on my right pants leg. Still holding Joyce, I
turned to confront this older man, who smacked me once on the elbow
with my truncheon. He was about to split my head open with it when

I drew my service revolver and shouted at him, "Drop the nightstick or I'll shoot!"

With that, he dropped the baton and it rolled away, but we continued tussling while I'm still holding onto Joyce Randall by the one handcuff. By now a mob of angry-looking onlookers had begun to close in on us. They aren't exactly good citizens coming to the aid of two police officers under attack.

Suddenly, I heard a gunshot behind me.

I look over and see Chapel laid out on the street. Erdelatz is standing next to her, gun in hand. I'm thinking, *Jeez, he shot her!* I placed the other half of my handcuffs on the man's wrist, locking him and Joyce together. Now I'm holding the center chain of my handcuffs with both suspects under arrest. I pulled them both toward the pay phone to call for backup. I dropped two dimes into the slot on the phone and dial zero. When the operator came on the line, I blurt out, "Operator, we are two uniformed cops getting the hell beat out of us. Please send help to the Booker T. Washington Hotel!"

"One moment, please," she said. *One moment, please? You've got to be kidding me.*

In less than a minute, cops from Northern, Southern, Park, and Richmond Stations came from every direction, sirens blaring, lights flashing.

I asked Eddie, "Did you shoot her?"

"No," he said. "I saw the crowd advancing at your back. Your nightstick had suddenly rolled toward me, so I grabbed it and hit her over the head and knocked her out. But the others were still coming toward you, so I fired a shot in the air. Everybody backed off. I saved your life!"

I was so relieved that Eddie hadn't shot Chapel. He had me going there for a minute. The paddy wagons came and carted away the three women and James Loyd, the man who had hit me with my nightstick. Eddie and I had our wounds treated at Central Emergency Hospital and went back to work. We continued to work together at Northern

Station for another three years.

Heroin use was on the rise in the mid-sixties, so we were on the lookout for dealers who we knew were operating in the Fillmore and particularly in the hotels. "The Manor Plaza was quite a hub of narcotics," Erdelatz, now eighty, says. "Whenever Frank and I walked in, the switchboard operator had some way to notify the crooks that cops were in the hotel, and they'd scatter. One night we were in the lobby waiting for the elevator. When the elevator doors opened there was a dead body inside. He was fully clothed and soaking wet from head to toe. We called the coroner. A week or two later, the same thing happened. Elevator arrives, doors open, dead body inside, fully clothed and soaking wet. It turned out they were drug overdoses. Their friends had put them into a bathtub full of water in an attempt to revive them. When it failed, they put the body in the elevator so someone would find it." I'd seen dead bodies before—suicides and overdoses at my previous station—but what shocked me about this was the callousness, the disregard for humanity, for a fellow human being, addict or not.

An enjoyable part of the Northern Station beat was being around the Fillmore Auditorium. In its heyday during the late sixties, the Fillmore gained national notoriety as the birthplace of psychedelic music with such rising bands as the Grateful Dead, Jefferson Airplane, Big Brother and the Holding Company, and many others performing on stage in front of swirling light shows. Elsewhere in the Fillmore, fans thronged to nearby jazz clubs for music and drinks. When most of the city was asleep, the Fillmore District was alive and jumping. Local businesses welcomed us stopping in from time to time to say hello, check on things, and assure their patrons' safety.

Eddie and I continued to make solid cases. We developed numerous confidential informants, mainly prostitutes and minor drug offenders who were easy to catch. To avoid jail time, they'd offer information on more serious criminals. If it happened in the Fillmore, Eddie and I most likely would solve the case. What was occurring was not going unnoticed by the new chief of police, Al Nelder, who had succeeded his former homicide partner Tom Cahill. Chief Nelder soon moved Eddie and me from Northern Station to the vice squad in the Bureau of Special Services, based on the fifth floor at the downtown Hall of Justice.

This 7:00 p.m. to 3:00 a.m. shift was the best job we ever had. We were the so-called "felony cars"—unmarked police cars looking for the worst criminals committing violent crimes—with citywide jurisdiction and one simple job: catch the bad guys. We'd make the arrest, write up the initial report, and our job was done. All the tedious follow-up work and court preparation was the responsibility of the men working at the Bureau of Inspectors.

After my first year at Potrero Station, several more at Northern Station, and a couple more working vice crimes, I was promoted in March 1970 along with Eddie to the Bureau of Inspectors on the fourth floor at the Hall of Justice. From my first day at the academy, this had been my dream. I was now working cases as a police inspector. I always knew my ultimate career goal was to be in homicide. Not just to be a homicide cop, working the big murder cases, the tough cases, but eventually someday to be the best in homicide. The Inspectors Bureau was a big step in that direction. Our first assignment on this job was to the General Work Detail, a catch-all unit for all crimes except robbery, burglary, auto theft, and rape. It was a great training ground for young inspectors.

After a year in General Work, I called the chief's office one day asking for an appointment to speak with Chief Nelder. When I walked into his office, Nelder was genuinely happy to see me and expressed his appreciation for the work we had done. But I was not there about police work. I was there to ask for his blessing to take our San Francisco Police Department All-Star softball team to South Lake Tahoe to participate in the statewide 1971 Law Enforcement Tournament. The chief was very receptive to the idea. The department encouraged physical fitness, the camaraderie was great for morale, and the games were played over a weekend, so we weren't playing on company time. The chief said, "Take your team, Frank, and bring back the winner's trophy."

I knew the department-wide team I had assembled was damned good, and I promised we'd win the tournament. We shook hands, and I started to leave his office. When I reached the door, I screwed up my courage, turned, and asked, "Chief, by any chance would you consider Eddie Erdelatz and me for the two openings in the homicide detail?" Chief Nelder hesitated and then answered, "As you know, Frank, we recently lost two good men to heart attacks." Walt Kracke and Telfred "Telly" Slettvedt had both survived but could no longer work in homicide, and they had both retired soon thereafter. Nelder continued, "Every inspector on the fourth floor wants those two positions. I do need to put younger men into those spots. I can't think of two better investigators than you and Eddie."

"Thank you, Chief," I said and left. I was very satisfied. He didn't say no, and he didn't say yes, but he sure as hell paid Eddie and me a huge compliment. At the time, there was no formal application or promotion process for entering the homicide detail. Those positions were strictly up to the chief. The very next morning, Eddie and I were transferred to homicide. My new lieutenant, Charlie Ellis, gave veteran Homicide Inspector Jack Cleary the choice of the three new men in the detail, Frank McCoy, Eddie Erdelatz, or myself, as his new partner to replace Kracke. I knew Jack well. He was my neighbor and nine years my senior. I had coached his son, Tom, along with my boy Dan in Catholic Youth Organization basketball from the third grade through the eighth grade. I respected Jack Cleary as one of the all-time best at solving murder cases. I was thrilled when Jack took me as his partner. I was going to be mentored by the best in the business.

And yeah, we did win that state softball tournament, knocking off the Los Angeles Police Department team seven to five in the championship final. What a great week.

State Champions 1971-72 Law Enforcement Softball Tournament

Back row standing L-R: Don Schneider, Dave Maron, Ken Sandstrom, Gary Lemos, Gerry Donovan, Gary Fox, John Sully, Tony Rodriguez, Roger Poole, Dennis Russell

Middle row kneeling, L-R: Joe Vigil, Frank Falzon, Dan White, Gary Bertucci, Gene Ahern, Harry Brown, John Portoni

Front row cheerleaders, L-R: Carli Casper, Sandy Larsen, unidentified, Janice McKay, Anne Harrington

CHAPTER 8
BODY IN THE BAY

A young couple was out for a summer stroll along the San Francisco waterfront early on the morning of July 10, 1972. They stopped for a few moments to take in the shimmering Bay and watch the ships glide under the Bay Bridge, some outbound through the Golden Gate for foreign ports, some inbound for the port of Oakland.

Coming to Pier 22½ at the foot of Harrison Street, the man and woman found a spot to sit on the dock, their legs dangling above the gentle swells that lapped against the pilings below. Screeching seagulls swooped overhead in the cool salty air, searching below for breakfast in the surf. It was 7:45 a.m. Just then, the couple noticed an odd shape under the surface of the water directly below them. At first, they weren't sure what it was, but, as it rose, there was no mistaking a human body.

The bloated corpse was floating about two feet below the surface. It was that of a fully clothed Black man, his hands and feet hogtied behind his back, a piece of cloth stuffed into his mouth, and a huge slab of concrete lashed to his waist with household electrical cords.

My partner, Jack Cleary, and I got word of the discovery and drove out to the pier. We had just been assigned to a brand-new four-door Plymouth sedan with forty miles on the odometer. When we got to the pier, I misjudged the unusual height of the curb when I drove over it.

We both heard the undercarriage of the car scraping the curb beneath us.

"Jesus, Frank, what the hell are you doing to our new car?" said Jack.

"Sorry, I said. "I didn't realize the curb was so high."

Fortunately, no serious damage was done. We proceeded to the edge of the pier where a crowd of onlookers had gathered.

By then I had been Jack's partner for two years. He was a great mentor. Jack never had a bad word to say about anyone. He was always the first to pay a compliment and to buy a round of drinks. He was good natured and took my teasing with a laugh and smile. I would say to Jack, "You're like Tonto's horse with a branch tied to your ass. No one can ever find out what you've been up to." I was referencing *The Lone Ranger* TV show. His Comanche sidekick, Tonto, would tie a branch to his horse's tail to sweep away its tracks in the dust as they rode so they couldn't be tracked by the bad guys. I had nicknamed Jack the "Monsignor." To Jack's credit, he is a loyal, faithful Catholic who attended church and Holy Communion services regularly.

He was always a gentleman, and everyone liked him. I learned a lot about being a good homicide inspector from Jack, but the biggest takeaway was that getting the job done right is important but never as important as your family. Family first, always.

Jack loved a good cigar after a meal. He would roll down the car windows so the smoke wouldn't affect me. When I occasionally complained, he would say, "Frank, go home, check your clothes in your closet. The reason why there are no holes in your clothes is because moths don't like cigar smoke." Now almost ninety, Jack gave up cigars long ago.

When I arrived at a crime scene with any of my partners, we always worked off a self-made checklist of tasks to make sure we gathered as much relevant information as possible. This was a daytime call, but for those times when you are yanked out of bed in the middle of the night, when your brain isn't always clear when you get to a crime scene, the checklist was vital. The list began with noting the location, date and time of day, weather, lighting conditions, the responding officers on the scene, which crime lab, photo unit, and coroner's staff were present, and any other details of the general scene. For a victim, we noted the approximate age, gender, race, physical description, clothing, personal possessions, obvious injuries, or other indications of the manner of death—e.g., location of and number of bullet wounds, possible caliber of the weapon, blood spray patterns, gunpowder residue or stippling, stab wounds, ligature marks, and other signs of trauma or restraints. Homicide inspectors are not to touch a body without the coroner's okay, so we rely on the coroner or his staff to empty pockets and purses, establish the victim's ID, age, address, phone number, and other relevant personal information. The responding officers will have spoken to any witnesses and given us their contact information. If witnesses were still at the scene, we would speak to them.

Occasionally, a senior commanding officer would show up at a homicide scene and scoff at the lack of evidence. "This is gonna be a round neck," he would say, an expression that meant it would never get solved. Those words only motivated me more. For me, it was like doing a jigsaw puzzle, fitting all the pieces together. You must take in all the clues and evidence and get into the mind of the criminal. You don't know what you don't know until you start digging into the person, his friends and family, his job, his daily calendar, his activities, his personal phone log. I was fascinated and motivated by the challenge of solving every puzzle I was assigned. In the office I would laugh and say "your job isn't complete until the murder suspect is in jail, rattling his cup against the bars."

As Jack and I got out of the car at the pier, firefighters from Station 35 were bringing up the body in a basket. Station 35 happens to be located at Pier 22½, with the city's fireboat moored alongside. Its crew responds to all calls for assistance along the bayfront. The man in the water was wearing a red and yellow sport shirt, black pants, black socks, and black shoes. He appeared to be in his mid-forties. His bloated skin was very light in color, almost pink from putrefaction, and his eyes were set back in his head. It appeared he'd been dead for several days, but as the firemen and coroner's aides placed him on a gurney, I noticed his shirt moving.

"Hey, Jack, I think he's still alive," I said to Cleary. Jack turned and looked down just as two baby crabs crawled out from under the shirt. They had been gnawing at the man's flesh. It was grotesque.

The victim's hands and feet were trussed behind his back with electrical cords that were also used to tie the block of concrete to his torso. The block was two feet by eighteen inches in size and weighed about sixty pounds. There was a sign of blunt trauma to his head. Nothing was found in his pockets. His only possession was a set of keys looped to his belt. We asked the young couple and others around the area whether they had seen anything that could help. Anything at all. No one offered any relevant information.

As we drove away from the scene, Jack said offhandedly, "Hey, Frank, I'll bet whoever dumped this guy probably had to drive over the same curb we did and may have scraped his undercarriage, too. You know what I mean, with all that weight in the trunk."

"Good point," I said, making a mental note for later.

Back at the Hall of Justice, we checked on recent missing persons reports and learned that the dead man was Colvin McCright, forty-four, a janitor with two jobs, one at the Standard Oil building and the other at a nightclub in San Francisco. He lived at 1001 Sunnydale Avenue, known as the Geneva Towers, a pair of twenty-two-story public housing buildings in the low-income Visitacion Valley neighborhood. His sister had reported him missing five days earlier after his supervisor at Standard Oil called her to inquire why he had failed to show up for work. The key ring found clipped to McCright held the keys for both of his janitorial jobs.

The autopsy concluded the cause of death was drowning, meaning McCright was still alive when he was tossed into the Bay. His killers hadn't realized that the gag used to silence him would also hold in bodily gases, offsetting the weight of the concrete and allowing the body to drift up to the surface.

Jack and I drove out to McCright's apartment. Part of the building was under renovation, with heavy equipment and tools staged in the garage. I noticed large pieces of concrete around the site and wondered if the demolition underway might be connected to our victim. We got the building manager to let us in the apartment, explaining that we were investigating a homicide. The manager told us that the only name on the lease was that of our victim, Colvin McCright. What we found in McCright's apartment prompted us to summon the crime lab and photo units right away. It was apparent to both Jack and me that this was our crime scene.

The first thing we noticed was that the cords on several lamps in the apartment had been cut off. The severed electrical cords were similar to those used to tie up McCright. I couldn't imagine how dumb someone had to be to leave the lamps in place with their cords cut. But criminals never cease to amaze me with their stupidity. I'm sure they were betting his body would never be found. Jack spotted a darkened area on the carpet. When the crime lab technician arrived, we had him remove the darkened patch for examination. On the underside was a water stain and a faded red patch. Someone had obviously tried to get rid of a bloodstain. We knew we were standing in the room where our victim was assaulted, tied, and gagged.

The crime lab collected the cordless lamps, the carpet sample, a bloody sheet, and a set of towels. On the way out of the building, I picked up a small chunk of concrete from the construction area that I asked the crime lab to analyze in comparison with the slab tied to McCright's body.

With the help of the patrol force, we were able to locate Colvin McCright's vehicle. We had it impounded and brought to the police garage for forensics analysis. Everything we turned up in the investigation was pointing to McCright's son, Calvin, and daughter-in-law, Harriet. We learned that Calvin and Harriet had recently moved into the apartment. That's a huge red flag. Why hadn't the son reported his father missing? Our investigation revealed that after the father disappeared, Calvin and Harriet were driving around in his father's car, using his credit cards, even cashing his paycheck. Calvin had forged his father's signature on one check for $223.98 shortly after his father had gone missing. Without eyewitness corroboration, however, we had to build the strongest circumstantial case possible. Many prosecutors will take a strong circumstantial case over eyewitness identification because eyewitnesses can often be mistaken in what they remember seeing.

Jack's suspicions about the car scraping the curb at the pier also proved to be prescient. The undercarriage of Colvin's car had evidence of damage like what we had experienced, and in the glovebox we found a receipt for $480 for repairs to the differential. In the trunk, we also found small pieces of broken concrete like that tied to the body, and a bloodstained throw pillow.

As a relatively new homicide inspector, I was still learning things about crimes and evidence every day. I hadn't been aware, for instance, that something as innocuous as concrete can have unique identifying properties. I had asked our crime lab, under the supervision of the renowned Shoji Horikoshi, to examine the slab of concrete tied to Colvin McCright and compare it with the pieces from the car and the sample I had picked up at the demolition pile at the Geneva Towers. I was fascinated when Shoji told us they were all of similar composition that included tiny particles of glass mixed with sand, gravel, and crushed stone. Those materials create cement, which is then mixed with water to make concrete. The glass particles, he said, gave the material its singular properties.

That determination, however, wasn't Shoji's most interesting contribution to this case. His background played a part none of us expected.

Shoji was born in San Francisco in 1926. During World War II, his Japanese family was interned in the Bay Area's Tanforan Racetrack Center Stables for eight months before they were sent to the Topaz Relocation Center in Utah, where four of them lived in a single room. Not long after they left the camp, Shoji enlisted in the Army in 1945 and served with occupation forces in Europe. He then enrolled at UC Berkeley and graduated in 1953 with a degree in criminalistics. He worked in Macy's warehouse until 1955, when he got an entry level position with the San Francisco Police Department Crime Lab. He rose through the ranks to become director of the lab, working under more than a dozen chiefs of police over thirty-eight years. Upon his retirement, the crime lab at Hunters Point was named the Shoji Horikoshi Crime Laboratory. He passed away in 2013.

It was Shoji's brief Macy's experience, as much as his forensic expertise, which contributed to the investigation. Towels, he told us, and later testified to at the trial, were typically sold in sets of six—two bath towels, two hand towels, and two face cloths. In McCright's apartment, we found such a set of matching towels, but one face cloth was missing. It was the one used to gag the victim.

Other evidence we gathered against Calvin and Harriet McCright was also circumstantial but contributed to the case overall. On the night Colvin McCright disappeared, the building security guard at Geneva Towers had been lured away from the front door by a false emergency. Also, sometime between the disappearance and the discovery of the floating body by the young couple, witnesses reported a man matching Calvin's description at Pier 22½, asking around if anyone had seen a body in the water. He was apparently making sure his father had sunk to the bottom.

During our investigation, we also learned that Calvin McCright was pandering his twenty-three-year-old wife, Harriet, as well as acting as a pimp for a young girl.

On August 29, the Grand Jury returned an indictment against

Calvin and Harriet McCright for the murder of Colvin McCright. We arrested them both and charged them with the crime.

The trial began on December 5 and lasted eleven days. During the trial, I sat beside Assistant District Attorney Tommy Norman. I noticed that Harriet McCright, from her seat at the defense table, was frequently looking in my direction with a menacing expression. Norman noticed it, too. "The jury is watching you and her," he said in a low voice. "Every now and then look back at her." I wasn't sure what he had in mind, but I knew our case against her was weak.

One day after lunch, while the defense attorney addressed the court, Harriet began staring at me again with a vicious expression. I looked straight at her and winked. Enraged, she flew out of her chair and started toward me, pointing an accusatory finger in my face. "I don't care how long it takes," she spat, "I'm going to get you!"

Nonplussed, Norman stood up, walked over to the jury box, and perched his butt on the railing. He looked back at me, smiled, and said for everyone to hear: "Frank, I think she just ordered another hunk of concrete."

The jury found both McCrights guilty on December 16, 1972. Two weeks later they were sentenced to life in prison.

CHAPTER 9
PAPER BAG KILLER

On the morning of October 16, 1973, Lorenzo Carniglia, a stocky, seventy-year-old, semi-retired painting contractor, was walking north on Third Street toward downtown San Francisco. The fog had dissipated, and the sky was clear and sunny. A native Italian, Carniglia was in good health for his age, but time and hard work had left him with a slight limp, a hitch in his stride that caused one shoe to brush the ground with each step. He carried with him the daily *Racing Form*. He often took a Greyhound bus to Bay Meadows, the popular horse racing track twenty miles south of the city. But on this day, there was no racing. No one ever knew where he was headed.

Shortly before 11:30 a.m., a slender young man with long blond hair, wearing faded jeans and a yellow shirt, ran up behind Carniglia and held out one arm with a small brown paper bag covering his hand and wrist. Gripping the butt of small handgun concealed in the bag, the man fired three shots through the end of the bag and into Carniglia's back, mortally wounding him. A nearby parking lot attendant saw the gunman run away going north, cut into a parking lot, and dash out of sight. Carniglia was taken by ambulance to the hospital, where he died a short time later.

Jack and I were on call that week. We were in the office when the report came in about the murder on Third Street. Despite its often-gruesome situations, the homicide detail was everything I had hoped for. I would not have traded jobs with anybody. I mean that. I know a lot of guys who can tell you exactly what they will be doing at twelve noon tomorrow. Being a policeman is never like that. You can be sitting somewhere having coffee one minute and be off on a hot call the next. That is the challenge. You get caught up in the chase, the hunt, the capture. You know you are doing something for society and, when you are an inspector, it is your case all the way. You are not going to make it unless you give it one hundred percent, like my dad always said.

For me, working homicide was like playing Major League Baseball. I was in the big leagues. Solving a case was like hitting a home run. It's a great feeling, but the next day you're in a new game, a new case, and the challenges are replicated time and again. Homicide work and the cops who are good at it are judged by their everyday performance. Great ballplayers are not judged by one game or one at-bat. It's a career of games and at-bats, the body of work, which determines your legacy.

Today, the so-called South of Market area where the Carniglia shooting had occurred is packed with hotels, apartments, shops, and a convention center. People scurry between work, lunch, downtown stores, the Giants' ballpark, and local transit stations. But back then, the area around Third Street near Folsom was a skid row, with more industrial buildings and warehouses than commercial offices, and sparsely populated. Shabbily dressed street people roamed the sidewalks and congregated under the nearby freeway overpasses.

When Jack and I arrived at the scene, two Southern Station patrolmen who had responded to the shooting, Alexander Barron and Thomas Burns, told us that the crime scene consisted of a small pool of blood and the crumpled newspaper on the sidewalk, with no other evidence to go on. No bullet shell casings were left behind, indicating the weapon used was a revolver. One witness we talked to was Anthony

Miller, who was in his third-floor apartment nearby when he heard the shots and went to his window overlooking the street. Miller said the shooter was still holding the revolver as he ran from the scene and into a parking lot. He stopped, Miller said, took off his shirt, tossed it on the ground, and changed into a green, short-sleeved shirt. Then he ran another half block to a white van parked on the street, got in, and drove away. We found the shirt where Miller said it was. It was tie-dyed yellow with a block chain pattern on the front. The van was too far away for Miller to make out the license plate, and white vans are a dime a dozen.

In addition to evidence, one of the first things we look for at the start of a murder investigation is motive, the reason behind the killing. Sometimes it's obvious, sometimes not. Money, revenge, jealousy, sex, drugs, pride—even sheer madness—are among the most common reasons. Beginning in the late sixties and early seventies, however, motive became harder to discern as more random killers struck for no apparent reason. There's always a reason, of course. The Paper Bag Killer's motive, we would find out, didn't fit anything we'd ever seen.

With nothing immediately pointing us toward a suspect, we turned to the victim for clues. Family and acquaintances told us that Lorenzo Carniglia lived on Texas Street in the blue-collar Potrero District, not far from where he was killed. Though retired, he continued to take small painting jobs. He had invested wisely in real estate over the years and owned eight residential buildings in the city. People who knew him seemed to respect him, characterizing him as honest but tough in his business dealings, and said he had an active social life. We considered the killer might be a disgruntled tenant or business associate, or a racetrack connection. We came up empty. All we had to go on was the discarded yellow T-shirt and a white van. Jack and I asked the local newspapers to publish a photo of the T-shirt with its distinctive artwork and a description of the killer, hoping someone might recognize it, or him. The papers did as we asked, as did local TV stations, but we did not get a single phone call from anyone about the shirt. Our leads had dried up. The case languished for weeks without a new development.

Nine weeks after the Third Street shooting, on December 20 at a few minutes before nine o'clock in the morning, Ara Kuznezow lingered outside the Lifeline Mission at Fifth and Folsom Streets, three blocks from the Carniglia shooting. He was fifty-four, heavy set, bald. His thick legs moved stiffly in the wind-whipped forty-degree weather, giving the appearance of a limp. He fished a newspaper out of a trash can on the sidewalk and pulled his shabby overcoat tighter around himself. The mission served a free breakfast with a sermon, and Kuznezow was waiting with a few other men for the mission to open. The Reverend Ralph Eichenbaum, who ran the mission, was sitting in his parked car nearby, contemplating his breakfast sermon. Kuznezow had been a regular at Lifeline for weeks.

From a gas station on the corner, a slender young man with long blond hair, wearing a hooded blue jacket and knit cap, approached Kuznezow. He carried what some witnesses later said looked like a broom in a large brown grocery store bag. He stopped three feet away, raised the bag, and pointed it at Kuznezow. It wasn't a broom in the bag. It was a shotgun. The young man fired once, the blast hitting Kuznezow in the face and head. He crumpled to the sidewalk, dead. The gunman turned and walked quickly back toward the service station, still holding the pump-action shotgun at his side. In an alley at the rear of the gas station sat a white Ford Econline van with its engine running. The young man jumped in the van and drove away.

Jack and I were in the office working on other cases that morning. We weren't on call. I was having my coffee and reading the *Chronicle*. Popular man-about-town columnist Herb Caen had a humorous item near the bottom of his column that caught my attention: "At the Hall of Justice, there has been a revival of 'The Bow Tie Boys,' as the homicide detail was known in the legendary days of Ahern, Cahill, and

Nelder," he wrote. "Inspectors Gus Coreris, Dave Toschi, Earl Sanders, Frank Falzon, and George Murray have blossomed out with big bow ties, despite denigrators who call them 'The Five Fruiters.'" Caen, and San Francisco's now inclusive society, were clearly not politically correct fifty years ago.

Because of the similarities to the Carniglia murder—the description of the young shooter, a lone male victim on the street, the white van, and the paper bag—Jack and I were assigned to investigate this new attack. We coined the name the Paper Bag Killer. You get so many cases that sometimes it's hard to distinguish one from the other. Jack and I will be talking across our desk about a case, and he might say, "What case are you talking about? The arson case? The Tenderloin murder? The Paper Bag Killer?" In this case, the media picked up on it when they asked us questions, and it stuck. The media, as everyone knows, loves to give killers or cases nicknames like that. It makes for great headlines, gets people talking, and sells more newspapers.

Although several people had witnessed the shotgun attack outside the Lifeline Mission, none of them got a good look at the killer's face. Only his general description and the white van matched up with Carniglia. And this time a shotgun was used rather than a handgun. But there were other similarities. Both shootings took place in broad daylight on a weekday morning on a public street in the same general neighborhood. Both victims were alike in age, body type, and the limp or skip-shuffle in their walk. Little was known about Kuznezow. No one around the mission knew his name. He had an accent but said little. In his pockets, he had eleven cents, a wallet with no money or identification, eyeglasses, a comb, a razor blade, a small pair of scissors, and a ballpoint pen.

After considerable legwork and phone calls, we found out that Kuznezow had been staying at a dodgy hotel at Sixth and Mission Streets, two blocks away. His room was bare and empty, save for a few pieces of clothes and a New York City welfare card. We learned from authorities in New York that he claimed to have a degree in architectural design but couldn't find work. It wasn't known when he had left New York or why he had decided to come to San Francisco. He had been in the city about six weeks, but we couldn't find anyone who knew him.

The paper bag recovered at the Kuznezow scene was a Safeway supermarket sack, like thousands of others given to shoppers at the big grocery chain's stores every day. It was made of glossy paper, and our crime lab technicians were able to get several good fingerprints from it. There were no immediate matches made, however, from the vast fingerprint file. The computerized fingerprint system did not yet exist. A fingerprint hand search was required, a painstaking hunt for a needle in a hundred haystacks. We couldn't find a match in the file. Unfortunately, we would find out much later that the killer's prints were indeed on file. Meanwhile, we focused our attention on the white van. One witness had seen the shooting in front of the mission, watched the gunman drive away, and tried to follow in his own car but lost him in traffic.

Like the Safeway bags, white delivery vans were ubiquitous in the area where both shootings occurred. We eventually ran checks on more than three hundred white vans and interviewed more than one hundred drivers. We kept coming up empty. Word had spread throughout the neighborhood that we were looking for a certain white van with a driver matching the shooter's description. Finally, on January 25, more than a month after Kuznezow was killed, a call came into the homicide office from a nervous-sounding man saying he might know something. "Hey, Falzon," said the inspector who answered the phone, "this guy's calling about the white van you're looking for." When I picked up the receiver, the caller told me a friend of his who drove a van had told him something we ought to hear. He was reluctant to continue over the phone and agreed to meet with us. At the meeting, the man told Jack, Lieutenant Charlie Ellis, and me that his friend, whom he called Bill, had shown him a couple of guns. Bill said he was trying to kill a man he believed was raping young women. Surprisingly, Bill said he had already killed the man several times, but that he kept coming back to life. Our informant, who described Bill as "a real good guy, straight and level," said Bill wanted him to help kill the man for keeps.

Jack and I were able to trace the van to a local delivery service. We talked to Bill's supervisor. He gave us Bill's full name—William P. Hanson—and confirmed the description we had. He said Bill was twenty-four and that he was a dependable employee who worked weekdays. Checking on Hanson's background, we learned of a strange case involving Hanson that had occurred a year before Lorenzo Carniglia was killed.

In December 1972, a man had been stabbed in the restroom of the Greyhound bus depot. The victim was a businessman in his fifties, stocky and bald, and walked with a limp. He was standing at a urinal when a man with a knife came up behind him, reached over his shoulder, and stabbed him in the chest. The assailant escaped. The victim, who was hospitalized for his wounds but recovered, never saw the face of his assailant. Six weeks later, that same businessman who'd been stabbed was walking along a busy downtown sidewalk when he saw a thin young man with long blond hair coming at him with a knife. After a brief skirmish, the attacker ran away, but two uniformed officers were able to catch him and place him under arrest. It was William P. Hanson. When the case came to trial, the victim was out of state on business and said he was too busy to come back to San Francisco to testify against someone who had simply menaced him with a knife. This victim had no idea that Hanson was the same man who had stabbed him in the bus station restroom. The charges against Hanson were dropped and he was freed.

But now that we had Hanson's fingerprints from the case, we matched them with the prints found on the paper bag at the Kuznezow murder. We secured a murder warrant for Hanson's arrest and another to search his residence. He lived with his parents on Lopez Avenue in the Forest Hill District, a wealthy residential neighborhood at the southern edge of the city. Hanson's father, Dr. Karl H. Hanson, was a prominent local psychiatrist. Dr. Hanson met us at the door. He was pleasant and showed us in. He could not believe us when we told him why we were there. He said his son wasn't home, but Jack heard sounds coming from an upstairs bedroom.

"It sounded to me like metal on metal, like a round was being chambered in a rifle," Jack recalls. "I told the father to go ahead of us up the stairs leading the way to where the sound had come from. At the landing, I told him to lie on the floor so he wouldn't be in the line of fire. Then I carefully opened the bedroom door. Bill Hanson was sitting on the bed. No gun was visible. He made no attempt to resist as we arrested him for the murder of Ara Kuznezow."

The case only got weirder from there. Hanson showed us to his closet, where we found a loaded shotgun, the weapon he used to kill Kuznezow. Hanson told us he had also killed Lorenzo Carniglia and that he had tossed the revolver he used in that murder into San Francisco Bay, but I found the gun under his pillow. Our search of the closet also turned up clothing that tied him to both shootings. Hanson's father told us he was unaware his son owned any guns and couldn't fathom that his son could kill anyone. Bill Hanson's boss, friends, and neighbors all had good things to say about him—good kid, no trouble, hard worker, no indication whatsoever that he would, or could, murder someone.

At the Hall of Justice, we read Hanson his rights and described the evidence against him. "I want to tell you everything," he said. As he talked, Hanson was being forthright and logical telling his story to Jack and me. After a somewhat lengthy admission and without warning, he abruptly changed his expression and personality in a heartbeat.

One minute he was a pleasant, smiling man trying to reasonably explain his killings, and the next he became something evil, something out of *The Exorcist* or like Anthony Perkins in *Psycho*. A complete change in character, voice, demeanor. He was so delusional that he'd gone to an altered state. His facial expression went from normal to cold, from a smile to a grimace. His eyes narrowed and his voice became guttural, almost like a zombie in a horror movie. I'd never seen anything like it in a suspect under questioning. For someone like me who considered himself a hardened inspector, the change in the suspect during our interrogation sent a chill up my spine. I could feel the hair on the back of my neck rising. I was face to face with a psychotic killer.

There was a man, Hanson told us, who was going around raping young women. He knew what the man looked like—stocky, bald, walked with a limp. The girls were innocent, Hanson said, and that's why he had to kill this man. He knew he had to kill and kill again until he finally put this man away. The man would always come back. No matter how many times he tried to kill him, this man would always be there again on the street. He said the man tried to disguise himself by wearing different-sized ears or a different nose or having sometimes thin fingers and sometimes fat fingers, but he could always tell because he could never change his height, his weight, the shape of his face and, in particular, his peculiar walk.

Hanson said during our questioning that as he drove around the South of Market area in the white van daily for work, he would notice beautiful women, dressed extremely well, wearing lipstick, rouge, and eye makeup. The closer he got to them, he could see they had tears in their eyes, and he *knew* that this balding man with the limp had raped them, too.

"I know at least four times I've tried to kill him," Hanson said. He described how he had stabbed this man in the bus station men's room and attacked him again on the sidewalk downtown six weeks later, and how he had shot him with a handgun on Third Street and with a shotgun on Fifth Street. "But he kept coming back," said Hanson, "so I had to kill him over and over again." It hit us like a bolt of lightning that the bus station victim and the businessman who was attacked with a knife on the sidewalk were one and the same. No one had ever connected the two attacks. When I contacted the businessman, he was astonished to learn the same assailant had attacked him both times. It had never occurred to him. Had he testified against Hanson about the street attack, the two subsequent murders might have been prevented.

Hanson's family hired Patrick Hallinan, the nationally recognized trial attorney and son of Vincent Hallinan, the founder of a powerful San Francisco family law firm known for handling complex and high-profile cases. According to Patrick Hallinan, Bill Hanson's former girlfriend had been raped in 1972. Bill somehow felt responsible, and he killed in the belief he was killing her rapist and saving other young women from a similar fate. "His imagination created a fantasy world in which he was a Don Quixote trying to rectify the wrongs that were done to a girl he loved," Hallinan said at the time.

In May 1974, Hanson was found not guilty by reason of insanity and sentenced to the Atascadero State Hospital for the Criminally Insane.

It was the latest heart-wrenching tragedy to befall the Hanson family. Dr. Hanson and his wife had previously lost a daughter in a car accident and another son to suicide. Dr. Hanson later came to see Jack Cleary and me in the homicide detail to thank us for the way we had handled the case and for treating his son fairly, considering the bizarre circumstances.

CHAPTER 10
CITY UNDER SIEGE

All hell was breaking loose in and around San Francisco in the early seventies. It was totally insane. The Bay Area, and especially the police, were under attack by radical extremists, counterculture terrorists, and just about anybody who had a beef with society or authority in any form. As a homicide inspector, I was not shocked by murder and death, but this period was murder and death on steroids. On the heels of the brutal Manson Family murders in Los Angeles in August 1969, the entire state exploded in homicides. From 1966 to 1969, the statewide number ran in the six hundred to one thousand range per year. From 1970 to 1975, the figure jumped to 2,200 per year. In San Francisco, there were twenty-seven murders in 1957—all of them solved. But by 1970 the total was 111, and that jumped to 129 in 1974 and 131 in 1975.

The rise of dissent against the Vietnam War and the emergence of violent groups like the Weather Underground, Black Panthers, Black Liberation Army, Symbionese Liberation Army, Zebra Death Angels, Tribal Thumb, and others coalesced into an explosion of violence that took many lives. Throw in serial murderers Juan Corona, Edmund Kemper, Herbert Mullin, and John Linley Frazier, who collectively killed fifty-one people from 1971 to 1973, and you get the idea.

It was a scary time to be a cop in San Francisco. We were vilified by these radical groups as "pigs" or "the man." We had targets on our backs every time we were out in the community. This surge in murders of cops, in San Francisco and nationwide, heightened the anxiety and fears with our families. These fears were most prevalent for our spouses and children. The daily newspaper headlines, followed by graphic television news reporting, only reinforced their worries. My wife, Donna, was concerned about me, but we kept the children in the dark about my work and the dangers of it as much as possible. We didn't talk about it at the dinner table. She watched the TV news at night and sometimes saw me on those programs, or in the morning newspaper, but she wasn't particularly inquisitive about it. She just didn't care to know the hellish part of my job. She trusted my good sense to survive in the jungle. I'd been threatened by suspects, parolees, and others over the years, and from time to time when I'd been threatened, Taraval Station cops made passing calls by my house in their patrol cars out of an abundance of caution.

The possibility of being killed in the line of duty comes with the job; I always accepted that. It was hard enough confronting and catching killers, let alone worrying about being ambushed at random for a political or racial reason. I really didn't think much about myself being killed in the line of duty. As a cop, that's not something you can control.

Nationwide, 2,260 officers died during the 1970s, the deadliest decade in U.S. law enforcement history. The worst year was 1974, when 275 officers across the country lost their lives. In just two years between January 1970 and January 1972, seven of my SFPD colleagues were killed in the line of duty. An eighth died in a helicopter crash. We lost four officers in 1970, beginning in the early morning hours on New Year's Day when patrolman Eric Zelms surprised two men during a burglary in the Mission District and was shot by one of them. A month later, a bomb at Park Police Station killed Sergeant Brian McDonnell and injured nine others. In June, Patrolman Richard Radetich was shot to death in his parked squad car while writing a ticket in Hayes Valley. A gunman walked up and fired three shots from a .38-caliber revolver through the driver's side window. Radetich died fifteen hours later.

"It was a really cowardly act of terrorism," former Chief Tony Ribera told the *San Francisco Chronicle* in a 2007 article about Radetich and the violent attacks against police. "He was an up-and-coming officer with a bright future ahead of him." Ribera said the string of police murders "really devastated the officers in our department. His assassination and the other officers who were assassinated in those years really hurt us."

When a cop in our department was killed in the line of duty, it was all hands on deck to do whatever was needed to solve the case. We had as many resources as we needed or wanted to bring the suspect to justice. It was like a death in your own family. At the funerals, I always thought, this could be *my* wife and kids grieving. When your fellow cops are killed, especially just because they're cops, you suddenly become part of the hunted group, a target. It becomes personal. And that made the job even harder. But I never thought of leaving. This was the job I knew I was made for. This was the ultimate career for me. One day one of the men in our homicide detail told the room full of inspectors, "The only way Falzon is ever leaving homicide is when they carry him out in a box." I reflected about that remark often over the years, always promising myself that I would leave on my own terms.

The carnage wasn't limited to the city. In August 1970, an attempt by seventeen-year-old Jonathan Jackson to free prison inmates, including his older brother, George, by kidnapping a judge at the Marin County Courthouse north of San Francisco ended in a parking lot shootout that left the judge, Jonathan Jackson, and two others dead.

In October 1971, SFPD Sergeant Harold Hamilton was gunned down as he responded to a bank robbery in the Richmond District. Days later a nail-filled bomb was set off at Sergeant Hamilton's funeral outside St. Brendan's Church. Fortunately, no one was hurt.

In the summer of 1971, motorcycle patrolman Arthur O'Guinn was shot to death at a routine traffic stop. He had stopped a car in the Bayview carrying two men, Robert White Jr. and Robert Hawkins, for a traffic violation. Art O'Guinn was a member of my class at the academy, one of six African Americans in our class of twenty-six recruits. He was a friendly guy with a smile and a pleasant greeting for all. I was still new to homicide, and this murder was one of my first cases. I was among a small group selected to join the hunt for O'Guinn's killers. Leading the group were two senior inspectors, Rotea Gilford and Sterling Weatherspoon. In a search of one of the suspects' homes, I found the murder weapon under a large pile of clean clothes on the floor of a bedroom closet. White and Hawkins were convicted in separate trials. White was sentenced to ten years to life in prison. But his life of crime didn't end there. In 1980, two years after he was paroled, and while free on bail from robbing a pharmacy, he was convicted for burglarizing a Wells Fargo bank branch. He was sent back to prison for another twelve years.

Just a month after O'Guinn's murder, on August 29, 1971, Sergeant John Young was killed by a shotgun blast during an assault by three Black Liberation Army gunmen on Ingleside Police Station. In January 1972, a despondent and unemployed man with a rifle opened fire from his window on two officers walking their beat, killing Sergeant Code Beverly. In all, there were more than two hundred murders in San Francisco in 1970 and 1971.

We especially had our hands full in the homicide detail over the winter of 1973 and 1974, when a group of extremist Black Muslims, who called themselves Death Angels, targeted white people at random to rise within their organization. These so-called Zebra attacks—named for the "Z" radio channel used in police communications about them—resulted in the murder of fifteen people in a series of random attacks on the streets of San Francisco. These were hate crimes. There is no other way to describe them.

A veteran homicide team, Gus Coreris and John Fotinos, was assigned to lead the investigation into the Zebra murders. Gus and John had been partners for many years and were the best team for the assignment. They worked so well together, like bacon and eggs or bread and butter. Throughout the department they were known affectionately as The Greeks. Added to the investigation team were two Black inspectors, Rotea Gilford and Earl Sanders. As the number of cases escalated and the volume of leads needing follow up increased, two burglary inspectors, Carl Klotz and Jeff Brosch, were brought in and assigned to help The Greeks, and rising star Herman Clark was reassigned from the robbery detail to work with Gilford and Sanders. Sanders, known for his stylish attire and ever-present fedora, later served as the city's first African American chief of police from 2002 until his retirement a year later. He and co-author Bennett Cohen published a book in 2011, *The Zebra Murders: A Season of Killing, Racial Madness, and Civil Rights.*

Jack Cleary and I got involved in one of the Zebra murders in a very direct and unexpected way. One night we happened upon what turned out to be the second Zebra attack moments after it happened.

It was just after 9:00 p.m. on October 30, 1973. Jack and I were out working on a case. We were driving along Haight Street and approaching Laguna Street. It was a warm night. We had our windows rolled down. Suddenly we both heard four loud popping noises from very close by. "That sounded like gun shots," Jack said. "Absolutely," I agreed. Jack drove around the corner toward where the sounds had come from. We saw a Ford Mustang parked in the driveway leading to the University of California Extension campus on Hermann Street. The passenger door was open, and a young woman was collapsed across the seat, falling halfway out of the passenger side of the car.

As I radioed in our location, Jack jumped out, went over to the car, crouched down, and cradled the woman's head in his lap as she slumped out of the vehicle. I grabbed our car radio microphone and put out a 406—officer needs assistance—call. This is the most urgent call an officer can make. I asked communications to send an ambulance Code 3—red light and siren—saying that a woman had been shot. I also reported that the suspect was still in the immediate area.

Frances Rose, twenty-eight, had been shot four times with a .22-caliber automatic, in the right side of her chest and neck and twice in the right side of her face. "She was bleeding from wounds to her face and neck but was still alive," Jack recalls. "She looked up at me but didn't say anything. She died right there in my arms."

A witness who lived in an apartment across the street had heard the shots and looked out to see the gunman walking away from the car. She described him as a Black man, about twenty-five years old, five feet, ten or eleven inches tall, with a muscular build and wearing a navy-blue watch cap, light-colored pants, an olive-green jacket, and gloves.

Within two minutes, the area was swarming with black-and-white police cars. Park Station patrol officers Tom O'Connell and Bill Kelly spotted a man matching the gunman's description walking at Waller and Steiner Streets, six blocks from the scene, and stopped him. He had discarded the cap and jacket and he was sweating profusely. The officers searched him and found a loaded .22-caliber automatic. They brought the suspect, Jessie Lee Cooks, twenty-eight, back to the crime scene. I took custody of him there, placed him in the back of our car, and took him to the Hall of Justice for questioning.

Once back at the Homicide Bureau, we found seventeen .22-caliber bullets in one of his pants pockets. I advised him of his rights and asked if he wanted to make a statement. Cooks told me he had been walking along the street when a woman pulled up in her car and offered him a ride. (A witness later told us that Cooks had blocked the car in the driveway and demanded a ride.) He got into the car, he said, but immediately became angry when she called him a "n----er." That made no sense at all to me. Why would a young woman offer someone a ride and then call him the n-word? It really didn't matter; he was providing me with a confession and trying to explain his reasoning for killing this young female. Cooks said, "She gave me no other choice" but to shoot her three, "possibly four" times. He told us where he shed his jacket and hat. Officers found them, and they matched the witness's description.

Unknown to us then, Cooks had participated in the first Zebra murder ten days before killing Frances Rose. He and two other men, Larry Green and Anthony Harris, were prowling the streets in a white van looking for white victims to kill. First, they unsuccessfully tried to abduct three young people, ages eleven to fifteen, who managed to get away. Later that same night, October 20, the trio came upon a young married couple, Richard and Quita Hague, out for an evening stroll, and forced them into the van at gunpoint. They drove the Hagues to a remote location, beat Richard with a lug wrench, then hacked his wife in the throat with a machete, killing her. They then drove off, leaving the Hagues for dead. Richard survived.

Again, we had no indication that Jessie Lee Cooks had been involved in the Hague murder when we interrogated him for shooting Frances Rose. Cooks had a record for bank robbery and other crimes and had served time in federal prison and at San Quentin, where he met Harris and other Death Angels. He pled guilty to the Rose murder in December and received a life sentence.

The capture and interrogation of Cooks, along with the cooperation of Anthony Harris, who was given immunity from prosecution, would become keys to breaking the Zebra case, although building an airtight prosecution in a very complex case took several more months. Meanwhile, thirteen more people were killed. The attacks terrorized the city with their randomness and level of violence. One Zebra victim who was shot and survived was future San Francisco Mayor Art Agnos. As he left a community meeting on Potrero Hill on December 13, a man walked up and shot him twice in the chest at point-blank range. Fifteen years later, Agnos succeeded Dianne Feinstein as mayor.

On May 1, 1974, police arrested seven Black men in connection with the string of killings. Among them, curiously, was a former high school classmate and football teammate of mine, Thomas Manney. In fact, Tom had gone to St. Michael's Grammar School with my wife, Donna, and my cousin, Kathy Fox. Tom was a backup halfback and kick returner on our city championship St. Ignatius football team in 1958. He went on to be an offensive star for three straight San Francisco State College Western Conference Championship teams and was drafted by the Pittsburgh Steelers in 1963. He signed with them as a free agent in early 1964 but was cut before he played any games with them. "They cut me because I'm a n----er," he told me at the time. "C'mon, Tommy, that can't be true," I said. In my view, although I didn't say it to him, at five foot eleven, 190 pounds, Tom was simply not big enough or fast enough to play in the NFL.

At the time of the Zebra arrests, Manney was the manager of the Black Self-Help Moving and Storage Company, where many of the Zebra killers met and worked. He allegedly provided transportation and guns for several of the Zebra attacks. Due to a lack of evidence, however, Tom Manney and two other suspects were released.

Four men were eventually convicted and given life terms. Jessie Lee Cooks, who received a second life sentence for the Quita Hague murder, died in prison in 2021 at the age of seventy-six. J. C. X. Simon and Manuel Moore predeceased him in prison. The fourth, Larry C. Green, remains incarcerated.

Homicide Inspectors and Assistant District Attorneys
who worked on the Zebra murders

First row, seated, L-R: John Fotinos, Gus Coreris, Steve Maxoutopoulis

Second row, L-R: Frank Falzon, Ed Erdelatz, Tim Simmons,
Jack Cleary, Gerhard Winkler, Lt. Charles Ellis, Asst. DA
Doug Munson, Carl Klotz, Diarmuid Philpott

Third row, L-R: Al Podesta, Jeff Brosch, Asst. DA Jim Lassart, George
Huegle, Earl Sanders, Ron Schneider, Gene Fogarty, Bill Armstrong

Back row, L-R: Dave Toschi, Cadet Mike Gonzalez,
Asst. DAs Bob Podesta and Bob Dondero

CHAPTER 11
CHINATOWN GANG HIT

On the evening of Sunday, June 3, 1973, I was taking advantage of the extra daylight to paint the exterior of my house on Wawona Avenue in the Outer Sunset District. Helping me were Mike Hughes and his wife, Terri. Mike was a close buddy who for six years was the assistant coach for my St. Gabriel's Catholic Youth Organization basketball team that included my son, Dan, and my partner Jack Cleary's boy, Tom.

At 7:30 p.m., my wife, Donna, called out from the front porch. "Frank, the Operations Center is on the phone for you." It was my last day of a relatively quiet week on call. There'd only been one other murder. A young woman, Rosa Vasquez, had been raped and smothered to death near the Conservatory of Flowers in Golden Gate Park.

I went into the garage and picked up the downstairs receiver.

"This is Inspector Falzon, headquarters. What do you have?"

"We have a shooting at Pacific and Grant in Chinatown," replied the dispatcher. "The victim is lying on the sidewalk. It appears to be gang related."

"Is he deceased?"

"No, Inspector."

The dispatcher was either new on the job or had forgotten an important detail.

"Homicide doesn't respond to attempted murders or aggravated assaults," I reminded him. "Tell the General Work detail to send their on-call team. You can call me back if the victim dies."

I went outside and climbed back up the ladder with my paint roller. It wasn't long before Operations called again to say the victim had expired. Jack had taken the day off to watch his daughter in her high school play, so Inspector Ron Schneider was assigned to fill in for him. Ron met me in Chinatown at the scene of the shooting near the Ping Yuen housing project, a multi-building complex with more than four hundred apartments. Ping Yuen translates to "Tranquil Gardens."

Seeing the dead man's body lying there on the sidewalk, we couldn't possibly know then that this case would stretch over the next ten years, involving a prison murder, a prolonged court battle, the dramatic reversal of a wrongful conviction, and a pot-smoking celebrity defense attorney who became the inspiration for a Hollywood movie loosely based on his character and the case.

The murder victim was identified as Yip Yee Tak, also known variously as Yip Yang or Dr. Ysung Yang. I don't recall which of those, if any, was his given name. At age thirty-two, he was an advisor to the Wah Ching youth gang. The Wah Ching were foreign-born gang members who had an ongoing feud with a rival gang, the Joe Boys, whose members had been born in the United States, most in San Francisco. Things had been heating up in Chinatown. At the time, it was the thirteenth gang-related killing in a three-year span. Within days, Mayor Joseph Alioto would urge Police Chief Donald Scott to crack down on youth gang violence in Chinatown.

Witnesses said the gunman walked up behind Tak, shot him three times, and then ran east on Pacific Avenue. Patrol officers had found three eyewitnesses to the shooting and two other witnesses who had seen a man fleeing the scene. All were asked to wait for us to arrive. One of the eyewitnesses was Andy Mill, a twenty-year-old professional downhill ski racer who would compete in two future Olympics and who later married tennis star Chris Evert. The witnesses all described the shooter as a clean-shaven Asian male between five feet six inches and five feet ten inches tall and weighing between 145 and 160 pounds.

One witness told uniformed officers that the shooter had discarded a gun in Beckett Alley around the corner from where Tak was shot. The officers were able to locate the weapon, a snub-nosed, five-shot, .38 Special revolver. The cylinder was empty. The gun had been stolen a few weeks earlier from a security guard at the Sun Sing Theater on Grant Avenue by seven Asian youths wearing masks. We had the shooting witnesses transported downtown to view mugshots. They were separated during the viewing, and each one individually identified a man named Chol Soo Lee from a mug book with thousands of photos of young Asian men. Two were positive identifications and one was tentative.

Meanwhile, we learned that the day before Tak was killed, police had responded to reports of gunfire in Chol Soo Lee's nearby apartment on Broadway. Lee, twenty years old, was a Korean American immigrant who had a prior history of juvenile arrests for burglary and narcotics possession. He claimed he had accidentally discharged a weapon in the room while cleaning it. Officers removed a bullet from a wall facing the window. It was a .38 caliber.

Based on the eyewitnesses' identification, Lee was arrested at 11:00 p.m. on June 7 as he returned to his apartment. He was carrying a Colt Python .357 revolver at the time and had forty-one rounds of .38-caliber ammunition in his pocket. "Go ahead and kill me," he told the arresting officer. "I would be better off." On the ride to the Hall of Justice, he said, "You guys are always picking me up. Last time it was robbery. This time it's murder. And I was just going home [to Korea] tomorrow."

Jack Cleary joined me on the case when he returned to the office after his day off. When Lee was brought into the homicide detail, we advised him of his Miranda rights before questioning him. In a subsequent live lineup on June 11, three of the five witnesses from the night of the shooting picked Lee as the killer. A few days later, a ballistics report from our crime lab tied the bullet recovered from Lee's apartment to the weapon used in the Tak shooting.

Eyewitnesses, the murder weapon, ballistics evidence—it was all there. We had a solid case, and Chol Soo Lee was held in the city jail for the murder of Yip Yee Tak. Public Defender Clifford Gould was appointed to represent him. Nine months later, after a seesaw battle over where to hold the trial, the San Francisco Superior Court prevailed in ordering a change of venue to Sacramento. Gould withdrew at that point, and a Sacramento public defender, Hamilton Hintz, took over as Lee's counsel.

Owing to the venue maneuverings and related procedural delays, the murder trial of Chol Soo Lee didn't begin until June 3, 1974, exactly one year to the day after the killing of Yip Yee Tak. Assistant District Attorney Jim Lassart and I went up to Sacramento and took rooms at the Mansion Hotel for the duration of the two-week trial. We presented what we believed was a strong case for a first-degree murder conviction. The jury agreed and convicted Lee on June 19, 1974. He was sentenced to life in prison and sent to the Deuel Vocational Institution in Tracy.

Three years later, prison officials classified Chol Soo Lee as a member of Nuestra Familia, a Latino prison gang. When he appealed, they withdrew their evaluation and cleared him of any gang affiliation. But suspicions among white inmates in a rival gang about his connection to Nuestra Familia lingered. On October 8 that year, Lee stabbed to death another inmate, Morrison Needham, during an altercation in the prison yard. Lee claimed he acted in self-defense when Needham, a member of the white supremacist Aryan Brotherhood gang, attacked him. This killing would send Chol Soo Lee to death row.

In early 1978, *Sacramento Union* reporter K. W. Lee took interest in Lee's case and began writing articles about him. In an interview years later, K. W. Lee said what piqued his interest in the first place was that he had a nephew named Chol Soo Lee, an astonishing coincidence. K. W. Lee's coverage of the case raised questions about the Chinatown murder and inspired several people in the Sacramento area and San Francisco to form the Chol Soo Lee Defense Committee. Within months, the committee filed a petition for a writ of *habeas corpus* with the Sacramento County Superior Court, alleging that key evidence had been withheld during the trial.

At the time, the right of "reverse discovery" did not exist for the prosecution in such hearings, meaning we were unable to know what new evidence the defense was planning to present at this appeal. When the hearing began in October 1978 before Judge Lawrence K. Karlton, Jim Lassart and I were surprised to see that a new eyewitness, Steve Morris, had come forward five years after the murder of Yip Yee Tak. The defense produced a document written by our colleague, Homicide Inspector Gus Coreris, who had taken a phone call from Morris the day following Tak's murder. Morris testified that he had called the homicide detail the day after the Tak killing to say he had been at the murder scene. He told Gus that he did not see the shooting take place, but saw the shooter run away. His physical description of the gunman differed substantially from that of Chol Soo Lee. Morris said Chol Soo Lee was not the man he saw. Inspector Coreris had specifically jotted "not an eyewitness" in the margin of the yellow legal pad with his handwritten notes and underlined it for emphasis. For that very reason, I never brought Morris in to view any photos or to participate in the live suspect lineup. We had several other eyewitnesses who identified Chol Soo Lee in both instances. Since he wasn't an eyewitness, Morris wouldn't have added anything.

Prior to ruling on this, Judge Karlton called me back into his chambers. "I want you to know that I have a dilemma here, Inspector Falzon," he said. "Your investigation is not in question. You did nothing wrong. But Inspector Coreris may have made a mistake. If you had followed up with Mr. Morris, you might not have charged Mr. Lee. I'm going to grant the appeal for a new trial."

As difficult as this was for me and my partner as the lead investigators, we could not disagree with the legal argument that Lee was no longer the killer beyond a reasonable doubt. That was incredibly frustrating, but we accepted the result. Jim Lassart and I returned to San Francisco with our tails between our legs, chagrined about having to retry a ten-year-old case and faced with questions about who this Steven Morris was. My subsequent investigation of Morris prior to the new trial uncovered that he suffered from a mental disorder, was dying of AIDS, and had experience with bestiality. All of this served to discredit him as a convincing witness.

At the same time this hearing was underway, Chol Soo Lee's murder trial for the prison yard killing of Morrison Needham had started in San Joaquin County Superior Court. In March 1979, a jury there convicted Chol Soo Lee of first-degree murder in Needham's death. The judge imposed the death sentence, and Lee was transferred to San Quentin State Prison's death row to await execution.

By now, the continuing coverage by journalist K. W. Lee, together with efforts by the Chol Soo Lee Defense Committee, increased the drumbeat of public interest in Lee's case and raised a hundred thousand dollars through rallies and fund drives. The money was used in part to hire new defense lawyers, J. Tony Serra and Stuart Hanlon.

The retrial began in August 1982, nearly ten years after the murder of Yip Yee Tak in June of 1973. Not surprisingly, the defense did not call Steven Morris as a witness, the very person they had used to win their appeal. Most likely the defense team learned how vulnerable Morris would be on the stand under cross examination by the prosecutor. However, the defense did produce an independent criminologist who testified that the original ballistics report tying the bullet in Lee's apartment to the murder weapon was flawed. Upon review, our lab had to recant its original finding. The defense did not produce a witness who could provide an alibi for Chol Soo Lee's whereabouts the night of the murder, or any other evidence proving he did not pull the trigger. If there was any compelling evidence whatsoever that Chol Soo Lee did not kill Yip Yee Tak, I would be the first to rise in defense of his acquittal. But there wasn't.

Tony Serra began his closing argument with a gambit that stunned me. He stood up, paced around the room a bit, then said to the jury, "Ladies and gentlemen, take a close look at this man."

I expected him to point to Chol Soo Lee, his client, and say something about his innocence. Instead, he pointed his finger directly at me.

"Take a good close look at *this* man sitting here. Look at his belt buckle."

What? Where is he going with this? I wondered. The belt buckle I was wearing was a registration gift I'd received at a recent annual conference of the California Homicide Investigators Association at the Silver Legacy Hotel in Reno. More than two hundred cops attending the conference had received the buckle. The center of the oval buckle was emblazoned with the number "187," the California Penal Code section for murder.

"You know what that stands for?" Serra said, his voice growing louder. "Murder! It stands for murder! This man is a walking indictment for you, for me, and for everyone else! He's so proud of who he is that he wears it on his belt buckle!"

I was staggered. *What the hell is he doing? He's defending a client in a murder case, and he chooses to focus his attack on my belt buckle? Give me a break. You don't have a defense for your client, so you argue to the jury about my belt buckle? Absolutely crazy.*

Later, outside in the hallway, Serra apologized for his dramatics. He was known for his boisterous and outlandish courtroom antics, but this was, in my opinion, a personal attack on my character and needlessly over the top. He told me he had taken drama courses at Stanford University and that he always wanted to be an actor. And now he was trying to convince me he meant no harm and wanted to be my friend. He elaborated how he had played football at Stanford and that his law partner was Jasper Monti, a good friend of mine. Jasper was my high school classmate at St. Ignatius and was the starting tight end on our

1958 city championship football team. Serra was always a smart and dedicated lawyer, and I respected him for his vigorous defense of his clients. But my belt buckle? C'mon.

I'll never know what part, if any, that sideshow played in the jury's ultimate decision on September 3, 1982, to acquit Chol Soo Lee of the murder of Yip Yee Tak. But it's worth noting that the jury foreman joined the Chol Soo Lee Defense Committee after the trial. The acquittal was hailed as a great victory in the Asian community, and I tip my hat to Serra and his legal team. And to K. W. Lee for his relentless work on Chol Soo Lee's behalf that included more than 150 articles. The *Bee* submitted Lee's work on the case for Pulitzer Prize consideration. K. W. Lee was the real true believer in this long saga.

A few months later, California's Third District Court of Appeal nullified Chol Soo Lee's death sentence in the prison murder case, citing an error in the trial judge's instructions to the jury and for allowing hearsay testimony in the death penalty phase of the trial.

In March 1983, San Joaquin County Superior Court Judge Peter Saiers ordered Lee released on bail. Five months later, Lee accepted a plea bargain to a lesser charge of second-degree murder in exchange for time served, and he was released from San Quentin.

Chol Soo Lee, center, convicted in two separate murder trials, becomes a free man. Photo: Documentary.org

It didn't surprise me that his life of crime wasn't over. Seven years later, he went back to prison for eighteen months on a drug possession charge. Back on the street, Lee had hooked up with Peter Chong, identified by police in court filings as the Northern California leader of the Wo Hop To Triad, a Chinese organized crime group. Chong's top lieutenant was Raymond "Shrimp Boy" Chow, another Chinese gang figure. In 1992, Chong hired Chol Soo Lee to burn down a family member's house in the Sunset District for the insurance money while Chong was in Lake Tahoe. Once inside the home, Lee doused the place with a flammable liquid. When he entered the kitchen and squirted the stove with the highly flammable fuel, the pilot light ignited the stream and sent it back to the gas can, which exploded and turned Lee into a human fireball. He ran screaming from the house into the street, where neighbors ran out with blankets to snuff out the flames.

Lee ended up at the St. Francis Hospital burn center near death with third-degree burns over 90 percent of his body. He survived but was horribly disfigured. He later pleaded guilty to the arson charge and was given probation in return for his testimony against Peter Chong in a federal racketeering case.

Chol Soo Lee lived another twenty-two years after the arson incident, many of them under different names as part of an FBI witness protection program. He died in 2014 at the age of sixty-two.

It is sad that this young Korean ended up being exploited by the very people with whom he had aligned himself. Society gave him multiple opportunities to turn himself around, but the lure of easy money in the criminal world was always there, and he was powerless to resist it.

The Chol Soo Lee case became the inspiration for the acclaimed 1989 film *True Believer*, starring James Woods as a fictional lawyer based on J. Tony Serra.

Hollywood has long had a fascination with San Francisco's killers and the police who pursue them, both real and imagined. From *The Streets of San Francisco* to *Nash Bridges* and *Bullitt* to *Zodiac*, our city, our murders, our department, and our homicide inspectors have given films and TV shows a steady trove of material that keeps us on the national stage.

My late former partner, Homicide Inspector Dave Toschi, was the inspiration for actor Steve McQueen's portrayal of Lieutenant Frank Bullitt in 1968, complete with Dave's signature upside down, quick-draw shoulder holster and tan trench coat. Actor Mark Ruffalo, playing the role of Toschi in David Fincher's 2007 film *Zodiac,* added Dave's trademark bow ties and his habit of munching on Animal Crackers. As for Clint Eastwood's antihero rogue Inspector "Dirty Harry" Callahan, well, let's just say Callahan was a rule-bender that only fiction would allow. But I always appreciated his integrity and willingness in high-profile cases to stand up to command staff interference when attempting to appease City Hall politicians. Whenever he did, it made my day.

I've had my own experience with the entertainment industry. In 2006, I served as a technical advisor on the film *Milk* about the assassination of San Francisco Supervisor Harvey Milk. I was the inspector in charge of the City Hall murders case, and their killer, Supervisor Dan White, was a former fellow cop and childhood friend of mine. I detail the events of that day and their aftermath later in the book. Actor Josh Brolin, who played Dan White, consulted with me. I have been interviewed for many true crime documentaries.

In 1972, my partner, Inspector Jack Cleary, and I became close to the two lead actors during the making of the film *The Laughing Policeman.* It starred Bruce Dern and Walter Matthau as SFPD homicide inspectors. Hard to tell from the title, but the story opens with a mass shooting on a city bus. One of the victims is Matthau's partner. Our relationship with Matthau and Dern enabled Jack and me to sit in the back of the bus during that scene. We were fascinated by Hollywood's staging. All the passengers on the bus had been outfitted in clothing wired with small blasting caps. When the shooting started, a technician sitting in the back of the bus flipped switches that set off the blasting caps. The charges blew holes outward from the body. In real life, the exact opposite occurs. Bullets create a small entry hole going into the body and a larger blowout hole exiting the body.

Matthau and Dern asked us to be present for the filming of other dramatic, violent action scenes. During our time together, Bruce Dern liked one story I shared so much that he asked director Stuart Rosenberg to add it to the script, which he did. When I was working for the Vice Crimes detail, I had told Dern, we kept tabs on an illegal gambling den in the tawdry Tenderloin District. One evening when we walked in, Dino the proprietor assured me the men were only playing cards for fun using wooden match sticks. No money was involved, Dino said. I looked at the table. Some men had big piles of matches while others had very few. I asked the players if it was true about the matches, and they all swore the game was for fun only. With that, I reached in and scooped up everyone's match sticks. "Let's be fair and split these matches more equally," I said as I divvied them up around the table. Some guys in the game started laughing but others were pissed off. I thought it was funny. For a moment there, I was the laughing policeman.

The *True Believer* producers imagined the film as the inspired story of a falsely accused murder suspect in a Chinatown gang hit being exonerated by his long-haired, pot-smoking hipster lawyer, San Francisco's renowned J. Tony Serra, a so-called "true believer" in his client's innocence. During the production, the script soon stretched so far from the actual story that Assistant District Attorney Jim Lassart, Coroner Boyd Stephens, and I threatened to sue for defamation. In the face of that, the filmmakers changed the setting from San Francisco to New York City and gave all the principals fictitious names. The movie was not factual at all. It was ridiculous. The homicide cops were corrupt, willfully documenting factious evidence with the collaboration of the district attorney and the coroner, all to convict an innocent man. Even Serra himself told the *San Francisco Chronicle* in 2014 that by the time the film was released, not a single frame was believable. Serra said he'd been promised a hundred thousand dollars fee for his story, but that disappeared once the producers backed away from the true characters and locale in favor of a fictitious storyline.

The movie did not mention anything about Lee's life after prison—a string of arrests for narcotics possession for sale and the botched arson-for-hire. Lee was hardly an innocent man.

Cast and crew of the Hollywood film, "The Laughing Policeman"
with our homicide inspectors, 1972.

Back row, L-R: Frank Falzon, Al Podesta, Gus Coreris, Jack Cleary,
Ron Schneider, Ed Erdelatz, Hobart Nelson, John McKenna,
Steve Moxoutopoulis, Frank McCoy, Dave Toschi,
actor Lou Gossett Jr. Bill Armstrong, Earl Sanders

Front row: actor Anthony Zerbe, unidentified, director Stu Rosenberg,
Homicide Lieutenant Charles Ellis, actor Bruce Dern,
actor Walter Matthau, Inspector Rotea Guilford

CHAPTER 12
NIGHTMARE ON POTRERO HILL

Barbaric. Atrocious. Savage. Horrendous.

These are the words used when people talk about what happened at Frank and Annette Carlson's Potrero Hill home on the night of April 18, 1974.

None is adequate. Not even using them all together. Truly, there are no words to describe it. I know I've said it before, as a homicide inspector you never know what you're walking into at a crime scene. But this was beyond the worst.

Amid all the public fears in early 1974 about the random Zebra murders, the Zodiac killer, the kidnapping of Patricia Hearst, underground extremists, radical bombers, and every other senseless crime San Franciscans were trying to cope with, this one took center stage. Many still rank it among the worst crimes in San Francisco history.

Every San Franciscan knows April 18 as the anniversary of the Great Earthquake and Fire of 1906. But the evil depravity of this terrible crime on that historic date in 1974 shook the Bay Area almost as hard and drove people into a new state of dread and revulsion.

Donna and I were sound asleep when the phone rang. It was 3:20 a.m. I reached over and grabbed the receiver.

"Hello?"

"Inspector Falzon, please," said the caller. "Operations Center calling."

"This is Inspector Falzon," I answered.

"We have patrol units on the scene of a 187-451 [homicide-arson] at 1301 Kansas Street. We've notified Inspector Cleary. He said to tell you he will pick you up shortly."

"Ten-four, headquarters," I replied. I hung up and went into the bathroom. I splashed cold water on my face, brushed my teeth, and got dressed quickly. On weeks like this when I was on call, I always had a suit of clothes prepared for middle-of-the night calls. I was ready in ten minutes. I was still a bit groggy as my partner Jack drove up. I remember it was a cool, clear night, stars twinkling in the darkness. We arrived at the scene fifteen minutes later, around 4:00 a.m.

Outside the two-story, yellow Victorian house, fire engine crews were picking up hoses and sweeping debris to the curb. Three black-and-white patrol cars were parked nearby as officers secured the scene from onlookers. Responding officers John Muckle, Louis Bacciocco, and Mark Potter briefed us on what they had observed upon arriving at the scene. The upper story was in flames. Fire fighters and witnesses had removed a young woman from the burning roof. The body of a man was found tied to a chair lying on its side, partially beneath the dining room table. He was bleeding from multiple head wounds. He'd been identified as Frank Carlson, twenty-five. The female victim, Carlson's wife, Annette, had been taken to Mission Emergency Hospital, adjacent to San Francisco General Hospital.

A strong odor of smoke and smoldering wood greeted Jack and me as we entered the house. There were burnt embers and ashes underfoot, and my shoes splashed in the water from fire hoses that had soaked the carpet.

The second I walked into the dining room, I saw Frank Carlson on the floor. His head had been so severely bashed in that it looked scarcely human. Around him in the room we found a blood-spattered broken claw hammer, a three-inch-thick chopping block with a bloody corner broken off, a shattered wine jug that had contained dozens of pennies, nickels, dimes, and quarters now strewn about the room, and a house plant in a broken pot. All these items, we would soon learn, had been used to bludgeon Carlson to death. A bloody shoeprint, likely made by some type of boot, was discernible in the carpet. The coroner had been notified and was on the way, the officers told us. The crime lab and photo unit had been contacted and were also enroute to the scene.

The fire had originated upstairs in the master bedroom, we were told. The walls, the furniture, clothing, and personal items in the room were all charred. A small, child-size rocking chair lay in pieces in one corner. Firefighters had piled debris in the middle of the room, which reeked of smoke.

"Holy Christ," Jack said. "We're going to be here for a week."

"No sense for both of us to stay here," I said to Jack after examining the scene for a while and talking to the officers and the fire captain. "I'm going over to the hospital to see if the woman can tell us anything." He agreed. I drove over to Mission Emergency Hospital just a few blocks away and parked the radio car in front. What happened there is something I will never forget as long as I live.

I walked into the emergency room and identified myself. Three nurses, all of them wide-eyed and visibly shaken, surrounded me.

"You have to catch this animal!" cried one. "Get that bastard off the street before he can do this to someone else!" plead another. At this point I still didn't know exactly what had happened at the house, and I wasn't sure what they were talking about. A doctor dressed in green scrubs came out from behind a door to greet me. "Hello, Doctor," I said. "I'm Inspector Falzon from the police department. I'm here to see Mrs. Carlson."

"She's still alive," the doctor said somberly. "I don't expect her to live. She wants to talk to you."

I couldn't believe this. *The woman is in critical shape, and she wants to talk to the police?* In all my years in police work, this just doesn't happen. Doctors have their job and cops have theirs, but never together like this, especially not inside the intensive care unit. I'm usually told to wait for doctors to finish what they're doing before I can talk to a victim.

"You can't go in until we prepare you," the doctor said. He guided me to a washing station to scrub my hands and arms. I was given a surgical cloth gown, a face mask, rubber gloves, and a cap to wear. With my notepad and pen, I walked into the room where twenty-four-year-old Annette Carlson was lying on a surgical gurney with two doctors tending to her. They were suturing lacerations on her head. Her face was badly bruised and swollen. Her head had been shaved and her face looked like a disfigured pumpkin, lumpy all over. The skin on her scalp was torn away, and her skull looked like a peeled orange covered in a spongy pith.

"Hello, Annette," I said softly. "I'm Inspector Falzon from the police department." I didn't say homicide detail right away because I wasn't sure how much she knew about her husband. "Can you talk?"

"Yes," she answered.

For the next several minutes, she made it very clear that despite her injuries, even as she was fighting for her life, she wanted me to know everything. In grunts, whispers, and halting words, she told me a nightmare story.

"I was asleep in bed upstairs," she began. "My husband was downstairs. Sometime between eleven and eleven-thirty, I woke up, and this man was standing next to the bed with his hand over my nose and mouth. I couldn't breathe. I could see the window was open where he had come in. He was a Black man in his twenties, medium build, maybe five feet eight to five feet ten inches tall. He had delicate facial features and a moustache. He wore a dark shirt and dark jeans. He was holding a knife with a dark brown wood handle. It was about three inches long, and the tip was broken. I screamed. My husband heard me and ran upstairs. The man told us, 'I need some money.' But he said it with a drawn-out sound, like 'monnay.' Frank told him he can have all the money we have, 'just don't hurt us.'"

I was blown away by her composure, her recall of so many details in her condition.

"The man took us both downstairs to the dining room," Annette continued. Frank Carlson was the assistant manager for a Safeway supermarket in San Mateo, she said, and had been working on the store's books. He had the stereo on low so as not to disturb her. "When we got downstairs," Annette continued, "the man asked us for some rope, but we didn't have any. He went into the front room and cut the cord off a lamp. He ordered Frank to sit down in a dining room chair and gave me the cord. He told me to tie my husband to the chair with his hands behind him. I did what he told me. Then he went over to check it and tightened it more."

Again, the intruder demanded money, she said, repeating the accented word "monnay." She told him the money was upstairs.

"Go and get it!" he had ordered. "And don't call the police or try any funny stuff." She said she went upstairs and retrieved the couple's credit cards, six dollars in cash, and an empty wine jug filled with coins, maybe one hundred dollars' worth.

"He told me to sit on the floor in front of the refrigerator. I said, 'Please don't hurt us.' He shouted at me, 'Shut up, bitch! Sit down and shut up!' He didn't believe it when I said we didn't have any more money. Then he asked me if we had a hammer. I went to the back porch, but I couldn't lift the toolbox down from the shelf. He came and got it and told me to sit down again. He went over to the stereo and turned up the volume. I could see through the doorway into the dining room.

"He started hitting Frank on the head with the hammer over and over until the head of the hammer broke off. I was screaming hysterically, but I'm not sure I was making any sound at all. I was petrified with fear. He started hitting Frank, this time with the butcher block.

That broke, too. Then he hit him with the bottle of coins until that smashed and the coins went all over."

Growing more ferocious by the moment, the intruder picked up a potted plant and bashed Frank over the head until it, too, broke, she said. Annette was horrified. She said that in his frenzy, as the intruder battered her husband repeatedly, the man shouted, "DIE! DIE! WHY WON'T YOU DIE, YOU BASTARD? DIE!"

I shuddered at this. The hatred in this evil person's heart was unimaginable.

Finally, Annette said, the chair toppled over on its side with Frank still tied to it. As far as she could tell, her husband was dead.

Now she knew she was next.

"He put a record on the stereo and turned it up real loud," she continued. "He came into the kitchen and tried to kiss me. I pushed him away. He said, 'If you are not nice, I will kill you.' He told me to go upstairs, sit on the bed, and take off my clothes. He followed me up to the bedroom."

Out of paralyzing fear for her life, she removed her nightgown and top. She remembered him taking off "heavy, dirty, black boots" and unzipping his pants.

"I'm high on coke," the man said to her. "When I'm high on coke, I can fuck for three hours."

And that's literally what he did. He subjected her to every depraved sex act imaginable, again and again, at length.

She told me his large Afro hairstyle reminded her of newspaper photos she had seen of Cinque, the leader of the underground Symbionese Liberation Army. The SLA had kidnapped newspaper heiress Patricia Hearst in Berkeley two months earlier, on February 4. At one point the intruder also told Annette he was the Zebra killer, referring to the recent series of random street murders in the city. The fifteenth Zebra murder within six months had occurred just two days before this assault.

At some point during the assault, Annette said, the suspect rummaged through the bedroom furniture drawers and pocketed several pieces of jewelry and a porcelain egg she kept atop her bedroom dresser.

When he finally stopped sexually assaulting her, he laughed and told her: "I have to kill you now. I have no choice. You know who I am, don't you? I've seen you before. You know me."

"But I don't know who you are!" she insisted, pleading again for her life.

Next, her assailant cut the cord off the telephone and started choking her with it. She promised that if he let her go, she would give police a totally different description of her attacker. He told her he'd been in jail before and if he let her go, he would end up in the gas chamber.

With that, she said, the man picked up her cherished childhood rocking chair and beat her on the head and face with it. She grabbed a pillow off the bed and tried to shield herself against the blows, but he continued his savage attack relentlessly. The beating inflicted ghastly scalp and facial cuts and fractured several bones. When the chair shattered into pieces, she said, he found a glass paper weight, wrapped it in a towel, and beat her some more. Finally, she collapsed in a balled-up heap.

"Let me die, please," she begged. "Just leave me alone and let me die."

The man said nothing. He took out his knife and sliced open the arteries inside her left wrist. Next, she said, he found a can of paint thinner. He poured it on the clothes in the bedroom closet and all around her bed. Then he set the room on fire.

We determined later that the man then went back downstairs, splashed paint thinner around the dining room where Frank Carlson lay bound to the chair, set that room ablaze, too, and left, most likely by the front door.

Miraculously, Annette Carlson was still conscious. She crawled naked, every move so painful, out the same window the intruder had used to get in and tumbled onto the adjacent gable, screaming for help.

Across the street at the Synanon Foundation Center, which had sixty-six residents, twenty-three-year-old Andy Rockwell was sleeping fitfully in his dormitory bunk. "I heard what I thought was a cat meowing," Rockwell told the *San Francisco Chronicle* later. He looked out his window and saw the woman on the roof, smoke pouring out of the window. He quickly pulled on trousers, ran barefoot across the street, scaled a fence, and climbed up to the roof.

A neighbor, photography student Joe Pearson, twenty-one, told *Chronicle* reporter Jerry Carroll, "It seemed like she had been screaming forever." Pearson, another Synanon resident, Mario Clairborne, twenty-five, and a third neighbor, Phillip Hornbeck, forty-five, all joined Rockwell and Annette Carlson on the roof. They wrapped her in a blanket and tried to comfort her as police and fire units converged on the scene. The first fire truck arrived at 3:14 a.m.

I finish my conversation with Annette by asking if the assailant had any identifying marks, scars, tattoos, or deformities. There were none, but she said she would be willing to help a sketch artist with a composite drawing of the suspect.

"I will never forget his face," she said. "I will always remember his almond-shaped eyes."

I left the hospital completely drained.

My God, I thought. What an amazing woman this is to have this kind of strength, resolve, and composure after everything she'd been through.

The nurses were right. We had to catch this monster quickly.

CHAPTER 13
STOLEN JEWELRY TRACED TO KILLER

The savage Carlson murder case stuck in my craw then, and it's still there, almost fifty years later. Hardly a day goes by that I don't think about what had happened to that beautiful young couple in the ordinary peace and quiet of their home.

This case reminded me of my own situation, my own home. Here was a young couple trying to get their start in life together. They had purchased a home and were working to remodel it to their style and comfort. I couldn't help but reflect on how Donna and I were remodeling rooms in our own home. There weren't a lot of differences between the Carlsons and the Falzons. Yet some animal felt he had the right to arm himself, climb through their bedroom window, and destroy their dreams.

After leaving the hospital, I went back to Kansas Street, picked up Jack, and we drove to the office as the sun was coming up. On the way, I related Annette's story of the sickening attack. When I mentioned the suspect's pronunciation of "monnay," Jack said, "He's Creole, Frank. That's how they talk." We brewed a fresh pot of coffee and got to work. We put out a teletype to all units with a description of the suspect and started checking for any similar recent crimes.

"You know," Jack said to me, "even though this guy demanded money and stole jewelry, that wasn't his main objective. I think we're looking for a sadistic rapist, not a burglar or a robber."

"That makes perfect sense to me, Jack," I replied. "After everything Annette told me, I'm sure money and jewelry were secondary. He went into the house with one thought in mind—raping Annette. Killing Frank allowed him to be alone with her for as long as he wanted."

The medical examiner who performed the autopsy on Frank Carlson told Jack later, "You could drop a man off a ten-story building by his feet and not cause that much damage to his head."

We went over to the rape detail and asked the inspectors there about any active cases that sounded like this one. There weren't any—we certainly would've heard about something this vicious—but they jumped at the chance to help us with this case in any way they could.

The fire and subsequent water damage at the Carlson house had degraded the possibility of retrieving any viable suspect fingerprints from the residence or the household items the killer used to bludgeon Frank Carlson and beat Annette. The boot print in the carpet wasn't much to go on. Fortunately, we had Annette's recall and willingness to describe the suspect for a composite sketch. She spent three hours with this sick bastard, mostly pleading for her life. I knew she would be able to describe him in detail to our artist.

The next day, April 20, Jack and I and Homicide Inspector Hobert "Hobie" Nelson went back to the hospital to see Mrs. Carlson. Hobie worked at a desk directly across from ours. Hobie was the department's official sketch artist, having drawn more than one hundred fifty portraits of suspects over the years based on victims' descriptions. The newspapers liked to call Hobie the "cop who caught crooks with his pencil not his gun." The majority of Hobie's sketches turned out to bear amazing resemblances to the actual criminal.

Hobie was a true renaissance man. Born in Sweden in 1923, he grew up in San Francisco. At one time or another, before he joined the police department in 1953, he was a farm worker, a Western Union delivery boy, a World War II soldier under General Patton in Europe, a Yellow

Cab driver, a singer, and a San Francisco fireman on the city's fire boat. In the SFPD, he spent thirteen years as a motorcycle cop and fifteen as a homicide inspector. After he retired, Hobie had a second career as a criminal investigator with the Sonoma County District Attorney's office and as a welfare fraud investigator for the Sonoma County Social Services Department. In his seventies, he raised and rode horses and was a dance host for different cruise lines, sailing around the world, dancing with ship passengers. Hobie was truly a man of many talents, not the least of which was his ability to draw.

Annette described her assailant's specific features in detail to Hobie as he sketched the man's likeness on an artist's pad. We added his drawing to our information bulletin and continued our hunt for the killer into the late hours that night. On Monday, April 22, the *Chronicle* ran an article quoting police officials that there was "absolutely no connection" between the Zebra killings and the "maniacal murder" of Frank Carlson and the attack on his wife.

Funeral services for Carlson were held that same day at St. Peter's Episcopal Church in the Richmond District. The church was packed to overflowing; some attendees had to stand outside in the courtyard. Cars were parked three deep in front of the church as motorcycle police directed traffic around the clogged street. Frank had grown up in the Richmond District, graduated from Washington High School, the College of San Mateo, and San Francisco State University, where he majored in journalism. Frank and Annette had met nine years earlier when they both attended Ebenezer Lutheran Church on West Portal Avenue. They were married in 1971 and bought the Kansas Street house two years later. Frank had worked for Safeway for seven years and was actively looking for a job in journalism. In addition to Annette, he was survived by a younger brother, Eric, and his parents, Sten and Elizabeth Carlson. The article pointed out that the family preferred memorial contributions be made to the Synanon Foundation or St. Peter's Episcopal Church.

Jack and I checked on several recent parolees known for violent rapes. We brought in a few of them for questioning, but all were subsequently cleared and released, most having verifiable alibis. We also looked at the residents of the Synanon building across the street from the Carlsons' home for potential suspects, even though several of its members had come to Mrs. Carlson's aid. At the time, Synanon was a drug rehabilitation program that offered live-in treatment for ex-convicts and others. Almost any of the residents could be considered possible suspects. We learned that ten of them had missed curfew the night of the crime. But we cleared them all. What looked at first as a likely place to find our suspect fizzled. We canvassed the surrounding neighborhood as well, hoping someone might have seen the suspect or recognized him from Hobie's sketch. Again, a dead end. We were coming up with a big zero everywhere we turned. It was disheartening, to say the least, and so frustrating.

Before the Carlson case occurred, Jack had scheduled some time off to tend to his ranch in Sonoma County, where he raised cattle and sheep. He wasn't eager to leave, but I urged him to go and promised that if there was any break in the case that I would call him immediately. I told Jack I would grab John Sully from our robbery detail to work with me. Sully was a skilled inspector who had helped us on an earlier murder case. He also happened to be the leftfielder on my police department all-star softball team and was fun to work with.

While Jack was away, John and I visited Annette often at the hospital to check on her progress. Her head and face were so heavily bandaged she looked like a mummy. One arm was in a sling. She was recovering gradually but had a long way to go. Almost every day that I visited, her father, Steve Gilson, was there, keeping a vigil by his daughter's bedside. Though she was sitting up and doing better, he was feeling distraught and powerless. "Inspector, I need to do something to help," he'd say. "What can I do?" I was at a loss what to tell him, but I promised to give it serious thought and get back to him.

It had been two weeks since the crime. The investigation had stalled. Then it hit me. One day I asked Annette's father, "You're an engineer, right? Engineers have artist skills?" He nodded. "Do you think with your daughter's help you could draw pictures of the jewelry items that were stolen?" I explained my thinking that the killer had almost certainly sold or tried to sell the jewelry or would soon. Gems could often be traced to a jeweler, a pawn shop, or a known fence.

"Of course," he replied. "A lot of it was my mother's, including her wedding ring, which she gave to Annette. I know exactly what they look like."

The following day, when I got to the hospital and saw what Annette and her father had produced, it far exceeded my expectations. The drawings were so perfect and detailed, they could have been photographs.

They had drawn pictures of six different pieces of jewelry valued at roughly three thousand dollars. One was a platinum wedding ring bearing the inscription inside, "Frank and Elizabeth, 2-4-44"—her paternal grandparents names and their wedding date. It had been passed down to the young couple through Annette's father. Also taken were two bracelets, and three other rings. One of them was another antique wedding ring with a blue-white, one-carat diamond flanked by baguettes and a full-cut diamond on each side. The sketches were all meticulously detailed. I couldn't wait to call Jack and bring him up to date. I was excited as I told him I was going to add the sketches to the back side of Hobie's composite drawing on the information bulletin. I further explained that I was also thinking about giving them to the media. Jack was in complete agreement with the plan and offered to come back to the city to help. I told him to wait to see if we turned up a solid break on the jewelry. Again, I promised to call him immediately if there was any major development from the media release.

I called Bob Popp, the *Chronicle*'s long-time police beat reporter, and asked him to come up to the homicide detail. Bob worked out of a third-floor room set aside for the press at the Hall of Justice. He was always a straight shooter with us and had helped us with many cases and articles over the years. Newsmen like Popp would work with the police for the common good. The same was true for Malcolm "Scoop" Glover, the *Examiner's* police beat reporter, whom I also called up to the detail. Finally, I asked Carol Ivy at KGO-TV, another reporter I trusted, to join the meeting.

"I'd like to ask for your help," I said when they were all in the office. I showed them the sketches depicting the stolen gems. "These items were taken from the Kansas Street arson murder crime scene. If you publish them and we go public with this information, maybe someone in a jewelry store or pawn shop will recognize them. We desperately need a break in this case." All offered their full cooperation.

Channel 7 aired Carol's story on the nightly news that same night. The *Chronicle* and the *Examiner* ran their stories and the drawings the next day, May 9. In less than twenty-four hours, we got a response. John Hurn, who worked at Gensler-Lee Jewelers downtown, had clipped the *Chronicle* article from the paper, placed it prominently at his workstation, and compared it to all the pieces he was currently working on. He called us right away.

"Inspector, I think I have one of the items you're looking for," he said. I thought this could be divine intervention. I decided not to call Jack, however, thinking it could also be a wild goose chase. I called Sully, and together we headed over to Gensler-Lee.

Hurn showed us an antique wedding ring that was a perfect match to one in the sketches, down to the inscription with the wedding date. I was more than excited. We signed a release form and took the ring. I tried to contain my emotions about this development, but it wasn't easy. We drove straight to Presbyterian Hospital, where Annette had been transferred to continue her recovery, and went to her room. Her father wasn't there. I told Annette I had something for her to look at and handed her the ring.

"Do you recognize this?" I asked.

She held the ring up to the light, examining it in silence for several moments. Tears began rolling down her cheeks.

"This is definitely my grandmother's wedding ring," she said. "Look at the inscription inside."

There are times in a stalled murder case investigation when something happens that jolts you into a new stratosphere. This was one of those moments. We left the hospital, returned to the office, and I immediately called Jack to fill him in. "Freeze everything," Jack said. "Wait for me. I'm heading down there now." He arrived within two hours.

Jack and I went back to the jewelry store to ask Mr. Hurn where the ring had come from. He said a customer brought it in to have it redesigned as a man's ring using the same stones. He showed us a copy of the receipt bearing the name Frank Whitfield, with an address of 120 Cashmere Street, out in the Hunters Point district. "That's our guy," I told Jack. Jack and I went out to Hunters Point to confront Whitfield.

Pumped up at having a solid suspect and with Annette's nightmare in mind, I was angry when we got there. When Frank Whitfield opened the door, I got in his face.

"What kind of animal are you?!" I hollered. "How could you do what you did to this beautiful couple?! You're a sick son of a bitch, you know that?!" Jack got between us and told me, "Calm down, Frank. Maybe Mr. Whitfield has a story he'd like to tell us."

"Listen," Jack said to Whitfield. "Just tell us what you know about this ring."

"Okay," Whitfield agreed, "but keep that other guy away from me."

We never planned what Hollywood likes to call the "good cop, bad cop" routine before we questioned a suspect, but this was a classic example of it. I would never intentionally harm a suspect, but I do have emotions and feelings. On this case, they had been stretched practically to the breaking point. I'm certain that was very clear to Whitfield.

Whitfield, realizing he was involved in some serious shit, opened up. "I got the ring from my brother-in-law, Gary Brown," said Whitfield. "Gary got it from a guy he works with at the post office." We got the brother-in-law's address, then booked Whitfield on penal code section 496, possession of stolen property. Jack and I both believed Whitfield was telling the truth. We told him that if what he was saying about the ring was found to be true, he'd be out of jail in less than forty-eight hours.

Jack and I contacted the brother-in-law, Gary Brown. He confirmed everything we'd learned from Whitfield. Brown told us he worked with a guy named Angelo Pavageau; in fact, they had been hired on the same day. Brown said Pavageau showed him a woman's ring with twenty-one blue diamond-like stones. Pavageau told Brown he "ripped off" the ring from someone and wanted to sell it to pay a phone bill. Brown did not want to buy the ring but thought his brother-in-law might be interested. Brown said he brought Pavageau to Whitfield's home. Pavageau introduced himself to Whitfield as Charles Jefferson to avoid using his real name in case Whitfield was ever caught with the stolen ring and was asked who sold it to him. Whitfield bought the ring from Pavageau for three hundred dollars, said Brown.

At last, after three weeks, we had a suspect. Angelo Pavageau had now been positively identified by two people as being in possession of the stolen ring. We did a workup on him. We were surprised to find out that Pavageau, twenty-five, a postal truck driver, lived at 1385 Kansas Street, at the other end of the same block as the Carlsons. They were practically neighbors.

The next morning, May 11, Jack and I staked out Pavageau's house, waiting for him to leave for work. We knew he had a wife and daughter, and we didn't want to risk any trouble by confronting him in front of them. The moment Pavageau stepped out of his front door at 11:15 a.m., in his postal uniform, we swooped in. I recognized him from Hobie's composite drawing immediately. He said nothing as Jack handcuffed him, but his forehead broke out in beads of sweat. We took him downtown and put him in the interrogation room.

Angelo Pavageau booking photo, May 11, 1974

Pavageau denied any part in the Carlson crime. However, when we told him we were going to obtain a search warrant for his home, he admitted to having the stolen jewelry. "I went outside for a cigarette between eleven and twelve o'clock that night," he said. "I know the time because Johnny Carson was on TV. I was sitting on my front porch smoking and watching my puppy. This Black guy came running down the street, dropped a bag, and kept going. I didn't get a good look at him. I opened the bag and there were all these rings and bracelets in there." He took the bag inside and put it in the nightstand next to his bed, he said. "Later I heard the fire trucks. The next morning my wife told me there was a murder down the street."

Pavageau said he sold two of the rings, but later admitted selling a third. The remaining jewelry was still in his bedroom. Pavageau signed a consent form for a search of his home, and we retrieved the remaining jewels from the nightstand. Jack and I booked Pavageau into city prison for the murder of Frank Carlson and the multitude of other charges relating to the crime.

We arranged for a live lineup and brought Annette Carlson

downtown to the police department show up room. "We had Pavageau and six other guys in the lineup," said Cleary, who ran the process. "I asked each one to turn left, then right, then walk downstage so our witness could get a good look at each guy. Then I said to them, 'Now I want each of you repeat these words: I want your money.'

"Number one, you start. Number one says, 'I want your money.'

"Number two, next. Number two says, 'I want your money.'

"Number three, same thing. Number three says, 'I want your money.'

"Now you, number four.

Number four was Pavageau. I was sitting next to Annette, who viewed the proceedings from a wheelchair in the audience area of the lineup room. The moment she saw Pavageau she identified him with certainty as the man who had killed her husband and raped her. But now she was hearing his voice for the first time since that night. She recoiled in revulsion as Pavageau said the words:

"'I want your monnay.'"

Me with Jack Cleary working on the Carlson murder

CHAPTER 14
LIFE SENTENCES

Pavageau was born in New Orleans, which explained the accent. Jack was right about his Creole background. Pavageau had served in the Army in Vietnam, received campaign medals, and was honorably discharged in 1971. He moved to San Francisco from Louisiana in June 1972. He worked for Pacific Telephone as a cable installer for five months, then for Young Patrol Service for four months before joining the post office as a part-time motor vehicle operator in November 1973. Oddly, after three months, the post office terminated Pavageau as an "unsatisfactory" employee but reinstated him on the same day because of his "potential." We weren't sure why. Perhaps a co-worker or supervisor had intervened on his behalf.

With Pavageau in custody, Jack went back up to his ranch, and John Sully returned to the robbery detail. I began wrapping up loose ends. I was at my desk contemplating what else, if anything, we could do to tie Pavageau to the crime. We had a solid evidentiary case already, but I wanted more corroboration. I went to the property clerk's office in the basement of the Hall of Justice, directly across from the cafeteria. I wanted to look through Pavageau's personal items that had been taken from him during the booking process. I signed out the property envelope containing everything that had been on his person when he was arrested. Maybe, just maybe, I'd find something we might have missed.

I dumped the contents out on the counter in front of the property clerk so I would have a witness in case there was ever any question later about something missing. There was a fifty-dollar bill, two twenty-dollar bills, a U.S. postal vehicle driver's license, a Timex wristwatch, a can opener, lip balm, four pens, a pair of eyeglasses, a Selective Service ID card, and a black address book. I was intrigued by the book. I wrote down six or seven names and phone numbers that were in the book, went back to the office, and started calling them one by one. Halfway through the list, I reached a woman named Lucinda Haley.

"Hello, Miss Haley, this is Inspector Falzon from the San Francisco Police Department homicide detail," I said. "I am investigating a murder that occurred in your neighborhood last month. I found your name and number in a phone book that belongs to an individual named Angelo Pavageau. Do you know him?"

Her reply caught me off guard.

"I knew you would find out about me eventually," she answered. "Yes, I do know Angelo. I call him Gello. If you come to my house, I will tell you everything I know." She lived at 24th Street and San Bruno Avenue, one block from the Carlsons.

I called John Sully and asked him to join me. We headed over to see Lucinda Haley that same day. She was a tough, streetwise woman. As we sat down in her living room, she said she was friends with Pavageau. We asked her if she had seen him on April 18.

"Yes, Gello came to my house about eleven. I know the time because the news was about to come on the TV. He was agitated about some confrontation he had with a punk on the street. He told me he had 'slapped the piss out of the guy' and had taken a knife away from him. Gello pulled the knife out of his waistband and showed it to me. It was thin and curved up at the end and the tip was broken. I went to a kitchen drawer and took out a much bigger knife. 'That Zebra killer better not come after me,' I told him.

"Gello asked me if I wanted to get high. I told him he looked high already. He said he needed five thousand dollars to buy a pound of coke. He wanted us to go into my bedroom. He told me that when he's loaded, he can fuck for three hours."

Sully and I looked at each other knowingly. She had just described the knife that Annette Carlson said her attacker used and repeated the exact phrase the suspect said to Annette about being high.

"He said he was going to have sex with me," Haley continued. "He said it to me twice."

"Then what did you do?" I asked.

"I was still holding my butcher knife and I told him, no, you're not. If you come near me, I'll cut your throat. I meant it. He just laughed and left."

"What time did he leave?" I asked her.

"It was about eleven thirty," she answered.

This was a bombshell, the exact corroborating evidence I was looking for. On the way back to the office, I said to Sully, "Now we've got the complete package for the D.A. It's like a Christmas present wrapped with a big bow. This is so solid he could call it in from a phone." What I meant was we now had a previously unknown witness confirming Pavageau having a knife with a broken tip, his identical statement about having sex for three hours when he's high on coke, and the time that he left Haley's place correlating with the time he entered Annette's bedroom. He would have to pass the Carlsons' house on his way home. All of it bolstered our case against Pavageau.

On May 17, Pavageau appeared before Municipal Court Judge Agnes O'Brien-Smith wearing his postal uniform. He was silent as his attorney, LeRue Grim, entered his plea of not guilty to all charges. The district attorney, Tommy Norman, asked that Pavageau be charged under state laws with a death penalty provision. Three days later, the grand jury returned an indictment against Pavageau, seeking charges including murder, rape, robbery, burglary, and assault with a deadly weapon.

Pavageau's trial began on July 22, 1974, before Superior Court

Judge Walter Calcagno and lasted twelve days. Tommy Norman presented the prosecution's case over the first week. Annette Carlson was a compelling witness as she related the overnight events of April 18 and 19. During cross-examination, defense counsel LeRue Grim referred to the intruder as the suspect or as the subject. Each time he uttered those words, Annette Carlson skillfully interrupted him. "Mr. Grim," she pointed out, "the suspect or the subject or the intruder is the man sitting next to you, Angelo Pavageau." Among the other witnesses Norman called was Lucinda Haley, who repeated the story she had told us. Norman concluded his case by playing the twenty-five-minute tape of our interrogation of Pavageau.

Attorney Grim declined to make an opening statement. Instead, he called Pavageau's wife, Harriet Adams, to the stand as his first witness. She testified that Pavageau had come home the night of the murder at 10 p.m., upset and trembling because of a fight he said he had with two other men who had attacked him. He left an hour later, she said, but returned between midnight and 12:30 a.m. and went to bed. He did not mention where he'd been or finding a bag of jewels.

Adams further testified that Angelo was unable to sleep and got up twice to walk his dog. The second time, she said, she heard the sirens of fire trucks. These trucks were arriving to put out the flames at the other end of the block.

Pavageau took the stand in his own defense. He testified that he had been drinking on the night in question but denied using any cocaine. He also said he had only a nodding acquaintance with Mrs. Carlson and had seen her on the bus.

On August 2, the jury—eight men and four women—found Pavageau guilty on all counts. Six days later, after sixteen hours of deliberations, the same jury decided that special circumstances prevailed in the crime, meaning that Frank Carlson's murder was willful, deliberate, and premeditated and caused by Pavageau during the commission of rape, robbery, and burglary. The finding of special circumstances under state law called for a mandatory death penalty. Judge Calcagno thanked the jury for its difficult decision and told them he "would have voted the same way, if it's any consolation to you."

Pavageau was sentenced to die in the gas chamber, plus fifty-four years for the other crimes. But the torment for Annette Carlson and both families wasn't over.

With Pavageau on death row, I heard little from Annette or Frank Carlson's family over the next few years. Occasionally Jack and I got a note from Frank's mother Betty Carlson thanking us again for everything we did, but that was rare and not expected. Jack and I both knew that the mutual respect generated during this case would last forever whether or not we maintained any contact.

Unless a victim or family member reached out to me after a case was closed, I made a point of not keeping in touch with them. Seeing or hearing from me would just bring up bad memories of the crime. Victims' survivors and families meet me under the worst circumstances in their life. Going through a traumatic incident together, we can form a bond, but once it's over, I realize that contact with me can bring up the tragic events again. I moved on to other cases and rarely looked back. I do still have contact with a few people I met during murder investigations, mostly surviving family members, but it's rare and it's their choice.

In 1980, a twist in the law that we didn't see coming thrust us all back into the Pavageau case with a jolt. A sequence of decisions on capital punishment by the U.S. Supreme Court and the California Supreme Court—including one ruling two years before the Potrero Hill crime—compelled the state to convert Pavageau's sentence to life in prison. Even worse for his victims and their families, he was now entitled to regular parole hearings.

It goes back to 1972, when the U.S. Supreme Court ruled five-to-four in a Georgia case that the death penalty in certain cases constituted cruel and unusual punishment and violated the Constitution. The decision caused all existing death sentences in the nation to be nullified and reduced to life imprisonment. Individual states were left to enact revised laws to reinstate capital punishment so it would not be administered in a capricious or discriminatory manner.

In November 1972, California voters amended the state constitution, making the death penalty mandatory in specified cases. But four years later, the State Supreme Court held that the California death penalty was unconstitutional under the United States Constitution. As a result, seventy condemned inmates had their sentences changed to a variety of terms other than death. The State Legislature, and later, California voters, reinstated the death penalty in 1977 and 1978, respectively. By then, Pavageau had slipped through a hole in the system and would avoid any future concerns about being executed.

Also in 1977, the state penal code was revised to include the sentence of life imprisonment without the possibility of parole. But that didn't apply to Pavageau. Under state law, he became entitled to routine parole hearings after serving a certain period of his sentence.

I was appalled when I heard from Betty Carlson in 1980 that Pavageau was up for parole just six years after his horrendous crimes. She and Annette Carlson asked me and the SFPD for help in fighting to keep Pavageau behind bars. I was more than eager to do whatever I could. I wrote a letter to the state parole board, the first of many I would write over the next four decades expressing my vigorous opposition to the prospect of Pavageau winning his freedom.

"The Carlson case was the worst possible crime," I wrote. "This man has avoided the death sentence but should never be released from prison."

In my mind, the day Pavageau climbed through that window into the Carlsons' home he made a decision that cost a man his life. By making that choice, Pavageau gave up his own freedom. His original sentence was fair and just. This crime was so heinous that life without parole is as lenient as the government should be for a crime of this nature.

On April 4, 1980, the state Community Release Board conducted a three-hour hearing on Pavageau's eligibility for parole.

Annette, who did not attend the hearing, also sent a letter to the board. "I have not yet rebuilt my life and the one who took it all away is having a parole hearing!" she wrote. "Good God, is there no justice left on Earth?"

Near the conclusion of the hearing, Pavageau told the three-member panel that he was "very sorry for Mrs. Carlson, and I hope that in her heart somewhere she may find forgiveness for me. I doubt it, but, being a God-fearing man, I ask that."

In a unanimous decision, the panel ruled that Pavageau was "unsuitable for parole on the basis of his offense." His assault on the Carlsons was "not only senseless and brutal" but was carried out in a "callous, dispassionate matter demonstrating a complete disregard for human life and suffering." The panel also cited a prison psychiatrist's report that "does not support release readiness."

Two years later, it all came back around with another hearing. *San Francisco Examiner* writer Guy Wright summarized it best in a column that ran, coincidentally, on April 18, 1982, eight years to the day after the crime:

> "Pavageau was caught, convicted, and sentenced to death. But when the State Supreme Court abolished the death penalty, he was among dozens of condemned killers who automatically became ordinary lifers eligible for parole. With his altered status he has been allowed to attend college, marry, and father a child, all the while in San Quentin.
>
> "Annette Carlson hasn't fared so well. 'I still sleep with the lights on,' she said. 'I still have nightmares. When I brush my hair, I can't help seeing the scars on my face and scalp. I can't get away from it.'
>
> "There is something grotesque," wrote Wright, "about a criminal justice system that requires this woman to make an annual plunge into psychological pain as the price for keeping her tormentor from returning to her world."

Pavageau was again denied parole in 1981, 1982, and 1983. During this period, Betty Carlson, who had been a registered nurse and managed retail stores, joined the administrative staff of Congressman Tom Lantos. She and her husband, Sten Carlson, used the crime and the subsequent parole hearings as a platform for activism on behalf of victims' rights. In 1985, the Carlsons founded Justice for Murder Victims. Working with other individuals and community organizations, they were successful in the late 1980s in making parole hearings bi-annual rather than annual.

Betty Carlson was beyond an exceptional woman. When she lost her son, I saw a woman use her steel fortitude to fight for victims' rights in the name of that son. Years later I introduced Betty to another dear friend, Harriet Salarno, who had suffered a similar fate when her daughter Catina was murdered on the campus of the University of the Pacific in Stockton in 1979. Harriet is the co-founder and board chair of Crime Victims United of California, which remains a strong political force. Both Harriet and Betty dedicated their lives to the fight for victims' rights. To this day, I have a special love for Betty Carlson, a dedicated mother, nurse, and friend. Betty Carlson was inducted into the San Mateo County Women's Hall of Fame in 2007, appeared regularly before the parole board, and remained active on behalf of victims' rights until she was ninety. She died in 2010 at ninety-three, followed a year later by her husband at the age of ninety-eight.

In 2013, the California Supreme Court ruled that a 2008 ballot measure increasing the time between parole hearings for inmates serving life sentences applied to all so-called "lifers," not just those sentenced after the law passed. The ballot measure, named Marsy's Law after murder victim Marsy Nicholas, expanded the legal rights of crime victims and imposed lengths of seven, ten, and even fifteen years between parole hearings for certain prisoners.

The Carlson family launched a website, JusticeforFrank.org, to memorialize Frank and bring attention to victims' issues. Frank's younger brother, Eric, who was sixteen years old at the time of the home invasion, shares his feelings in a video on the site, saying his brother's murder is "still incredibly difficult for me to talk about. It has caused me to question many things. Who could believe in a God that created Angelo Pavageau? My family finds itself appearing before this body on average every three years. We recount the event ad nauseum. It is almost as if the state of California gave the Carlson family the life sentence to relive the crime year after year. These hearings are cruel in every sense of the word. In forty-six years of incarceration, we still don't know why Mr. Pavageau did what he did. He has only offered lies and excuses that he's been forced to recant. There's been no acknowledgement of the gravity of his crimes, no attempt at an apology, no expression of remorse."

The website notes that "On April 15, 2020, the California Parole Board granted Pavageau's request to defer his next parole hearing for three years. This happened even though this was the first opportunity since Marsy's law was passed for it to be applied to Pavageau. Pavageau had tactically avoided the application of the fifteen-year rule by waiving his right to a hearing for his last three hearings. Pavageau, who has now fathered three children while in prison, will have another hearing in 2023.

"A panel of the prison's best and brightest psychologists concluded that Pavageau is a 'sadistic sexual psychopath whose condition is not amenable to treatment, although [it is] controlled' while he's incarcerated. Setting yet another parole hearing just three years out is an injustice to my family, to victims, and to the public," said Eric.

"The murderer refused to attend his hearing, as he has for over twenty-five years, and even stipulated through his appointed counsel that he is unsuitable for release. But so that he could continue to inflict this painful process on his victims, he offered to defer the next parole hearing only three years. We are deeply frustrated that, rather than make their own decision, the parole board took the path of least resistance and just accepted his offer. This means Annette and my family must relive this process again in three years. The Board could have done the just thing and postponed what even Pavageau believes is the pointless consideration of his parole for five, seven, ten, or fifteen years. They had the authority to give some small solace and time before my family and I have to relive this horribly debilitating process again three years from now. We are beyond distraught they chose not to.

"For anyone who has not had to live through a hearing of this nature, they are stressful, emotionally draining and a painful walk down memory lane. Victims are forced to confront, normally in person, the individuals who perpetrated the crime." Carlson said. "Preparing for this event takes many, many months, and is time consuming and draining as we rally support among law enforcement officials, elected officials, friends, and family to remind the parole board of the consequences of granting freedom to this person. And now we will have to do this all over again [in 2023]. Tragically, the prisoner is running the show and the board is enabling this outrageous behavior."

Carlson said more than two thousand California citizens sent letters and emails to convince the parole board that there is strong public support for the fifteen-year deferment of Pavageau's next hearing to keep him in jail.

"You and Jack are heroes to me," Eric Carlson said in a recent email. "One of the things that remains with me to this day is the support we have received from the SFPD." Just before the latest hearing in 2020, police officers were still calling Carlson to wish his family well. "They don't know me, but they had heard the story and wanted to express their support."

What Angelo Pavageau did to Frank and Annette Carlson was horrific. What the parole board is putting their families through is just as horrific. I sincerely hope that Annette and the Carlson family can find some peace someday, but as long as Pavageau, now seventy-three, is still alive, I doubt that's possible.

CHAPTER 15
LUCKY LUIGI

One night, a week before Thanksgiving in 1974, Luigi Aranda was celebrating his twenty-ninth birthday with friends at the Tip Top Club, his favorite neighborhood drinking spot in San Francisco's Outer Mission District. It was also a popular hangout for the local chapter of the Hell's Angels motorcycle gang.

As the night wore on, three Hell's Angels at a nearby table were getting rowdy. Luigi didn't appreciate the intrusion on his private party. He confronted the men and told them they weren't welcome at the Tip Top. The smallest of the three bikers, Jesse Galvin, known to his friends as "Little Bill," stood up and cold-cocked Luigi, knocking him to the floor. Staggering, Aranda got to his feet and squared off for a fight, but the biker quickly knocked him down again.

"You sucker punched me!" Aranda fumed, wiping blood from his mouth with the back of his hand. "C'mon, I'll take you all on, but let's make it a fair fight. One at a time!" Another punch flew, this time knocking Aranda unconscious. The next thing Luigi knew, he'd been stuffed into a trash can in the street outside the bar. When he came around and went back inside, the Angels were gone. Embarrassed and very angry, Luigi proclaimed loud enough for several in the bar to hear: "They made a big mistake picking on me. I'm gonna get them."

One week later, on Thanksgiving night, Little Bill Galvin was back at the Tip Top, enjoying his drink, when a young woman named Rachael Katz walked up behind him. Rachael was a local, known to most everyone in the bar. She was friendly and forward. "Ooh, I like your jacket," she cooed to Galvin, tracing her fingers along the back of his jacket. Galvin was wearing the Hell's Angels signature denim jacket with the gang's logo, or "colors," emblazoned on the back. This kind of move, Galvin made clear, was not tolerated under any circumstances.

"You don't ever touch a Hell's Angel's jacket," Galvin snapped. "Touch my colors again and I'll knock you on your ass."

Katz was being friendly. Galvin's response threw her off kilter and she felt belittled. She was known as a tough cookie who took no guff from anyone. She couldn't resist running her hand over Galvin's jacket again. "Fuck your colors," she said, laughing. Galvin made good on his threat. He swirled around on his bar stool and punched her in the face. The blow knocked out Katz's two front teeth. Witnesses told us she went to the bar's payphone and made a call, holding the bloody teeth in her hand. A short time later, Galvin left the bar and rode away on his Harley.

A couple of hours later, around 1:00 a.m., a car drove up alongside Galvin on his motorcycle at Dolores and 29th Streets, and the men inside forced him at gunpoint to pull over. Two men got out of the car, angry words were exchanged, and the two gunmen made the twenty-four-year-old Galvin kneel facing his motorcycle. They shot him twice in the back of the head. He pitched forward over the bike, dead. After shooting Galvin, witnesses said, the gunmen opened fire on two passing cars to intimidate any potential witnesses. The men jumped back in their car, with a third man at the wheel, and it sped away.

By the time Jack Cleary and I got the call and arrived at the scene, the intersection was swarming with police cars, Hell's Angels, and curious bystanders. Galvin was still on his knees, slumped over his bike. Two women in one of the passing cars that had been shot at, JoAnn

Webb and Linda Finley, had seen the Galvin shooting and called police. They described one of the shooters as a white man with black curly hair and said the attackers fled in a light blue compact vehicle.

Jack and I started asking around about the victim, and we learned about the incident with Luigi Aranda and the Hell's Angels the week before at the Tip Top Club. The bartender and other patrons told us about Aranda getting knocked out, being dumped into the garbage can, and vowing revenge on his attackers. Aranda became our primary suspect. The two eyewitnesses to the Galvin shooting got a very good look at Aranda's face. Both women, individually and separately, positively identified Aranda's photo as being one of the two men at the scene of the Galvin murder.

During our investigation of Aranda, we found out that sometime before his birthday, he was in the Tip Top Club showing off a gun. Witnesses described the weapon as a blue steel revolver. They said Aranda had unintentionally discharged the weapon inside the bar, the bullet hitting the wall opposite the bar. We knew from the autopsy that the bullets that killed Galvin were .38-caliber rounds. We went to the bar to see if we could find the stray bullet lodged in the wall. Sure enough, there it was. We called in the crime lab and the photo unit to recover the slug. The bar was open when they arrived, so all the patrons watched as they did their work. The lab tech dug a large hole around the entry point to avoid damaging the slug. The crime scene investigator carefully removed the bullet and dropped it into an evidence envelope. We had what we had come for. We thanked the bartender for his cooperation and started to leave.

"Hey, Inspector," the bartender called out. "You left a hole in my wall. Who's going to fix that?"

I looked over. He was right. The original half-inch hole where the bullet was lodged was now three inches in diameter. I thought about it for a moment.

"Do you have a hammer and a small nail?" I asked him. "Yes, I do," he replied. He turned to the mirrored back bar, opened a small drawer, produced the hammer and nail, and handed them to me. I walked over to the wall and tapped the nail into the wood paneling about two inches above the hole. "Hand me that sign over there behind you," I said to the bartender. He gave it to me, and I hung it on the nail. The sign said: "Nobody under 21 allowed." It covered the hole completely. I said to the bartender, "The police department is very pleased to know that this sign is much more prominent than it was before."

"Thank you, Inspector," he replied sarcastically.

The lab guys, Jack, and I all strolled out the door to uproarious laughter.

The bullet we took from the wall was a .38. It showed all the characteristics of the Galvin slugs, but it had been damaged on impact with the wall and wasn't a definitive match. Still, we had strong circumstantial evidence. One key to the case was finding out who Rachael Katz called from the bar after Galvin punched her.

We interviewed Rachael about her confrontation with Galvin the night he was killed. We learned that she and Luigi Aranda were good friends, and that she knew what had happened to Luigi on his birthday, but she would not tell us who she called. We still had enough evidence to charge Aranda with Galvin's murder. While he was in jail awaiting trial, his family suffered a tragedy of its own.

Early in the morning on February 12, 1975, Luigi's older brother, Frank Aranda, was walking on Justin Street near College Avenue when he was accosted by at least two gunmen who got out of a passing car, forced him to kneel, and shot him eight times in the back and chest. The killers fled in a light blue car driven by another man, according to witnesses. It was shortly after 1:00 a.m., close to the same time of night that Galvin was killed. We could only assume that it was retribution for Galvin's murder. Another team of homicide inspectors handled that case. Their investigation never resulted in an arrest and the case remains unsolved. Jack and I figured the Hell's

Angels had their revenge.

The murder of Frank Aranda devastated the Aranda family, especially Frank and Luigi's mother, Mary. When Luigi was first jailed, Mary vowed that his older brother, Frank, would solve the Galvin killing and set Luigi free. Frank was described as a decent, law-abiding young man. Now Frank was dead. There were reports that he had discovered who really killed Galvin—had even boasted about it to friends—but we were never able to confirm that.

Luigi's trial began in April, two months after his brother's murder, with Superior Court Judge Morton Colvin presiding. JoAnn Webb and Linda Finley provided key testimony for the prosecution, telling the jury they saw a man who looked like Luigi Aranda force Galvin to his knees and shoot him in the back of the head. They identified Luigi Aranda in court as the man they saw. The jury found Aranda guilty of second-degree murder and three counts of assault with a deadly weapon. On June 3, 1975, Judge Colvin, calling Aranda "contemptuous" of society and "not rehabilitatable," sentenced him to a term of twenty-one years to life. Luigi went to Soledad Prison, and Jack and I moved on to other cases.

Ten months went by. In September 1975, a woman named Dora Katz came to see Jack and me, saying she had new information about the Galvin murder case that we ought to hear. We listened incredulously as she told us that her husband, Mike, and his brother, George, were the ones who had killed Little Bill. Dora said Mike and his brother had tracked down the Hell's Angel after getting a phone call from their sister, Rachael Katz, saying that a Hell's Angel had just knocked out her teeth in the Tip Top Club. Dora also told us her husband was embarrassed about his baldness and owned two toupees of black curly hair. He was wearing one of them the night of the Galvin shooting, she said. When he got home and told her he and George had shot someone, she helped cut up both wigs and flush them down the toilet. He later bought a new wig, she said. She also helped Mike wash the clothes he was wearing, at his request, which they later dropped into a Goodwill collection box. She said that she and Mike loaned his brother, George, one hundred dollars to have his blue El Camino painted red.

Jack and I found her to be sincere and believable, and we asked why she waited all those months to come forward. "Because Mike told me if I ever told the police he would kill me and my son," she said. She finally decided to unload her burden of guilt about keeping quiet because she didn't want anyone else to die. We gave her a polygraph test. She passed convincingly as being forthright and truthful. In a photo comparison, her husband bore a strong resemblance to Luigi. We did what we could to follow up on her story, but we weren't able to find anything that would uphold her statement or that would refute the evidence used to convict Luigi Aranda. By law, she could not be required to testify against her husband. Without any corroboration, we had no reason to bring in the husband. At the same time, Dora could not say whether Luigi Aranda had been with Mike and George at the Galvin killing. There was a third man in the car, but Dora did not know who that was.

The Jesse Galvin murder case was now in total shambles. Jack and I had a hornet's nest on our hands. Neither of us ever wanted to see an innocent person go to jail. Or a guilty person go free. Here was a compelling development that raised enough questions about Aranda's guilt to warrant a review of his case. After many discussions, we both felt compelled to bring this new evidence to the district attorney and the court. Our logic was simple. Had any of this conflicting evidence surfaced during our initial investigation, the district attorney might not have charged Luigi in the first place.

We presented what we had to the district attorney's office and to the state parole board, recommending that Aranda be considered for release under the circumstances. District Attorney Joseph Freitas assigned Assistant District Attorney Thomas Crary to investigate the new evidence and make a recommendation. Crary compiled a thousand-page report supporting Aranda's release from prison.

At the same time, Luigi's and Frank's mother Mary Aranda had hired a private investigator to help exonerate her son. "We knew our Luigi was innocent from the start, and we had to pay a big price to prove it," she told the *San Francisco Chronicle*, referring to Frank Aranda's murder. "The police arrested Luigi quick enough and found him guilty, boom-boom-boom. They didn't believe him when he said he was innocent and spent the night at home with Shirley, his wife."

With the new evidence and the district attorney's call for a pardon, Mary had only praise for Jack and me and the other investigators. Her son, she said, would have continued to rot in jail for twenty-one years—"more than they give anyone convicted of first-degree murder"—if not for the help of "those fine men," meaning Jack and me.

On March 29, 1977, Freitas and Crary held a press conference at the Hall of Justice calling for a "full pardon" of Luigi Aranda by then-California Governor Jerry Brown. It was the first time in twenty years the D.A.'s office had made such a request. At the press conference, Crary called Aranda's conviction "a tragic case that involves mistaken identity by eyewitnesses along with a pinch of perjury." He said, "A new piece of physical evidence was found that clinched the case." He declined to say publicly what that was.

In my view, Joe Freitas, an elected official who was as much a politician as he was a law enforcement figure, turned this whole thing into a political circus to show voters his compassion for a man he believed was wrongly accused. But again, we never found anything to prove that Luigi wasn't present at the Galvin killing. None of the witnesses ever recanted their testimony. If this new evidence had been available at the time of his trial, he never would have been brought to trial, let alone convicted. This conflicting testimony would have confused any jury. There would be enough reasonable doubt to acquit him. We concluded the only just outcome was to let him out.

Still, springing Aranda wasn't a simple matter of unlocking his cell door. Aranda had a ten-year-old bad check charge that threw a wrench into the process. Under the state constitution, the governor could not grant a pardon to a felon with a previous record until the State Supreme Court considered the case. The parole board, however, could release him pending a reduction of that charge to a misdemeanor.

Even as Freitas was conducting his press conference, Aranda, now thirty-one, was giving an interview to *San Francisco Chronicle* reporter Kevin Leary from his cell at Soledad Prison.

"Get me out of here," he said. "That's my message. If they know I'm innocent, why should I have to stay here in prison just because of some red tape and technicalities? I got convicted because of the negligence of the San Francisco Police Department's homicide investigation. It was a half-assed job. On the day they arrested me, I told them to look at the facts, but they had already made up their minds and they wouldn't listen."

Speaking of the run-in with the Hell's Angels at the Tip Top Bar, Aranda said, "I got into a scuffle with Jesse ("Little Bill") and he decked me. I came to in a backroom and went back in to continue the fight. I'm kind of hard-headed. Then the Angels were all over me, and this time I woke up in the street. When I went back into the bar again, they asked me if I'd learned my lesson. I said, 'Yeah,' had a drink, and went home. I'm not a revengeful person. When you fight a lot, you win some and lose some. It's not a big thing."

This time he did not say the Angels were gone when he went back into the bar, nor did he mention the threat to "get them," as witnesses had reported. His remarks now were those of a man needing to sound contrite and not vindictive.

A month later, San Mateo County Superior Judge Alan Haverty reduced Aranda's bad check charge to a misdemeanor, removing the last roadblock to a pardon. Within a few weeks, the state Adult Authority

Board voted seven to two to recommend a full gubernatorial pardon for Aranda.

But justice moves at the speed of molasses. In late May, two months after the Freitas press conference, J. Anthony Kline, Governor Brown's legal affairs secretary, convened the first of several long meetings to review the case. Jack and I, along with six experienced prosecutors, a public defender, and investigators from the Adult Authority and the state Department of Justice, all attended that first meeting to evaluate the evidence and assist in defining the standard of proof necessary to make a recommendation to the governor.

It would be another three months before Kline made a formal recommendation to Governor Brown. Just before doing so, he told *San Francisco Examiner* reporter Larry Hatfield that, "This has been a tough case for us, for a number of reasons." It was unlike any previous case ever put before a governor, he said.

"In most of the previous cases, there has been 'overwhelming evidence' of an individual's innocence," the article quoted Kline as saying, "usually because the real murderer came forward and confessed." Kline told the newspaper there was "strong circumstantial evidence" of Aranda's innocence, but the burden of proof was on Aranda.

Another four months went by before Governor Brown expressed in an interview that he still wasn't quite ready to act. "It's troublesome," he said. "The pardon power is an expansive power, and that power must be exercised with great restraint."

Finally, on February 4, 1978, after eight months of deliberation, Brown commuted Aranda's sentence to time already served—two years, seven months, and twenty-nine days—but declined to grant a full pardon. In other words, Brown wasn't convinced of Aranda's innocence. That night, Aranda walked out through the Soledad gates to the joy of his wife, Shirley, his mother, Mary, his father, Ted, and his son, Teddy, then thirteen. Deputy D.A. Tom Crary, who accompanied the Aranda family from San Francisco to the prison, said his office was still working to gain the full pardon.

The pardon never came.

Frank Aranda's murder was never solved.

No one else was ever arrested for the murder of Jesse "Little Bill" Galvin.

I saw Luigi Aranda only once again in late 1985, seven years after his release. It was at a nightclub on Valencia Street, where several of my police buddies and friends went to see one of our favorite performers, the popular local singer and comedian Danny Marona. My wife and I had met Marona years earlier when he performed on a Mexican cruise we took, and we had become friends. I called ahead and Danny arranged for us to have tables right in front of the stage. When he took the stage that night, Marona introduced me in the audience as "his special friend, San Francisco Police Homicide Inspector Frank Falzon. He's the inspector who just broke the Night Stalker case!" I stood to acknowledge the politely applauding crowd and sat back down.

Then the owner of the place took the microphone from Danny and said he, too, wanted to introduce someone.

Gesturing to the back of the room, he said, "Please welcome my dear friend Luigi Aranda." Sure enough, there he was, standing against the back wall, waving to the crowd.

I almost spit up my drink. Which would have been okay, considering the waitress soon delivered a new round of drinks to our table. But she wouldn't take any money. "You can thank the man in the back named Luigi," she said as Danny Marona began his show.

When the show was over, Luigi came up to me, shook my hand, and said, "I want to thank you for everything you and Jack Cleary did for me."

I said, "You're welcome, Luigi. But seeing you here now after all this time, I just have to ask you one question. Remember, under the double jeopardy law you can never be tried again for the same murder.

But for my peace of mind, I would like to know, which one of you shot and killed Little Bill Galvin? What's the real story?"

I'll never forget his reply as he turned to walk away.

He took a deep breath, smiled, and said, "You know, Frank, someday you and I are going to have to have a long talk."

I'm still waiting for that…

CHAPTER 16
TOO CLOSE TO HOME

By 1975, I'd spent nearly five years in the homicide detail. I loved my job. Never boring, always interesting, and consistently challenging. At work I was constantly engaged in conversations. My colleagues kidded me that I was the office chatterbox. I could be loud, aggressive, funny, serious—but rarely quiet.

In a time before computers, I kept meticulous records of every homicide case assigned to me by creating a hand-written spreadsheet listing the victims, dates, locations, manner of death, suspects, and, most importantly, the court's final disposition and sentencing in each case. By the time I retired, I had logged more than three hundred cases. I still have those charts.

Away from the office, I spent much of my time coaching my oldest son Dan's Catholic Youth Organization basketball team or was out on the ballfield with my police inspectors' softball team. When there was spare time, I'd find my hammer and saw and busy myself with building or repair projects around the house.

I didn't bring the job home with me. I didn't talk about the non-stop dreadful crime scenes and murder cases I was working on. Dinner table conversations were about school, sports, activities—anything but "Dad's job." Donna didn't ask, and our kids were too young, except Dan, the oldest, who was fascinated by my career. He wanted to follow in my footsteps. I made every effort to discourage those aspirations. Not because police work wasn't a rewarding and honorable career, but because there was that dark side to police work that I didn't want him to see. In the end, I couldn't discourage him from becoming a cop. Upon his graduation from Santa Clara University with a four-year business degree, he had already applied to and was accepted by the San Francisco Police Department. He entered the police academy right after his graduation. I was certainly a proud dad when he did.

Donna and the kids were accustomed to the phone calls in the middle of the night and me being gone for hours on end. When I wasn't at the breakfast table, it was the elephant *not* in the room. The news brought constant reminders of the city's latest murder. My name was in the papers from time to time, occasionally with a photo. But for the most part, I was able to separate my job from my home life. Donna and I were very active parents with St. Gabriel's School and church. I coached the boys' basketball team; she was the girls' athletic director and coach of our daughter Debbie's CYO softball team. All in all, life was good. I had a beautiful home, a wonderful wife, and four terrific children.

Fourth grade CYO team, L-R, Dennis Sullivan, Tim Breen, Bob West, Greg Holl, Dan Falzon, Steve Spiers, Sean Roonan, Tom Cleary, Kevin McWalters

But that was all about to change with one phone call.

On January 13, 1975, a brutal attack on two young women from Ohio at San Francisco's Ocean Beach, barely two miles from our house, changed not only their lives and their families' lives forever but up-ended the Falzons' family life as well.

When I was on call, I always answered the phone during the night, knowing it was likely the Operations Center or my partner calling about a new homicide case. Most murders seemed to occur between midnight and 3:00 a.m., just before and after the bars closed. Sometimes, if I were in a deep sleep and didn't answer right away, Donna would pick it up. When the phone rang at 2:45 a.m. that Monday, she happened to reach over and answer it before I could.

"This is the Operations Center calling for Inspector Falzon," the dispatcher said. He must have known where I lived because he then added, almost flippantly, "Tell Frank he doesn't have to go very far for this one. It's right down the street from you." Without saying a word, Donna handed me the receiver and rolled over.

"This is Inspector Falzon," I said into the receiver.

"Inspector, we have patrol units on the scene of a 187-217 on Ocean Beach at the foot of Riviera Street near 48th Avenue," the dispatcher said, indicating a murder and attempted murder. "There are two young female victims with multiple gunshot wounds. One is deceased."

At the time, we were living at 28th Avenue and Wawona Street, twenty-five blocks away.

My regular partner, Jack Cleary, was off that week, so I was paired up on call with Inspector Eddie Erdelatz, my old partner from our early patrol days at Northern Station. The dispatcher informed me that the coroner's office had been notified and was enroute to the crime scene. I told the dispatcher to call Eddie at home and then roll the crime lab and the photo unit to the location. I got dressed and went outside to my radio car at the back end of the driveway. The overnight blanket of fog typical in the Sunset District had wrapped the entire car in a wet shroud of mist. I kept a garden hose in the back of the house for such days, and I used it to rinse off the car so I could see out of the windows. I got in and made the five-minute trip to the beach.

At the crime scene, I cringed at the sight of a young woman lying dead face down in the sand, a gaping hole in the back of her head big enough to indicate a shotgun blast up close. As hardened as I'd become on this job, it was always unsettling to see young people murdered so brutally and senselessly. The Taraval Station officers told us the other woman had been transported to San Francisco General Hospital with multiple gunshot wounds. After some time at the scene gathering information, we went to the hospital to see the surviving victim, a critically wounded but courageous twenty-year-old named Julia Kehling. The clarity of her memory of the attack and the description of their assailant was remarkable, considering what she had been through.

Kehling told us that she and Janet Rodgers, also twenty, two lifelong friends from Cincinnati, had come to San Francisco on New Year's Day. Julia was on vacation from her job as a nursing technician at Cincinnati's Children's Hospital, while Janet had come to enroll as a student at the San Francisco Art Institute. The girls wanted to see California and were told the best way to do that on the cheap was to hitchhike along the Coast Highway. Over the weekend they flew to Los Angeles and visited the beach community of Venice before hitchhiking back north on scenic Highway 1.

Julia said they had gone to great lengths to screen their rides for safety, trying to sort out drivers who looked suspicious "or like they were on dope." They turned down many prospective rides, she said. By late Sunday night, they had made it as far as Half Moon Bay, twenty-three miles south of San Francisco. A young, clean-cut, neatly dressed Black man driving a blue Datsun stopped to pick them up. He was "gentle, soft-spoken, and very friendly," Kehling told us. She said he made no sexual advances and spoke quietly of "the beauties of the city." He promised them "a grand tour" of San Francisco. It was well after 1:00 a.m.

with few cars on the road and the night air was chilly, so they got in.

Thirty minutes later they arrived in San Francisco via the Great Highway that borders the western edge of the city along Ocean Beach. The driver parked the car in a lot adjoining the beach and continued speaking enthusiastically about the beauty of the beach and the Pacific surf. He cajoled the girls to get out of the car to look at the beach. "Let's walk down to the shoreline and look at the ocean, the moon, the ship out there in the distance," he said to them. "This is a sight you'll never forget." The three of them strolled a few yards to the sand dunes alongside the roadway. When the man said to them, "It's kind of foggy and scary," the girls became apprehensive and turned back toward the car.

"I heard something that sounded like a shot," Julia said. She turned around and saw the man holding a gun with outstretched hands, taking aim at her. "I saw a spark and then I felt myself being shot. I felt a sting and warm blood on my cheek." She said she tried to kick sand in the gunman's face and turned to run. She felt a second sting, this time in the back of her neck. She fell face down onto the sand and heard another shot as her friend Janet ran toward her.

"She fell on top of me. I lay still. My ears were ringing. My head was under her waist. I could see the man pacing. Jan was crying and whimpering as the shooter walked away."

The "soft-spoken, very friendly man" had shot both girls with a .38-caliber handgun. He then returned to the car, opened the trunk, took out a 20-gauge shotgun, and came back to finish them off.

"I figured Janet was unconscious," Kehling said of her friend. "I poked her with my right elbow, and I said, 'Shut up,' hoping that would let her know I was okay. She kept whimpering. I heard him approach again, and there was another shot, really loud. He was really close. I thought he was going to kick us over to see if we were dead. When I heard the loud shot, Jan's body was pushed up against me harder, and he paced some more around us. Then he walked away. I laid still, hoping he believed I was dead. I heard a car door slam. Then

I heard the car drive away."

Bleeding profusely, her tongue feeling pieces of shattered teeth inside her mouth, Julia tried to take Janet's pulse. There was none. "I slapped her six times, trying to revive her, and then I laid her back down," she said. "I ran straight across the street to the first house I saw. A lady answered and I said, 'Please don't be afraid. I'm all bloody but I need help. I've been shot. Please call an ambulance.'" The people in the house had been drinking heavily and were in no condition to help, she told the reporting officers, so she found their telephone and made the call to police herself.

Back at the office, Eddie and I put out a teletype with a description of the gunman and the car, made some calls around about recent parolees or similar cases, and waited for the ballistics report. From everything we heard, this was a senseless, motiveless killing. This case had all the hallmarks of the racially motivated Zebra murders that had gripped San Francisco the previous winter and spring. In all, fifteen white men and women had been killed, and eleven others wounded in random attacks across the city. Four Black men, members of the local Nation of Islam Mosque who called themselves Death Angels, had been jailed back in May 1974 and were still awaiting trial. There had been no documented Zebra cases since April 1974. For all we knew, the danger had passed, or at least we were hoping that the Zebra reign of terror was over.

When I got home that night after being gone fifteen hours, Donna scowled at me. She had been unable to go back to sleep after I left, she said. In recent weeks there had been an attempted kidnapping of a young boy and two young girls by Black men with guns and sacks near Corpus Christi Grammar School in another neighborhood. The children were able to run away from their assailants and were aided by several off-duty firemen who heard their screams. Now this beach murder.

"This city's just getting too dangerous, Frank, and you're right in the middle of all of it," she said. "I'm going to start looking for a safer place for us to live. You can stay here and play cops and robbers all you want, but the children and I are moving."

San Francisco Chronicle

'Zebra
Style'

The two young women were shot on the dunes that fringe Ocean Beach near Rivera street

By Clem Albers

2 Hitchhikers Shot
By a Cool Killer

By Peter Stack

Two young women from Ohio, hitch-hiking along coastal Highway 1, were shot down on Ocean Beach early yesterday by a black man who had picked them up, police said. One woman died, the other was wounded.

Homicide inspectors likened the attack to the so-called "Zebra" slayings last year because the man who suddenly opened fire on the young white women was clean cut, pleasant to the point of being charming and absolutely cool.

The shooting took place about 2:13 p.m. on the dunes that fringe Ocean Beach along Great Highway.

The dead girl, identified as Janet Rodgers, 20, of Cincinnati, had come to San Francisco to enroll as a student at the San Francisco Art Institute.

Her companion, Julia Kehling, also 20 and from Cincinnati, survived the gunman's attack, apparently by feigning that she was dead.

She was admitted to San Francisco General Hospital for treatment of bullet wounds in her neck and face, and told homicide inspectors what happened.

Miss Kehling said she had taken a vacation from her job as a nursing technician at Cincinnati's Children's Hospital to accompany her friend to California. The dead girl, Miss Rodgers, had long aspired to study at the highly regarded art institute here.

The two women flew here on New Year's Day, and were staying at the YWCA Hotel, 351 Turk street. Over the weekend they hitchhiked to Venice, a bohemian seaside section of Los Angeles.

They started back Sunday.

Miss Kehling told officers she and her friend had gone to great lengths to "screen" their rides, trying to sort out

Back Page Col. 2

San Francisco Chronicle, January 14, 1975

I completely understood. I had no solid ground to argue about it. There had been 129 murders in San Francisco the year before, and this was already the fifth of 1975, barely two weeks into the new year. The last thing I wanted to see was one of my loved ones get hurt. I loved San Francisco; the city was the only life I'd ever known, and there was no better city in the world to me. Here she was, talking about giving up the city life that we knew and loved dearly and all its positive aspects for our children. But I had no choice but to support her wishes.

By then, civil service residency rules had changed, allowing city employees to live outside San Francisco if they were within thirty miles of the city limits as the crow flies. We had three options: south, down the Peninsula, much of which was too expensive on a cop's pay; the East Bay suburbs that just seemed too far; and Marin County to the north, which became the most logical choice. Many of my police buddies had already left the city and relocated to the small town of Novato. Initially, I wanted to be closer to the Golden Gate Bridge to keep my commute short, but towns like Sausalito, Mill Valley, and Larkspur were too pricey for us. Further north, new tract home developments were popping up in the fifty-thousand-dollar range, which we could afford. Novato was becoming a favorite relocation community for police, fire fighters, and other San Francisco city workers because it was exactly thirty miles north of the bridge. That's where Donna started looking.

We found a house and began the moving process. It was anything but smooth. Our children were extremely unhappy at being uprooted from their schools and friends. Dan, the oldest, took it the hardest. He was fourteen and about to enter high school. All he ever wanted was to go to St. Ignatius High School like me and where many of his friends were going. He'd already taken the admission test for St. Ignatius and passed. Now we were tearing him away. Some close friends of ours offered to have Dan live with them, but we decided that as difficult as it was for him, we were still a family and whatever we did it would be together. Dave and Debbie, I learned later, also took the move hard, but were just not as vocal about it as their older brother.

Dan excelled both academically and athletically at San Marin High School in Novato, but he never got over missing four years at St. Ignatius High School. I promised I would make it up to him, but I wasn't sure how. Eventually we were able to send him to Santa Clara University, a private Jesuit school in Silicon Valley where he was reunited with many of the guys he knew from elementary school and CYO sports.

All this family upheaval occurred as Eddie Erdelatz and I searched for the Ocean Beach killer. We scoured nearly every gas station receipt from Venice to Half Moon Bay looking for clues about the driver and his car. We showed photos of possible suspects to Julia Kehling. We checked on unsolved random shootings. At one point, a month into the investigation, we even hired a hypnotist.

Eddie had seen an article in *TV Guide* about Dr. Martin Reiser, the Los Angeles Police Department's first psychologist, who advocated hypnosis to help victims and witnesses remember elusive details. We hoped he might be able to help Julia Kehling recall more about her experience. Dr. Reiser told us he would come to San Francisco at no charge if we paid for his flight and hotel room. We asked Chief of Inspectors Charlie Barca for permission to bring Reiser up from L.A., and he consented. The three-hour session with Julia took place in a room at the Holiday Inn on Van Ness Avenue. The last thing she wanted to do was to relive the terror of that night on the beach, but her desire to help solve her friend's murder overcame her reluctance.

In the room with us was Inspector Hobie Nelson, our police sketch artist. Dr. Reiser spoke to Julia in a soft, reassuring voice. "Now, Julia, I'm going to hypnotize you, so I want you to relax. Just let all your muscles relax and go floppy, like a damp dishcloth," Dr. Reiser said to her. After a few test questions to determine the depth of her hypnotic state, Dr. Reiser asked her a series of questions about the events on January 13. As interesting as this technique was, it did not provide any new or useful details for our case. It did, however, help Hobie to fine tune the composite drawing of the suspect.

The year after our meeting, Dr. Reiser founded the Law Enforcement Hypnosis Institute, teaching more than a thousand attorneys, judges, and detectives about its applications. He said his research showed that Seventy-five percent of people under hypnosis provided valuable information—most of which could be verified. But critics of the practice doubted its reliability and suggested that investigators could use it to plant false memories. In 1982, the California Supreme Court called hypnosis "inherently unreliable."

On March 14, two months after the beach attack, we caught a break. Police arrested thirty-four-year-old Clarence E. Ferguson of South San Francisco on an auto theft charge for failing to return a rental car on time. Ferguson, who also went by Charles K. Frazier, said he was the business agent for a Muslim warehouse on Oakdale Avenue, but officials there said Ferguson was not employed by them. Ferguson had rented a 1975 Mercury from the Hertz rental car agency in downtown San Francisco on January 22 and dropped it off a week later than he was supposed to at an incorrect Hertz location, so it showed up as missing on the company's records.

There were enough similarities to Ferguson in Julia Kehling's description of her attacker for us to hold him until we could fly her back from Cincinnati for a lineup. She made a positive identification that Ferguson was the man who attacked her and her friend. We booked Ferguson for the murder of Janet Rodgers and attempted murder of Julia Kehling.

During a jail visit between Ferguson and his wife, Inspector Jack McKay from our Intelligence Bureau overheard him tell her, "You have to get rid of what's in the looker." When McKay relayed this to us, Eddie and I had no idea what was meant by "the looker," but we obtained a search warrant for Ferguson's house. My first thought was the looker could be a mirror, and we started our search in the bathrooms, looking behind every mirror. But then Eddie figured it might mean the television. He was right. When he looked behind the big screen TV, he found multiple guns. None was the murder weapon, but we soon figured out why he had so many.

During our investigation, Eddie and I reached the conclusion that Ferguson was a member of the Nation of Islam's Death Angels cult, sent from its Los Angeles Mosque to San Francisco with two missions. One was to bring new weapons to the San Francisco Mosque, and the second was to commit new Zebra-type murders that would draw suspicion away from the four men already in jail. If new killings occurred, they reasoned, it might lead to charges being dropped against the others. It was a failed plot. But along the way, he picked up the two hitchhikers and shot them.

Ferguson went on trial in June before Superior Court Judge Edward Cragen and a jury of nine women and three men. Julia Kehling was the star witness for the prosecution, conducted by Assistant District Attorney James Lassart.

"Julia Kehling was the greatest witness I ever had," Lassart says today. "She still had a bullet in her head when she was on the witness stand. I put an X-ray of it into evidence." She not only positively identified Ferguson visually, said Lassart, but "she remembered the way he spoke and specific words he used. She also described the interior of his car in detail—the dashboard, the lights, the colors. She was remarkable." Represented by Deputy Public Defender Gordon Armstrong, Ferguson did not take the stand and no defense witnesses were called.

On June 26, the jury found Ferguson guilty of first-degree murder and assault with a deadly weapon. The jury also convicted Ferguson, who had served a previous prison term for burglary in Los Angeles, of being a felon in possession of a concealed firearm. Judge Cragen sentenced Ferguson to life in prison.

That summer, the Falzons settled into our home in Novato. I bought a new car for the commute and began the daily thirty-mile trek to work. I wasn't happy about it at first, but I was certainly more at ease about the safety of my wife and kids.

Especially because there was no letup in murders in San Francisco.

1978 - 1979

187 | SOLVED | GLENN, LARRY | 11/8/79 | STABBING | 473 Ellis St. | Rudolph Pineiro | 79-3185345 | FALZON CLARK | ...

TYPE	SOLVED	NAME RACE-SEX-AGE	date	how killed	location	Suspect	REPORT CORONER# LAB#	INSP.	DISPOSITION
187	YES	PEACE, Donald NM23	9/2/78	Stabbing	110 Summit St.	Willie C. Beard NM32	78-2893971	FALZON MICHAEL	VOL. MANEL.
187		LEITH, WARREN	9/3/78	Stabbing	868 Valencia		78-2896903	FALZON MULLANE	
187	YES	TENNYSON, JOHN	9/3/78	gun shot	1169 Fitzgerald	Sonja McDowell TURNER	78-2898313	FALZON MULLANE	JENNHAH HOMICI
AC.	n/a	Wilde, Joseph	10/4/78	fall from bldg.	420 Castro St.	CASE signed out SUICIDE ½ ACCIDENT	CC# 1482 10/25/78	FALZON	
187	YES	MOSCONE, GEO. MAYOR	11/27/78	GUN SHOTS	CITY HALL	DANIEL WHITE	78-3221012	FALZON CLARK	VOLUNTN MANSLGT
187	YES	MILK, HARVEY SUPV.	11/27/78	GUN shots	City Hall	DANIEL WHITE	78-3221012	FALZON CLARK	VOLUNTN MANSLGT
187	YES	COLE, ERNEST E.	1/3/79	STAB WOUNDS	430 Stevenson	BOLDEN, CLIFFORD	79-2009102	FALZON CLARK	VOL. MANSLGY
187	YES	NAUMOFF, BORIS G.	1/3/79	gun shots	683 Portola Dr.	ROBT. LEE MASSIE	79-2009168	FALZON CLARK	PE degree N/SPEC C
37		PRINCE, WM.	1/4/79	STAB WOUNDS	240 JONES #206		79-2013341	FALZON CLARK	
INV. STING	YES	OFFICER RADOSEVICH, R.	2/15/79	G.S.W.	331 OCTAVIA ST.	DWIGHT P. CRESWELL	79-2175747	FALZON GUINTHER	GUILTY 2ND 2466 FE
37	YES	BURA, Eduardo	2/16/79	gun shots	Lake Merced @ BROTHERHOOD WY.	Rolando B. LUCHINI	79-2177323	FALZON GUINTHER	...degree RATE 6
37	YES	HEALY, Patrick	2/16/79	Gun shots	"	"	"	"	12 degree W/SPEC 6
AC	n/a	MACKIN, WM.	1/26/79	METHYL ALCOHOL	4216 - 22ND ST.	n/a SIGNED OUT 2/21 ACCIDENTAL	CC# 69	FALZON	
1	n/a	CUSENBERRY, JAMES	2/20/79	Subdural	3864 CALIFORNIA ST.	n/a Signed out 2/22 accidental	CC# 262	FALZON	
INV. STING	YES	OFFICER DONSBACH	3/31/79	GSW - during 211R att.	1418 Lombard St.	COURTNEY A. PEREIRA deceased	79-2346794	FALZON CLARK	JUSTIFIA HOMICID.
37	YES	SCOTT, ALFONZO	5/13/79	STAB WOUND	512 APT 4 FREDERICK ST.	JAMES McNALLY M. MOSENTHIEM	79-2504005	FALZON CLARK	1st degree 4/SPEC. C
37	YES	WERNER, BRADLEY	5/16/79	GSW - during 211R att.	1169 UNION ST.	WALLACE JOHNSON (deceased) ROBT. BLACKFORD	79-2520368	FALZON CLARK	JUSTIFI
37	YES	WONG, RAYMOND	7/5/79	G.S.W.	1359	JACK YEE, G. WONG TIM FONG, SHARA CHU	79-2676585	FALZON CLARK	VOLUNTAR MANSLAUG
37	YES	GLENN, LARRY L.	11/7/79	STAB WOUND	1889 - 46TH AV.	GERMAN Yamboa	792694850	FALZON CLARK	2ND o MURDE
1		ABRAMS, Jack	5/29/79	Beating	473 Ellis FRANKLIN ST.	RUDOLPH PINEIRO	79 3185345	FALZON	Volunta MANSLA
1		STANTON, Laura W.	8/1/79	RAPE - ROBBERY BEATING	REAR of 350 HARBOR Rd.	DAVID MCPENTER	79-1791735	FALZON GUINTHER	
34	N/A	SMITH, ROBT.	8/4/79	n/a	CENTRAL STATION	n/a	79-2800944 CC#1084	FALZON GUINTHER	natura death
1	YES	HANDLEY, GERALD	8/5/79	KNIFE WOUND	5160 MISSION	GAVEN SHINE	79-2805433 CC#1091	FALZON GUINTHER	NOT GUIL
1	YES	BIVINS, CALLE	8/5/79	STRANGULATION	111 Page St. #17	ROBT. JACKSON	79-2807633 CC#1094	FALZON GUINTHER	10/11/79 verdic ½ HOM
AV. MG	YES	OFFICER CEBALLOS, MARIO	8/6/79	n/a	400 LONDON ST.	Ricardo Colon	79-2807962	FALZON GUINTHER	guilty 2ets
1	YES	NOBLE, JAMES	8/7/79	STAB WOUND	6TH ST. @ NATOMA	ALLEN, CHARLES	79-2812444 CC# 79-1106	FALZON GUINTHER	2° MUL
1	YES	IRVING, MARVIN	8/9/79	STAB WOUND	500 Lyon St.	ANTHONY ADAMS	79-2784542 CC# 1112	FALZON GUINTHER	NOT GUIL
1	YES	SOLARNO, CATINA	9/5/79	GSW	U.O.P. CAMPUS	Stephen Burns	OUTSIDE INVESTIGATION	FALZON	2° ALLRO
1	YES	METCALFE, GARY	9/14/79	GSW	91 DRUMM	WILLARD MANNING	79-2958377	FALZON CLARK	ACQUIT

Sample page of the detailed charts I kept on
every homicide case assigned to me.

CHAPTER 17

WHO KILLED EX-CON POPEYE JACKSON?

Around 3:00 a.m. on June 8, 1975, a thirteen-year-old girl woke to noises like firecrackers going off outside her family's apartment on Albion Street in the heart of San Francisco's Mission District. She looked out her window and saw a thin, young adult Black man with a bushy Afro hairstyle standing beside a parked car, pointing a gun at the driver's side window. She saw him fire the gun into the vehicle and then run down the block toward Valencia Gardens, a racially mixed low-income housing project on the corner.

Inside the car, two people, an ex-convict and a Vallejo elementary school teacher, lay dead from multiple gunshot wounds fired at point-blank range.

This double murder thrust me into the workings of the radical violent underground in a way I never expected. This investigation would, over the next nine months, become a tangled web of competing New Left radical extremists, dueling motives, undercover informants, a discarded gun barrel, ballistics evidence, and multiple law enforcement agencies.

It would involve the prisoners' reform movement, a militant anti-police extremist group posing as "food activists," guns connected to a

Sacramento area bank robbery by Patty Hearst's kidnappers, President Ford's would-be assassin Sara Jane Moore, a coin store holdup on the San Francisco Peninsula, and a disguise using theatrical makeup and a wig.

My partner that week was Inspector Dave Toschi, known for his work on the Zodiac serial killer case in the late 1960s and early 1970s. He met me at the crime scene. The victims' car was parked in front of 43 Albion Street, a single block that runs between 15th and 16th Streets and parallel to Guerrero and Valencia Streets. Wilbert "Popeye" Jackson, a forty-five-year-old Black ex-convict and founder of the United Prisoners Union, was in the passenger seat. He'd been shot four times in the shoulder, chest, and head. In the driver's seat was a white woman, Sally Voye, twenty-eight, a teacher at Loma Vista Primary School in Vallejo, thirty miles northeast of San Francisco. She was slumped over with her head in Jackson's lap. She had been shot five times in the back and head.

When the coroner's deputies separated Jackson and Voye for transportation to the city morgue, it was clear they had been engaged in a sexual act when they were shot. Responding officers and crime scene technicians located five shell casings from a 9-mm automatic on the ground beneath the driver's side of the car, which belonged to Ms. Voye. The motive for the shootings was unknown, but we initially ruled out robbery; both victims had money and jewelry on them. Miss Voye's purse, with money and other valuables, was in the back seat in plain view.

One of the responding officers from Mission Station, John Hennessey, told us that other witnesses who were awakened by the shots saw a second man on the opposite side of Jackson's car but didn't see him fire any shots. Subsequent ballistics tests on the bullets recovered from the bodies showed that a .38-caliber revolver was also used in the murders, indicating a second shooter. Revolvers don't eject empty cartridges, explaining why no shell casings from a second weapon were found at the scene. Most likely a third man drove the getaway car. Hennessey said Jackson lived in a second-floor flat at 43 Albion with a woman named Pat Singer. She was nine months pregnant with Jackson's child. Miss Singer said Jackson and Ms. Voye had been to a party, though she couldn't recall where. We later learned the party was in the Lower Haight neighborhood in San Francisco for members of Jackson's prisoners' union and Vietnam Veterans of Foreign Wars.

"I heard the shots," Singer said. "They woke me up, but I didn't get out of bed or come downstairs." Singer had been living with Jackson and his three-year-old son from a previous relationship for the past year. She said she worked for the United Prisoners Union "doing whatever."

Jackson was well known in the community, and news of his murder brought friends and associates to the Albion Street flat throughout the day. Other members of the prisoners' union said they weren't aware of any threats against Jackson, but one man told reporters, "We were angry but not surprised. Popeye has had a lot of enemies, including the police. There are also right-wingers and racists."

Another witness said Sally Voye had been helping to arrange school lectures on prison reform for Jackson and other United Prisoners Union members. She was a graduate of the University of California at Santa Barbara and had earned her teaching credential from the University of California at Berkeley. Her father, Joseph Voye, told the *San Francisco Chronicle* that his daughter had "mentioned at one time that she was sympathetic" to the prison reform group but had not specifically talked about a man named Popeye Jackson. A friend of Sally Voye's told the newspaper that she "was sort of a political idealist, a good person" who had developed a strong sensitivity about social injustices.

Jackson had spent nearly half of his life in jail. He served nineteen years in prison for robbery and burglary before his parole in 1971. He was arrested again in 1973 for drug possession but claimed police planted the drugs in his car. He was acquitted after a jury trial. In April 1974 he was arrested again, this time on a misdemeanor charge of interfering with a police officer in the performance of his duty.

Jackson was elected to the board of directors of the California Prisoners Union in 1972 but left that group and formed the United Prisoners Union about two years before his murder. Both groups claimed to represent convicts and ex-convicts, advocating changes in the state and federal prison systems.

"We have been somewhat at odds with Popeye," John Irwin, a board member of the California Prisoners Union, told the *San Francisco Chronicle*. "We have kept our distance for the last few years for a variety of reasons. Popeye is a person who I would guess would have dozens and dozens of enemies, but I have been so far away from his personal life for so many years I would have no idea who they are."

The circumstances of the murders pointed to a targeted hit rather than a random shooting. The shooter was apparently lying in wait nearby for Jackson to arrive home and moved in once the car was parked. Sally Voye, from all accounts, was an unintended victim, killed simply because she was there. Dave Toschi and I canvassed Jackson's known associates, rivals, union members, neighbors, and others. There was talk of Jackson being "executed" for being a "snitch," a police informant. We had no knowledge that Jackson ever provided confidential information to any law enforcement agency. The FBI seldom confirms information about its confidential informants for obvious reasons. If Popeye were helping them, we would never be told.

The day after the shootings a citizen found the barrel of a 9-mm handgun in a trash bin eight blocks from Albion Street and turned it in to police. It was booked into the property clerk's office.

Two days after the murders, the New World Liberation Front (NWLF), an extremist anti-capitalist group that emerged in the wake of the Patty Hearst kidnapping in 1974, purportedly sent a communique to the *San Francisco Chronicle* claiming responsibility for the Jackson killing. The next day, however, the NWLF sent a communique to the *Berkeley Barb* saying the first was a fake attempt by others to pin the murders on the NWLF. While it praised the murder of Jackson, the second message denied any involvement in the attack.

A few days before the killing, according to a June 28, 1975, article in the *New York Times,* the NWLF ostensibly sent a letter to a local radio station, criticizing Jackson for wearing flamboyant clothes and driving a Cadillac. The group hinted that he was a police informer because earlier that year he "got off with a light sentence" for petty theft.

"All the assertions made against Mr. Jackson have been disputed by his family, coworkers, and Pat Singer, the woman he lived with," the article said. "According to Sleepy Bailey of the United Prisoners Union, 'Popeye was not a snitch,' the Cadillac was eighteen years old, Mr. Jackson and his three-year-old son lived on welfare, and he got the clothes from friends."

Meanwhile, the Weather Underground, a radical militant left-wing organization that had spun off from the Students for a Democratic Society in 1969, said in a statement that the only beneficiaries of the killings were "the ruling classes—those who exploit and oppress the people." The FBI described the Weather Underground as a domestic terrorist group that was responsible for a series of bombings of police stations, banks, and government buildings. Another organization, the Black Guerrilla Family, a "Black power" prison and street gang, said the murders were "the work of the pigs."

Why the hell is this in the paper? I wondered. *C'mon, this is stupid. These crazy people thought the cops were doing these killings? They are flipping it onto the cops.* This is the same thing that's happening today, as far as I'm concerned. The public needs cops to keep them safe. The cops are the ones who stand up to the bullies with the guns. What some of the public doesn't understand is when a police officer gives a citizen respect, he expects respect in return. When situations escalate and a suspect decides to confront the officer physically, the officer cannot afford to lose or be rendered unconscious. The officer is carrying a loaded weapon that, in the hands of the suspect, could mean the end of the officer's life.

Even with an eyewitness, shell casings, the gun barrel, potential suspects, and a possible motive, Dave and I were no closer to solving the case after three weeks. We deduced there was a connection to the rivalry among these militant groups but couldn't pin it down. Trust and power were at play between multiple violent groups. It's not unusual for one group to paint a jacket of suspicion on another group to cover their own guilt.

In November 1973, a group calling itself the Symbionese Liberation Army (SLA) claimed responsibility for killing Oakland Schools Superintendent Marcus Foster and wounding his assistant in a parking lot after a school board meeting. Cyanide-tipped bullets were used in the ambush. On February 4, 1974, the SLA kidnapped nineteen-year-old newspaper heiress Patricia Hearst from her Berkeley apartment at gunpoint. Two weeks later, Hearst participated in the SLA's robbery of a Hibernia Bank in San Francisco. The search for the SLA culminated in May in a wild shootout with four hundred law enforcement officers in Los Angeles. Six members of the radical group died in the gun battle and subsequent fire at a house in south central L.A. Hearst was not among the victims. Surviving SLA members brought Hearst back to the Bay Area and went into hiding again, traveling to the East Coast. They eluded a cross-country manhunt for more than a year. When they came back to California in April 1975, SLA members robbed a Crocker Bank branch in Carmichael, a suburb of Sacramento, killing a customer named Myrna Opsahl. Hearst was driving the getaway car.

In its months-long pursuit of Hearst, SLA fugitives, and other underground terrorists, the FBI focused much of its attention on the guns used in their various crimes. Guns are often traceable to their source or owner by serial number and through ballistics. The FBI enlisted a Sacramento-area gun collector and one of their confidential informants named Walter Handsaker to help. Walter was able to infiltrate the radical groups as a weapons instructor and source of untraceable firearms. He would teach the radicals how to assemble and disassemble guns, and to destroy or dispose of guns in parts.

Among the organizations that came to trust Handsaker was The Tribal Thumb, a collaborative of so-called "food activists" that ran a network of cooperative stores and businesses catering to paroled prisoners and refugees. It was founded in 1973 by Earl Lamar Satcher, a saxophone-playing ex-convict and former member of the Black Panther Party. The Tribal Thumb ran an eatery called Wellsprings Reunion in the South of Market neighborhood.

Handsaker was present when The Tribal Thumb conducted training sessions for its members on how to ambush and kill police officers during traffic stops or when being arrested. The plan was for a male member to drive a motorcycle with a female member riding in the seat behind. The bike would speed to draw police attention, then pull over when ordered to do so. As the officer emerged from his patrol vehicle or got off his motorcycle, the woman would get off the bike and walk back toward the officer with her hands raised in a sign of surrender. She would use a friendly smile to appear non-threatening and engage the officer in conversation. The distraction would enable the man on the motorcycle to draw his weapon and shoot the officer before he could react.

Another FBI informant at the time was Sara Jane Moore, a forty-five-year-old self-radicalized revolutionary. She had been a voluntary bookkeeper for People in Need, the food giveaway program organized by newspaper publisher Randolph Hearst in response to a demand from his daughter's kidnappers. Moore was a friend of Popeye Jackson and reportedly took target practice at a remote property owned by The Tribal Thumb in Arbuckle, an agricultural town one hundred miles north of San Francisco in Colusa County. On September 22, 1975, Moore fired an errant shot at President Gerald Ford with a .44-caliber revolver as he emerged from the St. Francis Hotel on Post Street in downtown San Francisco. She pleaded guilty to the assassination attempt and received a life sentence.

Dave Toschi and I went to the women's Federal Correctional Institution in the East Bay city of Dublin to talk to Moore about The Tribal Thumb, but she provided little helpful information in a rambling, mostly incoherent statement.

One day in late summer 1975, a Tribal Thumb member named Richard Alan London, a Caucasian-Latino man also known as Ricardo, brought two guns to Walter Handsaker for disposal. London said that one, a .45-caliber automatic, was "hot." The second weapon was the frame of a 9-mm handgun without a barrel. "This one is really, really hot," he bragged to Handsaker. "I'm a professional hit man now."

Both guns were among forty weapons stolen from a gun collector in Crockett, a small community on San Pablo Bay near Vallejo. The .45 had been used in the robbery of a coin store south of San Francisco on May 6, 1975, a month before the Jackson-Voye murders. A bullet from the gun matched one lodged in the ceiling of the coin store when the gun discharged during the robbery. The FBI was particularly interested in 9-mm guns because a 9-mm had been used in the Carmichael bank robbery by the SLA. When Handsaker told his FBI handlers about the 9-mm frame and London's comments, the FBI notified us that one of its informants might be able to help us in the Jackson case.

I remembered that the barrel of a 9-mm automatic was found the day after the Jackson-Voye shootings. I went down to the property clerk's office, located the barrel, and determined that its serial number matched the one on the handle that Handsaker had given to the FBI. Most people, criminals especially, aren't aware that a gun's serial number is engraved in two places, the barrel and the handle. The grip and trigger housing London gave Handsaker were a perfect fit with the barrel. We sent the barrel back to Washington, D.C., where FBI Agent Bob Sibert was able to match this so-called "dirty gun" with the shell casings and bullets recovered from the Jackson-Voye killings. This was the break we had been waiting for.

In our investigation we learned that London had been arrested in Napa County north of San Francisco for the coin store robbery in July 1975, a month after Popeye was killed. Napa police who stopped London's 1962 yellow Volvo van found two guns in his car that were traced to the Crockett burglary—a .380 automatic handgun and an M-1 carbine rifle. Neither was connected to the Jackson-Voye case, so we were not notified right away. More significantly for us, however, officers found an Afro wig in the glove compartment along with a receipt for theatrical makeup. Neither item drew much notice from the Napa officers, but they certainly got our attention.

The teenage girl who witnessed the Jackson-Voye murders had described seeing a Black man with an Afro as the shooter. It had never occurred to us that it might be a white man in disguise.

Now we needed to pick up Richard London to question him about the Jackson-Voye murders.

CHAPTER 18
THE NEW-AGE MAFIA

✦ ✦ ✦

Richard London wasn't hard to find. He had been locked up in the Santa Clara County jail for nine months awaiting trial for the coin store robbery in Mountain View, forty miles south of San Francisco.

During the first week of April 1976, Assistant District Attorney Jim Lassart presented the case we had compiled to the San Francisco County Grand Jury naming Richard London and five unindicted co-conspirators in the Popeye Jackson-Sally Voye murders. The Grand Jury returned a secret indictment of two counts of murder against London.

The Tribal Thumb/Wellsprings Commune took its name from the group's tribal organization and the idea that the human hand is useless without the thumb. The term Wellsprings was taken from a phrase in a book by controversial psychologist Wilhelm Reich, who once studied under Freud. With fewer than thirty members at its peak, The Tribal Thumb compiled a history of cold-blooded violence far out of proportion to its small size. Some of its members were convicted of first-degree murder, armed robbery, assault, and prison escape.

"Tribal Thumb is a revolutionary group that believes in violence now," Lassart told a reporter at the time. "They think that one wins a few, loses a few, and has to break a few eggs along the way." Broken eggs, in this context, meaning some people must get hurt.

"These guys are the cutting edge of a whole new type of organized crime," another investigator told the *San Francisco Chronicle.* "It's different from the old-line mob out of Chicago and New York, or any of the other organized crime groups most people are familiar with. These people came out of the counter-culture—revolutionary organizations, extremist prison reform groups, and so on. You could call it a sort of new-age Mafia."

The unindicted co-conspirators named in the indictment of London were Gary Johnson, Sandra Serrano, Ernest Kirkwood, Benjamin Sargis, and Elena Payne. This group constituted the nucleus of The Tribal Thumb.

Some or all of them, according to the indictment, met with London on two occasions near Arbuckle in January 1975. There they practiced firing weapons and continued their tactical training to avoid capture. They also bought guns stolen from the home of the Crockett gun collector.

Kirkwood, known as "Monster Mash," was thirty-four, six foot, five inches tall and weighed 235 pounds. He was an ex-convict and served as a lieutenant to Tribal Thumb founder Earl Satcher. We always suspected that Kirkwood was the second shooter at the Jackson-Voye murders, but we didn't have the evidence to prove it. Years later he would plead guilty to two other murders.

Sandra (Sandy) Serrano, then twenty-four, was Richard London's wife. She was widely known in Bay Area radical circles and frequently visited prison inmates. Elena Payne was active with Tribal Thumb as a writer and theoretician. Benjamin Sargis, forty-three, was a parole violator. Gary Johnson, twenty-nine, had been convicted of narcotics possession and attempted burglary in Sonoma County.

With London already in custody, Dave Toschi drifted away to other casework, leaving me to bring London back to San Francisco to be charged. Armed with the grand jury indictment, I asked Assistant District Attorney Jim Lassart to join me. Over time I had developed a deep respect for Jim. He was brilliant in the courtroom. We'd grown close as colleagues and friends. What I liked most was his intensity, his dedication, his fairness, and his willingness to fight the good fight for justice.

Jim, who was my age, had graduated from Santa Clara University, earned his law degree at the University of San Francisco, and was a Vietnam vet. Today Jim is a retired Brigadier General in the U.S. Army Reserve. We had a lot in common and shared numerous mutual friends. Many of these friends were athletes from St. Ignatius High School who had gone on to Santa Clara. Whenever Jim and I took on a case together, we would have dinner and tear into every aspect of the new case. "Frank," he'd say, "you're a cop, you think like a cop, and you know all the necessary elements of a crime to justify an arrest. All that comes naturally to you. Now I want you to think like a defense attorney and tear your case investigation apart. Find all the holes, the weak spots, and fix them. When you're finished, no defense attorney will want to cross-examine you. You will have all the answers and you will have done a complete investigation." I learned so much from him, and I like to think I helped to make him a better prosecutor by understanding the police inspector's point of view.

The day we were going to pick up London, April 7, 1976, Jim called me and asked if my former homicide partner, Jack Cleary, now chief of the district attorney's investigator staff, could go with us. "Of course," I said. It occurred to me that one way to break up the unpleasant prisoner transfer was to stop for a visit with legendary football coach Pat Malley at Santa Clara University. Malley had played on the Broncos' 1950 Orange Bowl championship team, then served in the Army before starting his coaching career at St. Ignatius High School. He had been my coach at St. Ignatius before he took the head coaching job at Santa Clara the year I graduated. Malley was a coach I respected, and a genuinely fine man revered by many of his former players. Jim Lassart, who had attended Bellarmine College Preparatory high school in San Jose, had been an outstanding linebacker for Malley at Santa

Clara. I called Malley. He was delighted to hear we were coming down, and he set up lunch for us on campus. It was a treat to spend time with him.

The rest of the drive down to the Santa Clara County Jail was uneventful. I can't say the same for the return trip.

We signed London out wearing his orange jail jumpsuit, handcuffed him, and placed him in the back seat of our unmarked car next to Lassart. I drove, and Jack sat beside me in the passenger seat. From time to time over my career, I have experienced a sixth sense about situations where I feel something's not right. I suppose it's natural for a policeman to be overly alert just because it's the nature of the job. But in certain situations, you pick up odd vibes. That was the case on this trip. It wasn't one bit lost on me that London belonged to an organization that trained in ambushing cops. I wouldn't put it past them to try something to free him.

The ride back toward San Francisco was quiet. We traveled up Interstate 280 and then cut over to U.S. 101 at San Francisco International Airport. No one said much, including London. I was thinking to myself that I was overreacting to my suspicions about possible trouble. Nothing was going to happen.

Just then, shortly after passing Candlestick Park on the way into downtown San Francisco, I noticed a California Highway Patrol car following us closely. Then he turned on his red light and motioned me to pull over.

What the hell? I thought. *What's he doing? I wasn't speeding.* I grabbed the radio microphone and called the Operations Center. "5-Henry-7 to headquarters," I said. "I'm returning to the Hall of Justice with a known terrorist political prisoner in the back seat, and I have a highway patrol car trying to pull me over. I'm not stopping. Please tell the CHP to have him back off." Given the political climate of the times and all the radical extremist violence in the Bay Area, I thought it wouldn't be that far-fetched for The Tribal Thumb to highjack a highway patrol car and uniform. The Operations Center dispatcher came back on the radio.

"CHP says negative on backing off, 5-Henry-7," he said. "He wants you to pull over."

Now all my senses were alerted. We were about a mile from the Sixth Street turnoff to the Hall of Justice. I pulled over to the side of the freeway, stopped, and told Jack and Jim to stay in the car. I got out and stood next to my door. I was holding my badge in my left hand and my service weapon in my right hand, down by my side. The highway patrolman got out of his car. I knew he could see my badge and my gun. He put his hand on his holstered revolver. *Could there be terrorists hiding in his back seat, ready to come out firing?*

In a strong voice I shouted, "You take out your gun, and that will be the biggest mistake you'll ever make!" Just then, Jim Lassart flew out of the back door and approached the officer. He explained who we were, where we were going, and most importantly, why we were being so cautious. The CHP officer stood down, got back in his car, and drove away. When Jim got back in our car, he said the officer told him he had pulled us over for speeding. "He said he clocked us at 75 miles an hour in a 65 zone," Jim said. It may have all been a big misunderstanding, but I wasn't taking any chances, not in this case.

When we pulled into the police garage a few minutes later, newspaper photographers were waiting for us. I don't know how they knew we were coming, but there were inspectors in our detail who liked to tip off reporters when something big was going on. There were also excellent reporters at the Hall who would pick up leads by routinely stopping by the homicide detail and listening to the police radio.

We booked London into the city prison on two counts of murder, conspiracy to commit murder, and possession of a firearm by a felon. Jim said that because two persons were murdered, special circumstances would be alleged under the state's new death penalty law, and the death penalty would be sought for London. He was arraigned the next day before Superior Court Judge Claude Perasso. London sat behind a bullet-proof glass partition alongside his attorney, Salle Soladay. Judge Perasso set April 22 as the date for London to enter a plea and issued a gag order forbidding all those involved in the case from discussing it. London was then returned to the Santa Clara County jail.

When London's trial began on September 12, 1978, Lassart told the jury of nine men and three women that London had bragged about killing Popeye Jackson, a reference to the statement London made to FBI informant Walter Handsaker about being a "professional hit man."

Another witness, Samuel R. Brooks, thirty-two, whose Santa Clara County Jail cell adjoined London's, testified that London had boasted to him about the murder. Brooks said that London claimed he was part of the hierarchy of The Tribal Thumb and was a member of a three-man hit team who "used a nine-millimeter to shoot the man."

Brooks also testified that London said he had used shoe polish and a wig to disguise himself as a Black man. London told Brooks, "Sally Voye was there, and because she was there, she had to go." London also told Brooks that he began disassembling the gun in the getaway car and that the barrel accidentally fell out a partially opened door.

Brooks was an ex-convict from Kansas who was arrested in San Jose in 1977 and was later sentenced to twelve years in prison after pleading guilty to charges of rape, kidnapping, burglary, forced oral copulation, and assault with a deadly weapon.

Gary Johnson, one of the unindicted co-conspirators who had been granted immunity, told the court that The Tribal Thumb ordered him to kill Jackson, but he did not carry it out.

In his opening statement, London's attorney, Alan Caplan, said he would prove that London was with his wife, Sandra Serrano, at the time of the killings.

Jim Lassart had asked Inspector Roy Hicks in our photo lab to work up a photo of London with darkened skin and wearing a bushy Afro. The modified photo was included in a lineup folder with photos of six Black men that included Ernest Kirkwood. When Lassart approached Sandy Serrano, who was seated in the witness box, he handed her the photos. "Who can you identify in these photographs?" he asked her. She picked out Kirkwood but could not identify any of the others. It was a very strategic move on Jim's part. Serrano could not identify her own husband in blackface makeup and wig.

London took the witness stand in his own defense and denied any part in the Jackson-Voye killings. He said he was with his wife at the time Jackson and Voye were killed. He also testified that the 9-mm gun used in the murders was given to him a week after the shootings by Tribal Thumb leader Earl Satcher. Satcher had died a year earlier, in April 1977, in a shootout at the San Francisco Food Cooperative warehouse in Hunters Point.

The London jury deliberated fewer than six hours before finding him guilty on all counts. Superior Court Judge Daniel Hanlon sentenced London to life in prison on October 20, 1978.

Law enforcement agencies had widely considered The Tribal Thumb/Wellsprings Commune defunct after the Satcher killing and the London trial. But they were wrong. It was still thriving. Its members were tied to a series of violent crimes over the next four years, including the murder of a customs agent, a Brink's truck robbery, escape from a federal prison, murder of a defected Wellsprings Commune member, a gun battle with police during a bank robbery, and explosives and firearms charges.

Ernest "Monster Mash" Kirkwood, who had been among the unindicted co-conspirators in the Jackson-Voye case, was the prime suspect in the murder of two men, Leonard Harris Jones, thirty-eight, and Cleophus Lovett, forty-six, and wounding of a third, Joe Coney, forty-four, in a McAllister Street apartment on July 24, 1982. All three were shot in the back of the head, execution style. Coney survived. My colleagues who investigated the case, Inspectors Napoleon Hendrix and Earl Sanders, put Coney under police protection, but he was unable to talk with them for four days, giving Kirkwood a head start to avoid capture. As the inspectors went through Kirkwood's belongings in his apartment, they found a picture of Kirkwood standing in front of the Eiffel Tower in 1980. That told them Kirkwood had a passport. They alerted Interpol to tag the name and passport number.

Using address books and telephone numbers also found in the apartment, Napoleon and Earl dogged Kirkwood for the next four months, tracking him to Florida, Puerto Rico, and Jamaica. In mid-November, Jamaican police were poised to arrest Kirkwood, but that same day he had taken a flight to London. Scotland Yard detectives were waiting for him at London's Heathrow Airport. The jury in his first trial for the murders deadlocked eleven to one in favor of conviction. On the eve of his second trial in 1987, he pled guilty to two charges of second-degree murder and was sentenced to seventeen years to life.

Assistant District Attorney Jim Lassart and me

CHAPTER 19
KILL OR BE KILLED

I was never a great shot.

I had a habit of flicking my right wrist when I pulled the trigger, so a lot of my shots were slightly off target. That's one reason I didn't like going to the firing range. Another was the noise. It was so loud. With thirty or more officers standing almost shoulder to shoulder, all firing at the same time, I would have splitting headaches for hours afterward. But if you wore any type of formal ear protection at the range back then, you were considered a wuss. Instead, I stuck a .38-caliber bullet in each ear. Today the SFPD is much wiser. All officers are required to wear sound suppressive headsets and eye protective glasses.

It seemed as if my partners could literally blow out the center of the target all day long. Carl Klotz and Mike Mullane were so good that I offered to buy them lunch if they would put their last bullets into my silhouette so my score wasn't so embarrassing. I had no choice, of course; regular practice with my service weapon was not only a department requirement, I knew that someday it could save someone's life, including my own.

As a police inspector, I carried a lightweight .38-caliber Smith & Wesson blue steel revolver on and off duty. It was easy to carry on my belt. However, it wasn't the most accurate weapon, more like a peashooter. Eventually, the department upgraded and issued all inspectors a heavier, more accurate, more powerful .357 Magnum with a two-and-a-half-inch barrel. I was one of the lucky inspectors to be issued a rare attractive stainless-steel model. Most others were given the blue steel model. My range scores improved dramatically. The range master taught us the technique of using the cup-and-saucer grip, using the palm of your left hand to steady your right hand holding the weapon. I loved this. It prevented my right wrist from flicking.

Working in plain clothes, I didn't wear the patrolman's bulky equipment belt. I wore a standard holster with a flap that tucked into my right waistband for support.

In thirteen years, I had only fired my weapon while on duty one time, when I was in uniform on foot patrol walking the Fillmore beat with another Northern Station officer, Charlie Tedrow. Our attention was drawn to the sound of a gunshot. A man had shot a person outside a Fillmore Street bar. I hollered at him, "Stop! Police!" The suspect turned and fired shots across the street at Charlie and me. We both fired back, then chased him down Fulton Street to Webster Street in the direction of a housing project known as the Pink Palace. He turned the corner and was out of our sight. When we reached the corner, we saw that he hadn't gone far. Two other officers, Charlie Beane and Bill Sheffler, with their canine unit on routine patrol, had the suspect in custody, spread-eagled with his hands on the rear of their vehicle. They were unaware of our pursuit and had made the stop when they saw a man running down the block, looking back at them with a gun. He tried to ditch the gun under their patrol car when they caught up to him.

In the spring of 1977, I signed up for a Thursday night class in horticulture at City College of San Francisco. I liked gardening and thought it would be an easy three units toward my Associate of Science degree in criminology. I knew a little about flowers and plants, but I sure didn't know their Latin names. It was a lot harder than I figured, but I liked the class.

After work on February 10, 1977, I drove out to Original Joe's Westlake, one of my favorite Italian restaurants. Westlake is in Daly City, just over the southern border of San Francisco. The vast development of multi-colored, lookalike houses in Westlake was the inspiration for Malvina Reynolds' hit song "Little Boxes" in the early 1960s. I knew the owners of the Original Joe's restaurants, and I never missed a chance to eat there.

I left Joe's at 6:30 p.m. for the fifteen-minute drive to City College. I took my regular route along Holloway Avenue, a wide east-west street that passes through the Ingleside District. At the intersection of Holloway and Ashton Avenue, Selmi's Market, a neighborhood grocery store, stood on the southeast corner. It had wood-framed glass double doors facing the corner and windows on each side of the store. When I came to the stop sign on the corner, I glanced at the store. I noticed both front doors were wide open, as they often were. My senses perked up. Something was off. I didn't know what, exactly. Just a feeling, like any cop gets now and then. I had no idea my life was about to change dramatically.

Driving slowly through the intersection, I glance at Selmi's once more. The open doors provide a clear view of the front counter and the cash register. I see a tall Black man in a camouflage military jacket standing at the register, his arm outstretched, as if he's throwing a punch. Then I see it, in his hand, the shape of a gun. An automatic, a .45 maybe. He is pointing the gun at people in the store. It's a stickup in progress, no question.

I pull past the store and double park. I'm in my personal Volkswagen bus, so I don't have a two-way radio to call headquarters. I reach for my gun in its holster but quickly remember it's under my seat because I never took my weapon onto the college campus with me. I fumble a bit under the seat before finding it. I get out of my car and crouch behind a parked car just beyond the grocery store entrance. My gun is in my right hand. My heart is pounding and my senses are now in high gear. My mind is racing.

I'll wait until the guy comes outside before confronting him so I don't endanger anyone inside. I'm reasonably protected here, crouched behind this parked car. When he comes out, I'll holler, "Freeze! Police!" If he comes up with his gun, I'll have to shoot.

I'm acting one hundred percent on instinct here. There's no time to think. It's all adrenaline. I think I'm in total control, but then I look down at my right hand holding the gun and it's quivering. Things are happening so fast, but in my head, everything is in super slow motion, almost like an out-of-body experience. Seconds seem like eternity. I don't feel afraid, but my body is smarter than my brain right now. Immediately I chastise my own reactions.

You're scared? How are you going to stop a holdup man with a gun? You'll be killed for sure. What a chickenshit you are! You're a coward! A loser!

This snaps me back. Suddenly my grip gets rigid on the weapon and I'm not shaking anymore. My plan is still the same. When I look up again, the double doors to the store are now closed. I can't see what's going on inside. Out of one eye, I notice a car pull up and park at the curb on Ashton Street, directly outside the store. Out steps a tall Black guy in a white linen suit and white shoes, a happy-go-lucky smile on his face, headed toward Selmi's. He's almost skipping, and he's whistling, like he's got a hot date and needs to pick up some booze at the market on his way to his girl's house.

I can't believe this is happening. If he goes into that store, he's either dead or he's a hostage. I can't shoot when there's a hostage. Now I'm dead. I gotta stop him from going into the store, but if I break my cover and that holdup suspect comes out of the store, he's got me dead to rights. Shit, I have no choice.

I step out from behind the parked car and walk briskly toward

White Suit until I'm just a few feet away from him on the sidewalk. I'm now holding my badge in my left hand, gun still in my right hand. I'm holding the badge up high so it's clearly visible, but he doesn't see the badge, only a white guy with a gun. He throws up his hands.

"Please, mister, don't shoot me!" he cries out.

"I'm a cop," I say. "There's a holdup in progress inside the market."

Just then, out of my left eye I catch movement at the front of the store. The doors are opening. The stickup man charges out, hunched over, head down, arms folded across his chest like a fullback going through the defensive line. I turn away from White Suit and face the guy head on. We're less than ten feet apart.

"FREEZE! POLICE!" I yell at the top of my voice, pointing my gun at him. With my badge in my left hand, there's no time for the cup-and-saucer, just my right hand holding the weapon.

He comes up with the .45, fires off two quick shots at us. Both somehow miss. That's the thing about a .45, it has a huge recoil so it's not the most accurate handgun. Thinking back on it now, he must have looked at White Suit and me standing together, got confused about who was the cop, and fired hastily, hoping to hit one of us. White Suit takes off running and disappears. I never saw him again.

I aim at the gunman and squeeze the trigger on my .357. I don't know where my shot goes, but I find out later that it grazed the top of his jacket and creased his left shoulder. He turns away from me and runs into the street, me in pursuit. It's still daylight, but the sun is setting. We are both in the street now. I pocket my badge, plant my feet, brace my gun hand with the palm of my left hand. I take dead aim at his back, but I don't fire.

He quickly spins and fires two more shots at me. With the kickback of his weapon, I see the explosive arc of the discharge spray out from the muzzle in a flash of exploding gunpowder, like tracer rounds. At this moment, I know I am going to die. But again, miraculously, neither round hits me. I have one thought.

Dear God, if I'm going to die, please let me take him with me.

He's now fifteen or twenty feet from me. I fire again, once. He falls onto his back in the middle of the street. I walk slowly over to him for a closer look. I have no clue where my bullet struck him. My eyes are focused on one thing—his gun. I'm not looking at his face. I wouldn't find out until the next morning that my second shot hit him in his forehead above the right eye. He is lying in the street, legs bent, right arm extended between them, still holding the .45. The bag of holdup money that he'd been clutching is on the ground beside him, a few bills spilling out of the top. I circle slowly, placing myself behind him, away from his weapon. I'm watching his hand. It's twitching. He's not dead.

If he comes up with that gun, I'll have to shoot him again.

Suddenly it hits me that this guy might still have a partner in the store with a shotgun who could come out any second and level me. I take my eyes off the wounded suspect's gun and look back at the store. The grocer sticks his head out the front door.

"HOW MANY MORE ARE IN THERE?" I shout.

"He's the only one," the grocer replies.

Alerted by the gunfire, people are pouring out of nearby houses, standing on their front porches and the sidewalk. I start shouting at the crowd.

"I'M A POLICE OFFICER!" I holler as I take out my badge again and hold it high in the air. "I NEED HELP! PLEASE CALL FOR HELP!"

Within a few minutes, I see a black-and-white patrol car barreling down Holloway, Code 3 with red lights flashing and siren blaring. It stops five feet from me and the wounded suspect. Out of the car bound two Ingleside Station patrolmen, Pete Maloney and his partner, John Sheehan. Maloney walks over to the wounded suspect, reaches down, and removes the .45 automatic from his hand. Pete finds that it still has a bullet in the chamber and three more in the clip. Sheehan radios for an ambulance, Code 3.

The paper bag from the robbery contains $279.

✳ ✳ ✳

The gunman was identified as Lloyd Henry Hill, twenty-six, an ex-convict with a record of grocery store holdups. He had served time in prison for the robbery of a Redwood City grocery store in 1970, during which a female hostage and a police officer were both shot. Hill had been convicted of kidnapping, armed robbery, assault with a deadly weapon, and two attempted murders. He received a sentence of fifteen years to life but served only a few years. He had been out of prison less than a week. Ironically, he was living in Novato, not far from my home.

Soon the intersection was crawling with police and other officials. Homicide Inspectors Eddie Erdelatz and Jeff Brosch, who were on call, responded to the scene. The homicide detail responds to all officer-involved shootings and takes charge of the investigation. Assistant District Attorney Doug Munson, Deputy Chief of Inspectors Clem DeAmicis, and Captain Don Taylor all arrived at the scene. The crime lab and photo lab also responded.

I followed Erdelatz and Brosch downtown to give them my statement. The department had already called my wife to let her know what had happened and that I was okay. She told the children, "Daddy was in a shootout with a holdup man, but he's fine." I called Donna from the homicide detail and downplayed the whole thing.

It was nearing midnight by the time I got home. Donna had taped the 11:00 p.m. news on Channel 7. Anchor Van Amburg opened the broadcast with the words, "Breaking News! San Francisco has a new hero tonight." I didn't feel much like a hero. As far as I knew, I had taken a man's life and almost lost my own. All for $279. We stayed up for quite a while talking. It was after 1:00 a.m. by the time we got to bed, and I didn't sleep well at all. On top of that, I got word that Police Chief Charles Gain wanted me in his office at 7:00 a.m. The *Novato*

Advance, our weekly newspaper, carried a front-page story about the incident under the headline, "Novatoans in Shootout." That was the epitome of the expression "all news is local."

When I went to see Chief Gain, he asked me to relate the details of the gun battle. When I was finished, he said, "I'm glad you're okay, Inspector. Congratulations. Job well done. You can return to your office."

That was it. No administrative leave. No psychological support. No PTSD counseling. No policy existed then to help officers after a tragic event. I simply went back to work. At 8:00 a.m. I was at my desk again, working my cases.

Later that morning, I heard Lloyd Henry Hill had died. I went downstairs to see Coroner Boyd Stephens and observe the body. Hill had lived for eleven hours before he succumbed from my gunshot to his skull, Dr. Stephens told me, but he was brain-dead from the moment of impact and never regained consciousness.

Months later I received a gold medal of valor for my actions. This is the highest honor the police department can bestow. It is usually given posthumously to an officer's widow. When I entered the Police Commission hearing room for the ceremony, all the department brass and other police officials present gave me a standing ovation. That threw me for a loop. It both surprised me and moved me. Over the years, I had received other meritorious commendations, but this was especially meaningful for me because I had survived the gunfight and no one else had been hurt. Later that same year, I was named the department's Policeman of the Year.

I still live with this experience almost daily, and I thank God I survived that day. The senselessness of it blows me away. All this for only two hundred seventy-nine dollars. Why does somebody arm themself and put their own life at risk by deciding to shoot it out with a police officer? One or both of them is likely to die. And for what? It just makes no sense. Eventually, law enforcement agencies implemented new policies to assist officers after a shooting or other traumatic incident.

I remember years later going with my partner, Carl Klotz, to interview two California Highway Patrol officers who had brought a suspect into our city prison. While he was being booked for drunk driving and possession of weapons, the man managed to swallow a concealed cyanide pill and died right there at the booking counter. When we arrived at the CHP offices to speak with the two arresting officers, their commander came out to meet us. "They're not here," he said. "I sent them both home on administrative leave. They're getting counseling for this tragic event they witnessed."

Administrative leave? Because they watched a man take a poison pill? I couldn't help but think back to my shootout with Lloyd Henry Hill and how I could have used some assistance coping with it. But when I think about that, I recall the story of my patrolman friend who accidentally hit and killed a young boy with his patrol car one Halloween Night while responding to a report of shots fired in the Sunnydale Projects. I can't imagine what it must have been like for him to live with that for the rest of his life.

Erdelatz and Brosch wrapped up the case of my shootout with Hill quickly and we all moved on to new cases.

I console myself about the exchange of gunfire with Hill by knowing I had no choice. Kill or be killed.

I never had to fire my gun again.

San Francisco Chronicle

Fatal Gun Battle

Cop Who 'Sensed' a Holdup

By Barney Peterson

HOMICIDE INSPECTOR FRANK FALZON
'I saw a .45 against someone's head'

By Robert Popp

Homicide inspector Frank Falzon said yesterday that a "sixth sense" made him stop Thursday evening at an Ingleside supermarket where he later shot it out with a holdup man.

The exchange of gunfire rattled the quiet neighborhood around Selmi's Market at Holloway and Ashton streets and brought death to Lloyd Henry Hill, 25, of 440 Alameda del Prado, Novato.

Hill was on parole from a 15 years-to-life term he received in 1970 for his part in a Redwood City supermarket holdup in which a policeman and woman were wounded.

"I was driving east on Holloway to attend a class at City College," said Falzon, "when I saw a man inside this market motioning with his hands. I didn't see a gun then, but a sixth sense, or something, made me stop.

"I parked the car ten feet away, and then I saw him plant a .45 against someone's head. I got out and got down behind the car and trained my gun on the middle of the door.

"I waited for him to come out, but he didn't, and it seemed like an eternity."

At this point, a passerby started to walk up to the store, so Falzon, fearing the robber might take the man hostage, left his cover to warn against entering.

"Then the guy came out, and I told him: 'Stop, I'm police.' He fired two shots at me and started run-

LLOYD HENRY HILL
He died in the shootout

ning. I fired once and I just hit his clothing by his right shoulder.

"We were both in the middle of the street by this time, and he turned and fired at me twice again. I assumed the cup-and-saucer position (cupping his left hand to steady .ne other fist holding the gun).

"I fired once and got him in the head and he went down."

Hill's body was lying over a bag containing $279 taken from the store. He had a .45 caliber pistol in his hand. There was one bullet in the pistol's chamber three left in its clip. Police found four shell casings in the area.

Falzon, who is 35, has been with the police department for 12 years, the last five with homicide.

San Francisco Chronicle, February 12, 1977

CHAPTER 20
MURDER AT CITY HALL

In early 1978, San Francisco was on the threshold of significant sociopolitical and cultural change. By the end of the year, the city would be transformed forever by two shocking and violent events a continent apart.

George Moscone was starting his third year as mayor, and Dianne Feinstein was the president of the city's eleven-member Board of Supervisors. Both were Democrats, but Moscone was viewed as a progressive who opened the doors of city hall and seats of power to women, minorities, and gays, while Feinstein was more centrist and pro-business.

The election in November 1977 marked the first time in San Francisco history that voters chose supervisors by district rather than citywide, so each member represented his or her own section of town. January brought the inauguration of four new board members. The newcomers included Harvey Milk, a forty-eight-year-old Jewish camera store owner and the first openly gay elected official in California history. Also taking their seats on the board were Carol Ruth Silver, forty, a lawyer and civil rights activist, and Ella Hill Hutch, fifty-five, the board's first African American woman. The fourth new member was my friend Dan White, thirty-two, a former Army paratrooper, police officer, and fireman.

I had known Dan since we were kids growing up in the same neighborhood. We attended the same Catholic grammar school and played at the same baseball field, though he was four years younger than me and went to Riordan High School. We had also been in the police department together and played on the all-star SFPD statewide law enforcement championship softball team that I managed.

Dan was a political neophyte, unaccustomed to the rough and tumble nature of partisan politics, pressure from outside influencers, and the give and take of dealmaking. When he told me he was thinking of running for office, I tried to discourage him, fearing he wouldn't fit in. In my view, Dan was simply too honest, principled, and naïve for that world.

Once Dan was in office, I rarely saw or talked to him. Cops paid scant attention to city politics unless it affected them or their paychecks directly. Some of our police chiefs had later become politicians—Frank Jordan was elected mayor, for instance, and Al Nelder and Richard Hongisto served as supervisors.

At first, Dan White and Harvey Milk got along quite well. Dan even invited Harvey to the christening of his newborn son. But as the year wore on, battlelines were drawn between Dan's work on behalf of his largely conservative Excelsior District and Harvey's advocacy for his predominantly gay and liberal Castro District. On November 10, after ten months in office, Dan capitulated to the stress of political gamesmanship and the financial hardship of his low pay as a supervisor and resigned. But days later, when community and labor union leaders in his district pressured him to reconsider, Dan attempted to rescind his resignation and asked Moscone for his board seat back. At first, Moscone seemed inclined to reinstate White. However, Milk and other influencers soon persuaded Moscone to fill White's seat with someone who would return the board to a six-to-five liberal majority.

Over Thanksgiving weekend, Moscone told reporters he would fill White's vacant board seat with Don Horanzy, a federal housing official.

When KCBS radio reporter Barbara Taylor called Dan White at home on Sunday night to get his reaction, Dan was caught off guard by the news, mumbled something about Moscone "breaking his promise" to give White his job back, but declined to comment for the record. Moscone scheduled a news conference to announce Horanzy at 11:00 a.m. Monday, November 27.

I had just begun a week on call with Herman Clark. We were working on our active cases. Herman was still relatively new to the detail, having been a cop for sixteen years, nine of those in the robbery detail. At 11 a.m., I was in a meeting in the district attorney's office with Assistant District Attorney Jim Lassart when I got a call from my boss, Lieutenant Jack Jordan, telling me to return to the homicide detail immediately. "Shut the door," he said when I walked into his office. That was unusual. Jordan rarely closed his door unless it was a serious personnel matter that he didn't want the other guys to overhear.

"There's been a shooting at City Hall," the lieutenant said to me. "It's in the mayor's office. You and Herman need to get up there right away."

"Look, Lieutenant," I protested. "I'm really busy. I don't have time for one of Erdelatz's practical jokes. He's pulled this one on me before."

Believe it or not, Inspector Ed Erdelatz had once tricked me into believing that a dinner guest had been stabbed to death at the mayor's home. He called me at home late at night with the news and I jumped out of bed. I was almost completely dressed when he called back. "Gotcha!" he laughed. "There's no stabbing."

"This is no joke, Frank," said Jordan. "This is the real thing." Jordan was no prankster, and I could see he was serious. "Now get up to City Hall," he commanded again.

Herman and I had no sooner stepped into the hallway when we saw Captain Bill Conroy, the head of communications. "Hey, Frank," he said. "Are you and Herman heading up to City Hall? There's been a shooting." Okay, now we believed it was the real deal. The adrenaline started pumping as we headed down to the police garage.

Herman, who is taller and has a longer stride than me, was moving fast. He reached the unmarked car first, went to the driver's door, realized he did not have the keys, and shouted to me to toss them over. Although I usually preferred to drive, we were in such a hurry that I didn't insist on it. We got in, and the first thing Herman did was grab the red light from its hook under the dash, hung it on a similar hook at the top of the windshield, and then turned on the light and the siren. And we were still in the garage. I couldn't remember anyone ever doing that. Clearly, we were both getting jacked up about this as we peeled out of the garage and headed up Sixth Street toward City Hall.

Herman was maneuvering through heavy traffic as cars were pulling over to let us by. Just as we crossed Mission Street, a huge, multi-wheeled flatbed truck was trying to get out of our way, and we were jockeying to get around it. But we ended up bumping into the rear of this truck.

The right front end of our car was banged up, and the hood was a bit crumpled, but the damage was minor and we were okay. With an oversized steel bumper on the flatbed, it had sustained no damage. Amid all the tension and adrenaline, Herman turned to look at me, his eyes as big as saucers. I'm sure he would've said the same about my eyes. We were heading to City Hall on a report of a shooting, and now we were in an accident. *Can our day get much crazier?* I thought.

He said, "What the hell are we going to do now?"

I looked back at Herman and said, "What do you mean 'we'? I'm not driving!"

We both started laughing uncontrollably. It was a crazy thing for me to say at that moment, but that's how cops are in a high-stress situation. Saying something funny breaks the tension. When reality set back in, I said to Herman to tell the driver we're on the way to a shooting at City Hall and to give the guy his business card. Herman got out, talked to the driver, and handed him a card. We never heard from the driver after that.

For the rest of the five-minute trip my mind was in overdrive. *What happened? What am I walking into?* I immediately recalled the Jonestown tragedy ten days earlier. The Rev. Jim Jones had ordered his men to ambush Congressman Leo Ryan, journalists, and others as they boarded planes to depart the Jonestown jungle compound in Guyana. Ryan and four others were killed, and several were wounded. After the airport ambush, Jones beseeched some nine hundred of his followers, most from the San Francisco Bay Area and including three hundred children, to commit "revolutionary suicide" by swallowing a cyanide-laced fruit drink. (This tragedy created the term "drinking the Kool-Aid," although the actual drink used was Flavor Aid.) Those who didn't comply were shot. A few escaped. Jones shot himself to death.

We had heard that disciples of Jones were going to target politicians in San Francisco whom they considered enemies. The day after Congressman Ryan's funeral, a week before this, a man had anonymously telephoned the *San Francisco Chronicle* to say his brother "was just back from Guyana" and that the mayor should be warned "to have someone with him at all times." Asked for his or his brother's identity, he replied, "If I told you that, I wouldn't see tomorrow. Just tell the mayor to take care of himself." Moscone had also confided to friends that he might be in danger but wasn't specific. I figure this was all going to tie into Jim Jones somehow, and I already have in my head some potential suspects.

Had Dan White entered my thinking at all? Absolutely not. No way the clean-cut all-American boy that I knew would kill someone. Never.

We pulled up to the Polk Street side of City Hall at 11:10 a.m. Crowds were gathered on the sidewalk and on the stairs leading up to the building. We flashed our badges to the security guard at the door, bypassing the metal detector, and ran up the stairs to the mayor's office on the second floor.

I was just about at the top of the landing when I saw Jim Molinari, the SFPD sergeant assigned to Mayor Moscone's security detail, waiting for me. His eyes were bigger than Herman's were at the accident.

"Frank," said Jim. "The mayor is dead."

"Do we have any suspects?" I asked.

"Dan White."

I felt like Jim had just hit me over the head with a sledgehammer. *Dan White? He must be mistaken. It can't be Dan White.*

Like I said, my relationship with Dan went all the way back to grammar school. We both attended St. Elizabeth's at Wayland and Somerset Streets, although he was four years younger and I didn't know him then, and we shared a mutual love for the game of baseball.

I remembered the opening day of the SFPD Softball League in 1969. Our first game was at Portola Park, my ball field as a kid growing up, against Southern Police Station. I had helped form this league four years earlier. I was the commissioner of the league and the playing manager of the Northern Station team. The rules were simple: you had to love the game and be assigned to a police station to participate.

In 1965 and 1966, the first two years of the league, Park Station's powerhouse team won the championship. The following two years, 1967 and 1968, my Northern Station team took back-to-back titles, and in 1969 we were looking forward to a three-peat. This league had really caught on. The games were serious and had the support of the police administration. It was great for morale, and the interest was real throughout the department. All the teams played to win, except for the Central Station B team. The Central A team played to win. The B team would show up with a case or two of beer.

In fact, I'll never forget the day Police Chief Al Nelder, a cop's cop in my view, said to me, "Thank you, Frank. You've done what I couldn't do."

"What do you mean?" I asked. "You're the chief."

"You've got my men out of the bars and onto the ball field," Nelder said. Nelder himself had a genuine love for the game, having been a star player at Mission High School. I was never an excessive drinker, as I mentioned earlier in the chapter about my first day as a patrolman, but I knew what he meant. I liked an occasional cocktail and wine with dinner, but for me, playing ball was natural, healthier, and more fun.

Back to the opening game in 1969. I was about to hit infield practice when an athletic, good-looking young man walked up to me. He was wearing a baseball cap, had a baseball glove tucked under his left arm, and a pair of baseball cleats, with their shoestrings tied together, draped over his right shoulder. He looked me in the eye.

"Hi, Frank, I'm Dan White," he said. "I want to play on your team."

I laughed. "You have to be a cop to play," I said.

"I *am* a cop," he said.

"But you have to be a cop at Northern Station."

"I *am* at Northern Station," he said. I looked at him quizzically. *Who is this guy?* "Don't you remember me, Frank? Right here on this diamond, when we were kids, I would shag balls for you and your friends all day long. You were a few years older, but at the end of the day you guys always let me hit a few."

Ah, yes, the rite of passage. I remembered being that kid that would shag balls all day for local college players Joe and Ron Gaggero and some of the U.C. Berkeley varsity ball players who would occasionally work out on their own at Portola Park. The Gaggero brothers lived across the street from Portola Park. What a thrill it was for me at the end of the day to hit against college pitching. When I was older, we'd do the same for the younger kids that shagged balls. Dan was telling me he was one of those boys.

Dan started that day at second base. I moved him to shortstop the following week. I was playing in the outfield. We went undefeated that season.

1969 San Francisco Police Softball League Champions, Northern Station

Front row, kneeling, L-R: Tom Boyd, Dan White, Frank Falzon,
Gary Lemos, Jim McMahon, Tony Novello

Back row, standing, L-R: Police Chief Al Nelder, Tom Gordon,
Tom Vigo, Jim Sullivan, Art Ritter, Joe Chiamparino

I would later assemble an all-star police team. On that squad, we had plenty of good outfielders, but we needed a second baseman. I moved myself into that spot. Dan's skill and instincts were so good that he and I became a stellar double play combo, regularly turning two with the best of them. Our SFPD All-Stars went up against the very best teams from Los Angeles, Sacramento, the FBI, and a multitude of police, sheriff, and probation departments in the state, and we'd win consistently.

For two straight years our all-star team never lost a game. We won two straight State Law Enforcement Tournaments held annually in South Lake Tahoe. We had terrific ballplayers, some even had major league experience, but none were as good or as talented on the ball field as Dan White.

At the end of the 1971 season, having won the state championship for the second time, there was a huge banquet for the players, their wives, family, and friends. The banquet was held in one of the major South Lake Tahoe resort banquet rooms. I invited the three umpires who had worked the games to join us. At the dinner, the senior umpire came up to me and said, "Frank, I've been umpiring games for over twenty years, and I want you to know the finest player I've ever seen is that shortstop of yours, Dan White."

During the dinner, Dan took the podium and called me up to present, on behalf of our team, a plaque thanking me for what we had accomplished for the second year in a row. I returned to my seat with everyone standing and clapping, I was embarrassed but so appreciative for what they had done for me.

How had we come from those glory days just seven years earlier to this moment, with the mayor dead and Dan White suspected of killing him? Standing there, staring in utter disbelief at Jim Molinari, I couldn't process what he had just told me.

I knew Dan had quit his job and was planning on going back to the fire department. It was a smart move, I thought at the time. I knew he would be out of his element in a world of big city politics. Most cops would be, especially those raised in the city who had lived through the socially changing times. But I knew nothing about the interactions between White and Moscone and Milk in recent weeks, so this really knocked me for a loop.

I paid very little attention to the day-to-day scrimmages of City Hall politics. As I said, cops hate politics. We are mostly simple people on the job. Most police officers have a spouse, a home, a mortgage, children. All we care about is law and order. Protect and serve. That's pretty much our job. All the other stuff at City Hall was always so chaotic. Protests and civic disobedience were the most challenging. We hated situations that put us in riot helmets and batons, or hats and bats, as we called it. Nobody enjoyed that part of the job. It pits you against the people who are your friends and neighbors.

Molinari led me through the mayor's suite of offices. I stopped briefly to talk to George's assistant, Cyr Copertini, who said that Dan White had come in that morning, asking to see the mayor. Moscone had willingly showed him in. Cyr said that after a few minutes, she heard what she thought was a car backfiring, but when she looked out her window, she saw nothing and went back to work.

Jim and Herman and I walked into the anteroom behind the mayor's main office. There was a sofa, a coffee table, some chairs. On the table were two highball glasses and a bottle of liquor, bourbon or Scotch, I think. Moscone was on the floor, a partially smoked cigarette still between his fingers. He had two wounds in his upper body that I could see, one in the back of his right shoulder and one in the right side of his back, and two bullet wounds to the head. Herman and I could see pockmarks on his face caused by bullet fragments and powder burns. That told us the shooter had fired at very close range. To me, they were clearly *coup de grace* wounds. Later, Coroner Boyd Stephens, who conducted the autopsy on Moscone, confirmed that Moscone was shot four times. One bullet had entered Moscone's head through the right earlobe and traveled upward, and another penetrated the bony mastoid region behind the right ear, a fraction of an inch below the first. Stephens could not say whether the head wounds were fired after the two shots to the back, but said it was likely, and that they were the fatal shots. If not for the head wounds, Stephens said, Moscone would have had a good chance of surviving.

None of this made any sense at all. The mayor dead on the floor. A reliable police friend telling me Dan White was the suspect. No way I could fathom Dan White putting two bullets into the mayor's head. Like I said, I thought of Dan as my kid brother. He was a hard-working, dedicated family man who excelled at almost anything he tried to do. He was just not capable of murder.

I went back out into the main reception area to use the phone. I was going to put out an alert to all units to pick up Dan White for the shooting of George Moscone. Deputy Chief Jeremiah Taylor was there, hanging up the phone. "Frank," he said, "Dan White is at Northern Station. He turned himself in." I went back into the anteroom where Herman was making notes. "Do you mind if I leave you here?" I asked. "I understand Dan White is in custody." Herman gave me the car keys and I headed out, joined by two assistant district attorneys, Tommy Norman and John Rowland, who happened to be in the building at the time of the shooting.

As we left, Norman informed me that Harvey Milk was also dead from multiple gunshot wounds in his office, across the building from the mayor's office. The coroner said later that Milk had two similar execution-style side-by-side wounds to the left ear area of his head. His other wounds included one through the right wrist and into the abdomen, one that passed across the left chest, out the left side and into the left elbow, and a third in the small of the back, nicking the vertebral column. He, too, could have possibly survived if not for the head wounds, said the coroner. He recorded the official times of death as 10:50 a.m. for Moscone and 10:55 a.m. for Milk.

Early in the afternoon, when then-Board of Supervisors President Dianne Feinstein came out of her office to announce the assassinations to the press, she was in such a state of shock by the events that she had difficulty getting the words out. She managed to steel herself by focusing on my co-author, *Chronicle* reporter Duffy Jennings.

"I will never forget Duffy Jennings," says now U. S. Senator Feinstein about that moment. "I remember going out into the City Hall rotunda to make the official announcement. I saw Duffy, and I don't know why but I kept staring into those blue eyes and that innocent face of his. I couldn't speak for what seemed like a long time. It was like the world stopped. By focusing on Duffy, I was finally able to say those terrible words."

Outside, the scene was chaotic. Officers had sealed off the entrance. The coroner's wagon was there, and people were rushing around. We got in the car and drove up Van Ness Avenue to Northern Station at 841 Ellis Street. We were met there by Sergeant Paul Chignell, who told us that White had walked into the station on his own after meeting his wife, Mary Ann, at St. Mary's Cathedral four blocks away. Chignell said he read White his Miranda rights and put him in a holding cell, but that Dan had refused to make a statement.

Before Norman, Rowland, and I got to Northern Station, two of my other colleagues, Homicide Inspectors Howard Bailey and Carl Klotz, had picked up White and taken him to the Hall of Justice to wait for my arrival. They weren't aware I was coming to Northern Station, but they knew that as the inspectors on call, Herman and I were officially in charge of the investigation.

CHAPTER 21
A TALE OF BETRAYAL AND REVENGE: DAN WHITE CONFESSES

When I got back to the Hall of Justice, it was bedlam outside the homicide detail. Reporters were crowded in the hallway, peppering me with questions. I declined to comment. All the doors to the unit that were normally open were now closed and guarded. Inside, Gene Fogarty and Ed Erdelatz were the only other homicide inspectors there. "Dan's in the back," said Erdelatz, tilting his head toward one of the interrogation rooms along the back wall of the office. I walked back and unlocked the door. As I entered, White stood up from his chair behind a small table. He was dressed in a three-piece tan suit with the jacket off and the vest open, white dress shirt, dark necktie. His short dark hair was tousled, bangs drooping messily across his forehead. He was not in handcuffs.

When he saw me, somebody he'd known for so long, somebody he had great respect for as a friend and mentor, his weary expression grew even more downcast. This guy who had been so tough—Army paratrooper in Vietnam, fireman, cop, athlete—was now shambolic, defeated. I looked straight at him.

"Dan, what the fuck happened?" I said. "How could you be so stupid?"

He scrunched up his face. He looked like he was going to explode like a pressure cooker about to blow its top. Tears were streaming down his face. He took a deep breath.

"I wanna tell you everything, Frank!" he blurted. "I want you to know the truth!"

"Stop, Dan," I cut him off. "If we're going to do this, we're going to do this right. I'm going to get my tape recorder and take a statement." I was being a cop first, friend second. We both knew that. I had a job to do, no matter how I felt about him. At that point in my career, I had investigated two hundred homicides, obtained thirty first-degree murder convictions, and sent four men to death row. I knew what I was doing. I left Dan locked in the interrogation room, went to my desk, removed my service revolver, and locked it in my desk drawer. Rule number one, never interrogate a suspect wearing your gun, for obvious reasons. I grabbed my tape recorder and a fresh cassette and returned to the interrogation room.

While I was getting my recorder, I asked Erdelatz to help me. It's always best to have two cops in the room when you're taking a suspect's statement. It not only helps to corroborate what's said, but another inspector can think of questions you might miss. Ed and his partner, Inspector Jeff Brosch, were pretty tied up with new cases. They had just come off a week on call and had picked up three murder cases over the weekend. But he agreed to help me with White. That just shows how tight most of the guys are in homicide, how we stick together. It can be a grueling job when cases turn up in bunches, so we all do what we can to help each other. Besides, I'd known Ed since we were young street cops together in the mid-sixties.

Before Ed and I went to question White, we were informed that public defender Jeff Brown was in the foyer telling our secretary Marge Lundquist and Inspector Fogarty, a big likeable fellow I had nick-named "Lurch," that he wanted to represent Dan White. No one had officially requested Brown, as far as I knew, but now I knew we needed to move quickly to get a statement because it wouldn't be long before Dan's lawyer showed up. I learned early on from my mentor and former homicide partner Jack Cleary that any statement was better than no statement. If a defendant wants to lie, let him lie. Once you have a statement you can tear it apart looking for inconsistencies and for veracity. Showing those inconsistencies and lack of candor and truthfulness plays out big in a courtroom before a jury.

Erdelatz and I went back into the room with Dan and shut the door. I told him I was going to Mirandize him again and he could tell us anything he wanted to tell us. I realized that at any moment an attorney representing Dan could walk in and shut us down. As much as everybody in San Francisco wanted to know why Dan White had done what he did, nobody wanted to know more than me.

"It made sense to get what we could as soon as we could," Erdelatz recalled more than forty years later. "This wasn't a whodunit. This interview was no different than any other when you already have your perpetrator. What you want to know is why, what was going through his mind. What was his mental state, his intent? Was he on medication? You're anticipating possible defenses."

I turned on the recorder and began: "Today's date is Monday, November 27th, 1978. The time is presently 12:05. We're inside the homicide detail, room 454, at the Hall of Justice. Present is Inspector Edward Erdelatz, Inspector Frank Falzon, and, for the record, sir, your full name?"

"Daniel James White."

After I read Dan his Miranda rights, I asked if he wished to tell us about the "incident involving Mayor George Moscone and Supervisor Harvey Milk."

"I do," White replied.

"Normally in a situation like this, we ask questions," I said. "I'm aware of your past history as a police officer and also as a San Francisco fireman. I would prefer you do it in a narrative form as to what happened this morning, if you can lead up to the events of the shooting and then backtracking as to why the shooting took place."

What followed was a long, rambling, now famous statement from Dan about the pressure he'd been under—at home, financially, politically, emotionally. Why he'd resigned his seat on the board of supervisors, how he tried to get it back, that Moscone promised to reinstate him but then double-crossed him, how Milk worked behind his back to keep White off the board. Dan was sobbing, choking back words. His whole body was convulsing. Eventually he admitted to leaving home that morning with his gun and extra bullets, being driven to City Hall by his aide, confronting and shooting Moscone in his office, reloading as he walked across the building to the supervisors' offices, calling Milk into his old office to talk, then shooting Harvey five times when he "smirked" at him.

White said he then asked his assistant for the car keys and left the building. He drove to the Doggie Diner restaurant nearby on Van Ness Avenue and called his wife, Mary Ann, from a pay phone. He told her what he'd done and that he was going to kill himself but wanted to say goodbye. Mary Ann pleaded with him not to take his own life and begged him to meet her at St. Mary's Cathedral a few blocks away. They would work it out together, she promised. Dan consented and drove to the church. There he prayed until Mary Ann arrived. She was able to convince him to turn himself in, and they walked together back to Northern Station on Ellis Street.

I would take a considerable amount of criticism and derision for allowing White to narrate his own statement. Criticism not from my co-workers, police department brass, or prosecutors, but from the community and supporters of Moscone and Milk. People thought I was cutting Dan slack because of our relationship, that I was too soft on him.

Whatever skills I had as a homicide inspector, I would rank my ability to communicate as my best asset. I was able to converse with all people, all persuasions. I almost always get the suspect to talk. A confession proved you had the right suspect. That alone gave me peace of mind, knowing an innocent man wasn't wrongfully convicted. You're looking for *why* he killed two people. Everyone wants to know why. I was no different. I wonder if no statement had ever been taken what the end results might have been. Dan, when he saw me—I know for a fact he wanted to tell *me* why. We were that close.

Erdelatz and I had zero knowledge of why Dan would kill. George Moscone wasn't particularly liked by the rank-and-file cops. When he was running for mayor, I remember the day he addressed a roomful of several hundred San Francisco police inspectors and administration brass and promised that if he were elected, he would appoint Ray Canepa as chief. We heard that vow with great relief. Canepa was a cop's cop, admired and respected by me and most other officers. But Moscone broke that promise after he won, appointing outsider Charles Gain to the top job. That didn't go over well with us at all. But it certainly wasn't a reason for murder.

My logic in starting the interrogation was to let Dan do a narrative, gaining knowledge of why the crime occurred and work off of what Dan was voluntarily sharing. My plan worked but there were those who thought I should have taken a tougher approach, firing short questions like Sergeant Friday from the TV show *Dragnet*.

During the questioning, Dan denied intent, but our follow-up work showed that was not truthful. He brought his loaded .38-caliber weapon and a pocketful of extra rounds in his pants pocket. This was a betrayed, angry man, armed and on a mission. Until the interrogation, I was unaware he had reloaded the gun between the two killings.

By letting Dan narrate, we allowed him to virtually hang himself. In the end I was satisfied we had done our job professionally, especially considering the trying circumstances. There was no need to browbeat or hammer on a willing, talkative suspect who had admitted that he killed two people and gave the reason why.

Minutes after the interrogation concluded at 12:30 p.m., attorney John Purcell, hired by the White family, arrived and requested no further questioning of White. He also refused to allow lab technicians to perform neutron activation tests to determine whether Dan had fired a gun. We could have done this test before Purcell showed up, but there wasn't time. As Dan's lawyer, he could stop us from conducting any test that might put his client at risk of self-incrimination.

I did not learn until talking with Inspector Jeff Brosch at around 2:00 p.m. that when White arrived at City Hall that morning, he had avoided the metal detector at the public entrance on Polk Street by climbing through an open window on the basement level at the McAllister Street side of the building.

By the time we were done with the interrogation, most of the inspectors were back in the office. Ed and I gathered several of them to form a tight huddle around Dan as we escorted him to the elevator and up to the county jail on the sixth floor for booking on murder charges. Ed and I both were convinced that Dan had committed two first-degree murders with the intent to kill. It was 3:15 by the time I went downstairs to the coroner's office to inspect the wounds on both victims.

That night I had to do one of the most difficult and emotional tasks I've ever had in this job. Herman and I went to Dan White's house to serve a search warrant. I apologized profusely to Mary Ann at the front door.

"It's all right, Frank," she said. "I understand you have a job to do."

Perhaps because she'd been married to a policeman or because she was simply relieved to know that her husband was still alive, or both, she was surprisingly accommodating. After all these years, I truly admire Mary Ann White and Gina Moscone, too, for their strength in the wake of that horrible tragedy. Both have maintained their privacy, cared for and protected their children, and gone on with their lives as best as they could.

Herman and I went downstairs to the den, where Dan had separated himself from his family for days. On a small table, we could see that he had been mulling over old newspaper articles about his father's heroics as a fireman. I thought back to the many times that Dan and I talked about how we both lost our fathers at an early age, about being told as young boys that we were now the man of our family. To both of us our fathers were our heroes. They each had set a high bar. We both attended Catholic schools where the Ten Commandments were etched into our mind by Catholic nuns and reinforced at home by good, loving Irish mothers.

It was both heartbreaking and revelatory to realize that Dan must have despaired, thinking he had let his father down by quitting his job as supervisor. And that he was ashamed of his failures in politics, business, and at home. But he probably felt he could fix all that if only he could get his supervisor's job back. The police and fire department unions, along with the Chamber of Commerce, had Dan's ear and had been urging him to reclaim his seat on the board.

But Dan was only talking to Dan, and this time he was betrayed by his own conscience. Dan was definitely not giving Dan good advice.

It upset me to acknowledge my own failure as a friend to have not known or understood anything Dan was going through at City Hall after he resigned. I've always felt that if Dan had reached out to any of his dear friends—and I include myself on that list—before November 27, 1978, maybe none of this would ever have happened.

But it did happen. And Assistant District Attorney Tommy Norman felt from day one he had a slam dunk case for two counts of murder in the first degree.

The trial would produce an entirely different outcome.

Me with Dan White

Escorting Dan White to city prison after our interrogation.
L-R Behind me, Insp. Ed Erdelatz, Me, Dan White,
unidentified uniformed officer, Insp. Ray Hilvert

CHAPTER 22
SHOCKING VERDICT

Assistant District Attorney Tommy Norman was one of the best prosecutors I ever knew. I sat beside him, shared my thoughts on choosing jurors, and testified in dozens of the four hundred murder cases he had tried before juries during his thirty-seven-year career. But the trial of Dan White for the murders of George Moscone and Harvey Milk would be the one that brought him both the most attention and the greatest disappointment.

Known as Tommy to all his friends, me included, he was beloved by prosecutors, defense attorneys, and public defenders who worked at the Hall of Justice. The son of a doctor, Tommy went to Washington High School but never attended college. His brilliance, skill, and dedication, however, served him well enough to earn his law degree from Lincoln Law School in San Francisco and to join the district attorney's office in 1960.

I adored him. I remember sitting at my first trial with him in the early 1970s, waiting impatiently for the jury to return a verdict. "This is a dead bang case," I said to Tommy. "What's taking so long?" He smiled and looked at me. "I'll tell you what's taking so long," he said. "They're spending the first hour talking about me and trying to decide if I'm a gay man."

He wasn't, but he had a way about him, certain mannerisms, and he would seem to sashay around the courtroom. He would somehow manage to convince a jury that if you disagreed with him, you didn't have a brain. Put another way, when Tommy died in July 2009, criminal defense attorney Michael Gaines told the *San Francisco Chronicle* that Norman "knew how to dance. He had this way of waltzing in the courtroom—it was a combination of taking his work seriously and still having a glimmer in his eye." Tommy ranked right up there with the best of courtroom performers.

The Dan White trial began on May 1, 1979, six months after the City Hall assassinations. Tommy thought educated, wealthy people made the best jurors, but I didn't agree. I think you want a man or woman who puts in eight hours of work five days a week, understands their community, and wants their city to be safe.

The thing about the initial jury panel for the Dan White trial was that it looked like they emptied out every Lions Club, Rotary Club, and country club in town. This was like no jury panel I'd ever seen. Very middle America. They would eventually look at Dan like he could be their son or brother. But Tommy was going for the death penalty. He and I and many others were certain we had an airtight case for two counts of premeditated murder, and many in the city wanted Dan White to pay the ultimate penalty for the killings. I felt that Dan, too, knew he should pay the ultimate price for what he had done. Guided by that goal, Tommy eliminated potential jurors who were against capital punishment. It was during that *voir dire* process of jury selection that Tommy was eliminating those who might be sympathetic to George Moscone and Harvey Milk. Most San Francisco liberal thinkers won't support the death penalty under any circumstances. Even these.

But I never saw a defense attorney as well prepared as Dan's young lawyer, Douglas Schmidt. He did such a great job presenting a strong reasonable doubt alternative for a sympathetic jury to consider. Schmidt produced a parade of mental health professionals to establish that Dan's mental condition had deteriorated so drastically from stress, sleep deprivation, and a sugary diet that it rendered him with "diminished capacity" to kill intentionally, despite his own confession.

In fact, several jurors wept as they listened to Dan's emotional tape-recorded confession. Even Dianne Feinstein, who had become mayor upon Moscone's death, shed tears during her testimony.

When Schmidt cross-examined me about the tape on the witness stand, he asked me what I thought of Dan White before the killings. My immediate response was easy. I had a great deal of respect for Dan as a person with integrity and a genuine love of people. "He was a man among men," I replied.

My logic was simple. I had known him for many years. Dan had been an Army paratrooper fighting for his country. After his discharge, he joined the San Francisco Police Department to protect and serve the city he loved. He then joined the city's fire department, partially to honor his firefighter father. Finally, he ran for supervisor to represent his neighborhood and community. Every one of these jobs took dedication, loyalty, and self-sacrifice—all terms that fit Dan White to a tee.

When I sat down at the prosecution table after testifying, Norman was clearly annoyed by my answer. He felt I had prepared that response in advance. I assured him I had not.

Meanwhile, Schmidt's co-counsel, Stephen Scherr, was a master tactician who countered every move by Norman. I sat through many trials, almost all of them interesting and many of them dramatic at times, but none compared with the Dan White trial. I felt I was watching a masters chess match, except with real people in place of knights and pawns. White did not take the stand in his own defense. The trial lasted nearly three weeks.

The courtroom was packed every day. So many media wanted to attend that an auxiliary room down the hall was outfitted with closed-circuit cameras to handle the overflow. Throughout the trial, Judge Walter Calcagno permitted only two reporters to sit inside a thick sheet of bulletproof glass separating the spectators' gallery from the trial participants. They represented the city's two largest daily newspapers. One was *San Francisco Chronicle* reporter Duffy Jennings, my co-author for this book, and the other was Jim Wood from the *San Francisco Examiner.*

"I don't recall anyone in the media expecting anything other than two first-degree murder convictions," said Jennings. "In fact, while the jury deliberated, I wrote a lengthy summary of the trial on that assumption. It was set in type but not published. This saved time in case the jury came in late in the day, close to my deadline. All I needed to do when the verdicts were announced was write a few lead paragraphs." The *Chronicle* later submitted Jennings' trial coverage for Pulitzer Prize consideration, calling it an "arduous reporting job well done."

By the time the jury finished its deliberations after several days, the entire city was on edge, waiting to hear White's fate. It was Monday, May 21, 1979. Just before the verdicts were read, District Attorney Joe Freitas entered the courtroom and took a seat at the prosecution table between Tommy and me. Joe looked at me and asked, "Frank, what do you think the verdicts will be?" I told him that I thought the jury might consider diminished capacity and drop the Moscone murder to voluntary manslaughter, but Harvey was a different story. Dan reloaded and sought out Harvey to kill him, that would be a first-degree murder. Norman was irate. He looked at Freitas askance. "Frank has it all wrong," Tommy said. "He will be convicted of two first-degree murders." Tommy and I were the so-called experts and neither of us got it right.

The jury found Dan White guilty of voluntary manslaughter in both killings. When the decision was read aloud, the gallery erupted in gasps of shock and verbal outbursts of disbelief. Outside the courtroom, word spread like wildfire. Across the city people were stunned and outraged by the leniency shown to White. Angry mobs collected in the predominantly gay Castro neighborhood and descended on the Civic Center. In the ensuing revolt, rioters shattered windows at City

Hall and set several police cars afire. Every available cop was put into hats and bats to control the chaos, but I was excused. The verdict and subsequent White Night Riot, as it came to be called, drew headlines around the country and was national news on television.

Afterward, I'd see cops in the hallway at work or at crime scenes or at Irish community events who'd say things to me like, "Thanks for what you did for our Danny boy." They treated me like some kind of hero. But I sure didn't feel like one. Between the day of the City Hall murders and the verdict, Herman Clark and I had logged 480 hours on the investigation and were absolutely satisfied that we had done everything possible to perform our duties professionally and to assure a thorough and fair outcome.

District Attorney Joe Freitas, who called the trial outcome "the worst day of my life," lost his re-election bid that November. He died of lung cancer in Paris in 2006. The case destroyed Tommy Norman, and he wasn't quite the same after that. He stayed in the D.A.'s office another eighteen years before retiring in 1997. When he died in 2009 at the age of seventy-nine, then San Francisco District Attorney Kamala Harris called Norman "an iconic figure" and said his passing was "a great loss for the legal community."

CHAPTER 23
DEATH WISH

Robert Lee Massie, who had been condemned to die three separate times between 1965 and 1985, fought so long and hard to have his death sentence carried out that he became the national poster boy for both sides of the argument on capital punishment.

At San Quentin State Prison, he became known as "The Killer Who Wants to Die." By the time he was finally given a lethal injection in 2001—after a last meal of extra crispy fried oysters, French fries, and two vanilla milkshakes—Massie had been on death row for a total of twenty-two years.

"I'm tired," Massie said in his final hours. "I just don't want to live the rest of my life in prison."

I had helped put him there, and I was there for his execution.

Inspector Herman Clark and I were on call for the week beginning New Year's Day, 1979. Herman, who held a bachelor's degree in administration of justice from the University of San Francisco, had become a close friend and valued partner since we joined forces six months earlier. Black, smart, tall, and athletic, Herman cut an impressive figure in the detail. He was good-looking and fit, with a thick moustache that framed a set of brilliant white teeth. He reminded me a little of

Denzel Washington. Herman was also an impeccable dresser, always in tailored suits with silk pocket squares, monogrammed shirts with cuff-links, color-coordinated neckties, and polished shoes. He was so stylish that Grodin's, a popular men's clothing store, used Herman as a model on its billboards around town.

Homicide Inspector Herman Clark, my partner from 1978 to 1981

Things had been relatively normal in the weeks following the Jonestown tragedy and the Moscone-Milk murders. There had been seven murders since that awful day at City Hall, one the day after and six in December, an average month for San Francisco. The holidays were winding down and San Franciscans were looking forward to the new year with hope for a more peaceful one than 1978 had been.

It didn't last long. We caught three homicides in two days.

On Wednesday afternoon, January 3, Herman and I were dispatched to the city's first murder of the year. The victim, Ernest Cole, forty-two, had been nearly decapitated in an alley just south of Market Street. We would learn that his killer was Clifford Bolden, twenty-five, a six foot, eight inch, 260-pound former Marine, Vietnam veteran, and martial artist. Bolden had been drinking wine with his girlfriend, Frances Ned, when they encountered Cole around 2:30 p.m. Ned told us that Cole had offered Bolden twenty dollars to have sex with her, which outraged the jealous Bolden. The trio walked a block to Stevenson Street, where Bolden produced a machete from under his coat. He held Cole's head from behind and drew the blade across his neck from ear to ear, severing both carotid arteries and the airway. Cole died instantly.

Bolden had escaped from the scene by the time police arrived. Despite our considerable efforts to track him down, he remained a fugitive and killed again in May, stabbing a San Jose man to death. In early September, he was finally caught in downtown San Francisco after he wounded another man with a knife. Bolden went to prison on voluntary manslaughter convictions in both killings. He was paroled in 1986. He hadn't been out long when he stabbed Michael Pederson, forty-six, to death in a Twin Peaks apartment. Bolden was sentenced to death for the latest murder but eventually was able to get the death sentence lifted on appeal. He remains in prison.

As Herman and I examined the Cole murder scene and talked to witnesses, my pager buzzed with the number for headquarters. I went to our car, started the engine, and grabbed the radio microphone.

"This is Inspector 5-Henry-7, headquarters," I said. "What've you got?"

"We have Ingleside Station patrol officers on the scene of a 211-187 [robbery-homicide] at Miraloma Liquors, 683 Portola Drive, Inspector," said the Operations Center dispatcher. "One victim is deceased from multiple gunshot wounds and another one is wounded. Please respond."

"Negative, headquarters," I replied. "I am currently 10-7 [out of service] with 5-Henry-12 at the location of an earlier homicide. Please send a backup team from the homicide detail to the Portola location to take charge of the investigation and stand by until we can get there."

"10-4, 5-Henry-7. Let us know when you are en route to the scene."

"10-4, headquarters. We should be able to wrap things up here in the next thirty minutes or so."

By the time Inspectors Carl Klotz and Howard Bailey arrived at the liquor store and began their initial investigation, responding officers had cordoned off the area with yellow crime scene tape. When Herman and I arrived, the deceased owner, Boris Naumoff, had been transported to the morgue and a wounded clerk had been taken by ambulance to the hospital. There was disarray and signs of a struggle at the front of the store. Carl and Howard filled us in.

A man had been seen hanging around the liquor store and the adjacent grocery store earlier in the day. Witnesses said he appeared "jittery" and made jerky movements, looking up and down the street. Just before 3:45 p.m., employee Charles Harris came in to begin his regular evening shift at Miraloma Liquors. Harris saw Naumoff talking to a man he assumed was a customer. Harris continued walking toward a back storage room. At the same time, a female customer, Sandy Bateman-Collins, entered the store and saw Naumoff standing behind the counter, handing money to a man, who then started to walk out. Naumoff followed him, said Bateman-Collins, mumbling what sounded like, "A guy can't make a living anymore." She and Harris both heard a scuffle. Harris turned and saw Naumoff holding the man face-to-face in a bear hug. Harris began to approach the two men, then heard three quick gunshots followed a second or two later by a fourth, which struck Harris in the leg. Naumoff, a sixty-one-year-old Greek immigrant who had owned the liquor store for nearly thirty years and was well known and liked by many in the neighborhood, fell to the floor with three bullets to the chest, two in his heart. He died at the scene.

Witnesses gave a description of the man who shot Naumoff as white, slightly built, late thirties to early forties. He was seen getting into a parked Chevrolet Vega and driving away. Later that evening, a woman named Laura Garnett-Young saw a car stop outside her San Francisco home. A man got out, looked around, took off his shirt and jacket, put them into her garbage can, and drove away. She jotted down the license number of the car, 119 TGL, and notified police. Officers retrieved a blood-stained shirt and jacket from the trash can. The blood evidence would later be a match for Boris Naumoff's type. In the meantime, Herman and I were back in the office putting out an all-points bulletin on the liquor store robbery and homicide with a description of the suspect, the car, and the license number. "Suspect is armed and dangerous," we noted on the bulletin.

The next night, just before ten o'clock, San Francisco Police Officers Michael Pearson and Jeffrey Morlock were on routine patrol when they saw a Chevrolet Vega with a license plate of 119 TJL, one letter off from the one that Garnett-Young had reported. A man was the only occupant. The officers radioed for backup, then followed the vehicle on an erratic route through the Haight-Ashbury District as it changed directions frequently. When other units arrived, they finally stopped the car at Divisadero and Oak Streets and arrested the driver, Robert Lee Massie, age thirty-seven. Herman Clark responded to the location to confirm that it was Massie in the car. Massie had a loaded Ruger .357-caliber revolver in his waistband, a cocked and loaded .380-caliber Mauser automatic in his coat pocket, several boxes of ammunition, and a buck knife in the car. The professional diligence of officers Pearson and Morlock in carrying out the stop and arrest of a dangerous suspect most likely prevented a possible hot pursuit with shots being fired. The SFPD uniformed force—the backbone of every department—executed a precise tactical maneuver to seal off his escape and to apprehend an armed and dangerous suspect. Our ballistics expert, Rich Grzybowski, was later able to match the .380 with the four bullets fired at the liquor store. The officers brought Massie to the Hall of Justice shortly before midnight and delivered him to the homicide detail.

Herman and I put Massie into an interrogation room. I read him his Miranda rights and asked if he wanted to make a statement.

"I want to think about it," he said. "I'm hungry. Can you bring me some coffee and something to eat?"

"I'll see what I can do," I told him. We almost always had a pot of fresh coffee brewing in the office, but I wasn't sure where I was going to find any food at that hour. I went into our office kitchen and looked in the refrigerator. Our boss, Lieutenant Jack Jordan, was a frugal brown-bagger who regularly brought his lunch to work rather than go out or downstairs to the building cafeteria like many of us did. Luck would have it that he had left a sandwich in the fridge. I don't remember what kind it was, but it looked a bit stale, like it'd been there for a few days. I brought Massie a hot cup of coffee and Lt. Jordan's old sandwich. You'd have thought I gave him a steak dinner the way he dived into it. When he finished, he decided to talk to us.

He told us he'd been drunk and high on cocaine the day before when he went into the liquor store, pulled out his gun, and told the man behind the counter, "This is a holdup." Massie claimed the man gave him twenty or thirty dollars but attacked him as he was trying to leave. "So I shot him."

Massie seemed bright and was even-tempered but distant, like a lost soul. He asked to be put in a cell separate from other prisoners. He was afraid that the Aryan Brotherhood, a white supremacist prison gang, was trying to kill him.

"We can't promise anything," I told him, "but we'll see what we can do."

We booked Massie in the city prison on robbery and murder charges.

We pulled Massie's police jacket and found he had a record of robberies and assaults dating back fourteen years. And this wasn't his first murder. He had been sentenced to death for the 1965 shooting death of Mildred Weiss, a forty-eight-year-old mother of two, when she was getting out of her car in front of her house in southern California. At the time, he fired his lawyers and said he wanted no "intervention" in his scheduled execution. He called prison "hell" and said it was "the most monstrous system ever devised."

He was just hours from the gas chamber in 1967 when then-Governor Ronald Reagan stayed the execution so Massie could testify against an accomplice in the case. He returned to prison to await another execution date, but in 1972, the California Supreme Court banned executions. Massie's sentence was commuted to life in prison with a possibility of parole. He made parole in 1978 and had been out eight months when he held up the liquor store, killing Naumoff. On January 16, before Municipal Court Judge Frank Hart, Massie pleaded not guilty to the murder of Naumoff and the wounding of Chuck Harris. He later fired his public defenders and changed his plea to guilty over their objections.

At his trial, Massie testified in his own defense. He admitted killing Naumoff but denied what he had told us about the robbery. He told the court he bought liquor and cigarettes in the store, but outside he discovered that he'd been shortchanged by thirty dollars. He went back inside, he said, and confronted Naumoff, who gave him the correct change. When he was leaving, according to Massie, someone grabbed him from behind in a bear hug and "slammed" him in the face. Thinking it was someone from the Aryan Brotherhood who was attacking him, he drew his gun and fired without aiming, he testified. On the witness stand, he did acknowledge telling me and Herman that he had shot Naumoff during a robbery but insisted that he did so because he believed if he told us what we wanted to hear that we would protect him from the Aryan Brotherhood by placing him in a separate cell. The taped confession Massie had given us was played for the jury. It would be their decision which of Massie's statements to consider when rendering their verdict.

It was not uncommon for suspects to change their story in court from what they said during an interrogation. Once they hear how incriminating their own voice sounds on a tape confessing to a crime, they often backpedal the truth under questioning during the trial.

Massie did offer evidence that he had been stabbed twice in the chest with a sharpened screwdriver and was seriously injured while at San Quentin in 1974, an assault he attributed to the Aryan Brotherhood. A former member of the gang also testified that it had wanted to kill Massie for years, and prison officials testified that Massie had been moved at various times to Kansas, Nevada, and Washington for his protection, even though his sentence was for a crime committed in California. After the stabbing, officials transferred him to Soledad Prison. He impressed prison officials there with his "unusually good work record," according to a state community release board member. Upon his parole in May 1978, Massie got a $750-a-month job as an executive assistant with the San Francisco law firm of Smith, Snedeker & Commiskey, a group of attorneys that worked with prisoners. He left that job after a few months, traveled to Florida to visit his mother, then returned to San Francisco during the Christmas holidays.

Massie was convicted of the Naumoff murder and sentencing was scheduled for May 21. But a quirky convergence of cases in the superior courts caused the judge to delay his final ruling until the end of the week.

Two other well-publicized murder trials were in progress at the same time. In one court, the jury was deliberating the case of Dan White in the City Hall murders. In an adjacent courtroom, jurors were being selected to try Roland Luchini for the fatal shooting in February of two San Francisco Water Department supervisors, Patrick Healy and Eduardo Bura, over a poor job rating.

I had been on call on February 16 with Inspector Ora Guinther, who went by the nickname Whitey because of his Scandinavian heritage (pale skin, light hair, and blue eyes) when we were notified that Healy and Bura had been gunned down at the Lake Merced pump house where they worked. A surviving witness, James Chamberlain, who had been shot twice in the assault while grappling with the gunman, identified the shooter as Luchini, a city stationary engineer. "He didn't say a word. He just started shooting," Chamberlain had told the responding officers. We put out an all-points bulletin on Luchini and patrol units arrested him at his apartment without a struggle forty minutes after the shootings. We also recovered the weapon alongside the Southern freeway.

The Luchini case drew parallels to the Dan White case because a disgruntled city worker had killed two others at their workplace. Both men acted out of revenge for perceived backstabbing. Both shot their victims in the head within minutes. Both carried extra bullets and reloaded. Both mounted a psychological defense.

Because I was the homicide inspector on all three cases—White, Luchini, and Massie—I found myself shuttling from one courtroom to another, lugging all the case files with me, trying to keep track of which trial I was testifying in from day to day. It's hard to explain how unusual this was. This simply doesn't happen, that one inspector has three capital cases all in trial at the same time. Court proceedings were being recessed in one or another courtroom until I finished testifying in the adjacent courtroom.

In the Massie case, Superior Court Judge Daniel M. Hanlon delayed the sentencing because he did not want the imposition of a death sentence on Massie to influence either of the other two cases. On the afternoon of May 21, the White jury returned its voluntary manslaughter verdicts against Dan White, shocking decisions that touched off a city riot. Luchini, meanwhile, was tried, convicted, and sentenced to life in prison without the possibility of parole.

When court reconvened for the Massie sentencing on Friday, May 25, 1978, Judge Hanlon began by noting that there was no evidence of mental impairment, and that Massie had shown no remorse for the murders. "Except for the fact that you are a fellow human being, I find no basis for mercy," said the judge. "You were given a chance [parole] to start your life anew, without guns and without violence. You have shown a callous regard for human life." Judge Hanlon sentenced Massie to die and added fourteen years for Massie's guilty plea to three counts of robbery, four counts of carrying a concealed weapon, and one count of assault with a deadly weapon.

"Robert Lee Massie," said the judge after passing sentence, "may God, whose guidance the court has sought, have mercy on you."

Massie, ever defiant, stood up, looked at the judge, and said, "And may God have mercy on Your Honor."

Massie then moved to have attorneys appointed to defend him and that the judgment be set aside. Both motions were denied.

Every death sentence in California comes with an automatic appeal by law. Massie opposed any appeal, but the California Supreme Court, led by then-Chief Justice Rose Bird, overturned his conviction on the grounds that Massie had pleaded guilty over the objections of his attorneys. A new trial was ordered, and in 1989 Massie was convicted of murder and sentenced to death a third time. The California State Supreme Court upheld the sentence in 1998. For a time, he sought freedom through state and federal courts, while his case became a *cause célèbre* for many anti-capital punishment organizations as well as victims' rights groups. Massie ultimately gave up the fight and advocated for his sentence to be carried out.

Although California reinstituted executions in 1976, it had not executed anyone since 1967 and would not put another convict to death for almost thirty years. Executions resumed in 1996 and eight men were put to death over the next four years.

I had retired from the police department in 1992 and was working as a vice president for a title company when I received a call from the California Department of Corrections in early 2001.

"Inspector Falzon, we're calling to ask if you wish to attend the upcoming execution of Robert Lee Massie at San Quentin Prison," the caller said.

While I had solved cases that sent nearly a dozen men to death row, none had been executed during my career.

"Yes," I replied. "I would like to be there." It was not only that I had never attended one before, but because of the national debate around executions being cruel and inhumane, and because I had a strong belief in justice, I wanted to see for myself what it was like.

The execution was scheduled for midnight on March 27, 2001. My old partner, Carl Klotz, and I made the short drive from Novato to the prison late in the evening of March 26. We were escorted to a waiting room where we joined some fifty other people. They included Boris Naumoff's children and grandchildren; Ron Weiss, the son of Mildred Weiss, Massie's 1965 murder victim; lawyers; other law enforcement officials; and news media.

This execution was the first time that witnesses were allowed to view the lethal injection procedure from beginning to end. The night before, the U.S. Supreme Court had affirmed a federal judge's order to end San Quentin's practice of opening the death chamber curtain only after the condemned inmate was strapped into the gurney.

Massie, in shackles, seemed calm and alert as five guards led him into the old green gas chamber that had been converted for lethal injections after 1993 when the courts ruled death by poison gas was cruel and unusual punishment. As *San Francisco Chronicle* reporter Jim Herron Zamorra wrote in his account of the event, "Patients waiting in the dentist's office usually look more worried than Massie."

Massie's arms and legs were tied to the gurney with leather straps. He did not resist as officials swabbed his left arm with alcohol before inserting the intravenous lines into his arm. I remember thinking it seemed a little odd to me that they were concerned about infection. Massie flexed his fist several times to enlarge his veins for the injection and expressed no emotion. At 12:17 a.m., Warden Jeanne Woodford asked Massie if he still wanted to forego his appeals and proceed.

"Yes," he replied, nodded his head, and spoke his last words: "Forgiveness. Giving up all hope for a better past."

The drugs began flowing into his arm at 12:20—sodium pentothal to render him unconscious, followed by pancuronium bromide to stop his breathing, and concluding with potassium chloride to paralyze his heart. His body shuddered a few times, his back arched, and his feet jerked as the drugs took hold. Massie stopped breathing at 12:25 and was pronounced dead at 12:33 a.m.

"The Killer Who Wants to Die" finally got his wish.

The occasion was the first time some of Naumoff's relatives had seen each other in twenty-two years.

"I'm glad this is done," Naumoff's grandson, Menck Rickman, told the *Chronicle*. "This ruined our family. It ripped us apart."

Boris Naumoff's son, Rick, said Massie's death would help the family to put the murder behind them. "This execution marks the end to a sad and tragic chapter," he said.

On the way home, Carl and I were somber about what we had witnessed, but neither of us was particularly upset. To us it was as humane as possible, much like putting a sick or dying animal to sleep. The gallows, the electric chair, the gas chamber—all were without a doubt extreme ways to take someone's life. Most people, we agreed, are okay with assisted death for those with incurable diseases. In our minds, Massie had an incurable disease and no longer wanted to live. He went to his maker asking for forgiveness, but on his terms.

CHAPTER 24
PLAYING COPS AND ROBBERS

By 1964, when I joined the police department, Inspector Robert Donnelly had risen to a senior position in the traffic bureau. I first met Bob near the end of my police academy training, during the Christmas holidays that year. The members of my recruit class were assigned to fixed-post traffic duty, serving as added help with the increase of shoppers in the downtown area. I somehow lucked out and was assigned to the Union Square Garage. My job was to present a police presence, assist with the traffic flow in and out of the huge parking facility, and offer guidance to shoppers. We were finally out of the classroom and on the streets.

I realized right away that traffic wasn't an assignment I desired. Like many other young patrolmen, I craved more action, but this was a required part of our training. Every morning that week as we walked from the Hall of Justice to our assignments, I would see Bob Donnelly at his post at Market and Fourth Streets, chatting with store proprietors, shoppers, pedestrians. Bob was the perfect fixed-post traffic officer. He was a good-looking Irish cop with an ever-present smile. He looked sharp in his uniform, a perfect example for young would-be police officers to emulate. Women found him charming and would call out "Good morning, Officer Bob" when they saw him. He was a veteran cop and a recipient of the SFPD's Gold Medal of Valor. Bob was fourteen years older than me. As a rookie, I looked up to him for his experience and reputation. He must have been a strong and positive influence on his seven children as well; three of them went into law enforcement. Unfortunately, Bob Donnelly was injured on the job in 1977 and took a disability retirement in 1979.

I had what would turn out to be an ironic encounter with Bob Donnelly in the mid-seventies at the St. Francis Fountain, a throwback diner and classic soda fountain at 24th and York Streets in the Mission District. It was San Francisco's oldest ice cream parlor, dating back to 1918, and was popular with police as a local coffee shop and lunch spot. On any given day at the St. Francis Fountain, you could find several tables filled with cops, usually seated in groups of co-workers—traffic and solo motorcycle guys at one table, robbery inspectors at another, fraud detail cops at another.

I was having lunch there one day with a few of my fellow homicide inspectors. I got up to use the restroom. On the way back to my table, I walked past a table with several veteran traffic cops, including Bob Donnelly. He had his back to me, so I'm sure he didn't notice me. But I saw him gesture toward our table and say to the guys he was with, "There's your new young breed of homicide cops over there. How'd you like to have one of those guys investigating the murder of someone in your family?" Several men at his table laughed.

At first, I took it as a putdown, but I quickly understood where he was coming from. Every business or profession has its hierarchy of senior level staffers who look down on eager newcomers seeking to make their mark. Many of the veteran homicide inspectors at the time were getting near retirement or were already gone—Gus Coreris, John Fotinos, Rotea Gilford, Bill Armstrong, Ken Manley, Dave Toschi, Hobie Nelson. These were the men in homicide that Bob Donnelly knew and respected. The younger inspectors, guys like me, Eddie Erdelatz, Frank McCoy, Herman Clark, and Earl Sanders, with our relative inexperience handling high-priority homicide cases, represented the changing of the guard. Bob Donnelly's comment about our table was his way of saying we still needed to prove ourselves. I'd heard jabs like it before about the new guys, so I said nothing and sat back down with my buddies.

What I never expected was that Bob's flippant remark at the St. Francis Fountain that afternoon would one day become a reality for both of us.

Bob's youngest son, Sean, and Charles McKelvie were best friends. The two sixteen-year-old juniors at San Francisco's McAteer High School liked to spend time driving around together in McKelvie's car after school and on weekends.

McKelvie's white Ford LTD sedan was similar to the Crown Victoria model used by many police departments as unmarked radio cars. McKelvie had even attached a fake microphone to the glove compartment of his car. Sometimes, the boys got their kicks pretending to be police officers talking into the microphone to fool other drivers into thinking they were plainclothes cops.

It was an odd prank for Donnelly, considering his father was a cop.

Sean was tall and thin and liked to play basketball and waterski. I don't know if he ever thought about being a cop like his siblings and his dad. Whatever Sean's dreams were, he didn't live long enough to pursue them. Late on the night of Friday, January 30, 1981, Sean and Charles were cruising around the Inner Sunset District, Donnelly at the wheel of the LTD. They had just left a party where both had been drinking. They were headed to another party when they came to a stop sign at 11th Avenue and Lawton Street at a few minutes past midnight. A dark green Volkswagen bug came to a stop behind them.

In the VW, which had been stolen four days earlier from in front of a house on 17th Avenue, were Stephen M. Thompson and David Lam, a soldier in the Wah Ching youth gang based in Chinatown. Thompson, who had met some Wah Ching members while he was incarcerated in the California Youth Authority, was driving. He and Lam, both nineteen, were on a mission from Allan Wong, leader of a ten-member cell in the Wah Ching, which then had fifty to sixty members.

Wong had instructed Thompson and Lam to rob the house of a young woman on 33rd Avenue in retribution for her testimony against him in a court case. Wong gave Thompson and Lam ski masks, surgical gloves, rope, and two guns, a .38-caliber Smith and Wesson revolver and an RG .38-special revolver. They were on their way to carry out their assignment when they stopped behind the Ford driven by Sean Donnelly.

Thompson honked the horn and shouted for the Ford to get out of the way. Donnelly motioned for the VW to pass. Thompson backed up, pulled around and passed on the left going north on 11th Avenue, swearing at the two boys in the Ford on the way by. Enraged, Donnelly sped up and caught the VW a block away at 11th Avenue and Kirkham. As the Ford drew along the driver's side of the VW, McKelvie shouted, "Hey, motherfuckers!" He appeared to be talking on a microphone.

Thinking the young men in the Ford were undercover police radioing for backup, Thompson feared he and Lam were about to be arrested in a stolen car with loaded weapons. He grabbed one of the guns and fired five shots in rapid succession at the Ford. The first bullet hit McKelvie in the shoulder. As the VW sped away, McKelvie looked over to see Donnelly outside the car, lying in the street. That's where Officer Mary Rose Nilan, the first patrol officer to respond to reports of shots fired at the intersection, found Donnelly when she pulled up to the scene at 12:13 a.m. Donnelly had been shot once in the back. He died a short time later.

Herman Clark and I had already been to two other homicide scenes that night, the robbery and shooting death of a man on Laguna Street and the strangling of a prostitute by her pimp near the Golden Gate Park Panhandle. We were finishing up at the second one and were about to call it a night when we got word of the shooting at 11th and Kirkham, about ten minutes away. When we pulled up at the intersection, the Ford was still parked there. Before being taken by ambulance to the hospital, McKelvie told Officer Nilan that there were two assailants in the Volkswagen, both in their late teens. A Caucasian male with facial acne and black hair parted in the middle was driving and there was an Asian male with a sparse moustache with him, McKelvie said.

After spending some time at the crime scene, Herman and I were back in the office putting out an all-points bulletin with a description of the suspects, the Volkswagen, and the caliber of the gun used. After McKelvie was treated for his wound, we showed him a large book that our Asian Gang Task Force maintained which contained hundreds of police photos of possible suspects, but he was unable to identify any specific individual. The stolen Volkswagen was found abandoned on Cole Street in the Haight-Ashbury neighborhood two days after the shooting.

Four months went by without much progress in the case. Other than McKelvie, there were no eyewitnesses, and the Volkswagen hadn't yielded any useable fingerprints or other evidence. When all our efforts weren't producing results in a case like this involving Asian youths, we would turn to our Asian Gang Task Force for help.

I was sitting at my desk one morning when police officer Dorree Donnelly, in full uniform, came in and sat across from me in Herman's chair. Dorree was Bob's daughter and Sean's sister; she'd been named after her mother. She asked how our investigation into her brother's murder was progressing. I told Dorree the truth, that it was slow going.

"I know what the suspect looks like," she said.

"What do you mean? How do you know what he looks like?" I asked.

"I had a dream, and I saw the man that murdered my baby brother," she said.

I was about to say, "Are you kidding me?" Then I took a good look at Dorree and could see she was dead serious. I could tell she had not been sleeping well. Her eyes were bloodshot, and she looked tired. This dream suspect was real to her and was her way of trying to help solve her brother's murder case. I sure as hell was not going to compound Dorree's pain by discounting her dream. She offered to meet with our police sketch artist to draw the suspect she saw in her dream. I told Dorree the artist would be contacting her and thanked her for her help. After she left our office, I called John Sterling. He had replaced our previous artist, Hobie Nelson, after he retired. I explained the situation and asked John to contact Dorree, draw her suspect, and give me the sketch for the file. The next morning, I was called into the captain's office.

"You authorized overtime for John Sterling to draw a suspect seen in a dream?" asked Captain Joe Lordan. "What were you thinking?"

Captain Lordan and I knew each other well. He was a prince of a man who had been my sergeant at Northern Station years before. We had a mutual respect. When I explained to him about Dorree Donnelly's dream, he got up from his chair and shook my hand. "That was very compassionate, Frank. I would have done the same thing."

Unknown to us during that time, Stephen Thompson was busy figuring out how to kill McKelvie to keep him from identifying him or testifying against him. Thompson had gone to the library to look up McKelvie's home address in the Polk City Directory, a reverse phone book. He also went to McAteer High School, where he found a picture of McKelvie in a yearbook. Thompson had purchased an M-1 rifle at a gun shop on Judah Street. He believed he would be able to shoot McKelvie in front of his house using the rifle from a nearby hillside. But first, he needed to practice.

On the afternoon of February 16, two weeks after the killing of Donnelly, police were called to investigate reports of gunshots on Mount Sutro, a wooded open space not far from the Donnelly murder scene. Patrolmen Anthony Fotinos and John Cleary Jr., two excellent young officers, responded to the call. Tony Fotinos was the son of Inspector John Fotinos, one of my colleagues in the homicide detail.

John Cleary was the son of my former partner, Jack Cleary. John Cleary, incidentally, had been Charles McKelvie's swim coach at the Olympic Club, and remembers him as an accomplished boxer there as well.

"Driving up Seventh Avenue toward Warren Drive, we could see two guys way up on the hill," John Cleary recalled. "We couldn't see if they had a gun from that far away. When we got up to the location, it was heavily wooded. We had our guns out and we were walking through the heavy foliage, but we had no idea where they were. Just then, one of them tripped and fell. That noise helped us find them, and we were able to identify ourselves and take them into custody. They had a big rifle, an M-1, fully loaded with a banana clip. If they hadn't made that noise, they would have had me and Tony dead to rights."

The two officers arrested Stephen Thompson and the other man, William On, and took them to Park Station to be booked for firing a weapon within the city limits. While the two young suspects were sitting on a bench at the station, On pulled a handful of bullets out of his pocket and threw them into a nearby trash can. Both Thompson and On were then taken downtown to the city jail.

Here we were, me and Herman, working like crazy to find our suspect in the Donnelly murder without having any idea that he was upstairs in the city prison on the gun charge. There was nothing at that time to tie Thompson to the Donnelly case. He eventually made bail and was back on the streets. Herman and I were frustrated. Every case is important, but the murder of a fellow police officer's child brought added pressure to solving the case.

In April, Bob Donnelly and his family joined the San Francisco Chamber of Commerce in offering a $4,000 reward in the case, hoping to draw out anyone who might have information that would help find Sean's killers. But it wasn't until late June, when Allan Wong was in the county jail and facing multiple unrelated charges, that we caught a break. Wong was the Wah Ching gang leader who planned the robbery that Thompson and Lam were on their way to carry out when

Donnelly was killed. Wong was being held on five charges unrelated to the Donnelly murder: burglary with use of a firearm, receiving stolen property, possession of burglary tools, possession of tear gas, and credit card forgery. Since three of the charges were felonies, he felt he was likely to go to prison on the burglary charge at least. He decided to try to make a deal to avoid spending any more time behind bars. On June 25, Wong called Inspector Leon Crouere of the Asian Gang Task Force from the jail. "Do you want to solve the Donnelly murder?" he asked. Inspector Crouere called me that same day to tell me Allan Wong wanted to cut a deal.

Inspector John McKenna of the Gang Task Force had deep knowledge of the Wah Ching. He and I met with Allan Wong the next day. He told us that Stephen Thompson and David Lam were the ones responsible for the murder of Sean Donnelly and the shooting of Charles McKelvie. Wong denied, however, that he had ever given Thompson or Lam a gun or that he had planned the robbery, claiming it was Thompson's idea. Wong told us that Thompson had tossed the murder weapon into the Bay near Pier 24. He also showed us the location in the 600 block of Cole Street where Thompson and Lam had abandoned the Volkswagen after the murder.

As it happened, both Thompson and Lam were again in police custody. They had been arrested the previous day in separate cases and were still locked up. Thompson had been charged with driving a stolen vehicle, malicious mischief, resisting arrest, and arson. Lam was being held for extortion.

Wong worked out a deal with the district attorney's office to plead guilty to felony burglary and have his other charges dismissed. He was also guaranteed to receive probation and no further jail time if he testified in the August 25 preliminary hearing in the Donnelly murder case.

Both Wong and David Lam testified at the hearing and at Thompson's trial in November. Wong told the jury that Thompson had called him after the shooting asking for help. Wong met up with

Thompson and Lam at a sandwich shop in the Haight-Ashbury a short time later.

"I just dusted a cop," Wong said Thompson told him. Just as Wong had told us when we interrogated him, he testified that he helped Thompson and Lam dispose of the murder weapon. Wong said that when he learned from the newspaper the next day that the victims were not police officers, he told Thompson, and Thompson responded, "Well, they shouldn't have been playing cop." Wong told the court that Thompson wanted to obtain a rifle to kill McKelvie so he could not identify Thompson.

Defense attorney Manton Selby argued that Thompson was being framed by the Wah Ching and that we had acted inappropriately with the gang to secure their testimony against his client. That argument fell on deaf ears.

Bob Donnelly was overcome with emotion when the verdict was announced. "Sure, I'm satisfied," the retired inspector told the *San Francisco Chronicle*. "Even from inside the system I can now see that it works."

During our investigation, we had turned up a letter Thompson had mailed a few weeks before the Donnelly murder to *Warbonnet*, a militant magazine and weapons mail-order company based in Wyoming.

"This letter is in response to an advertisement in *Soldier of Fortune*. I am interested right now in buying an Uzi or Ingram and a 9-mm or a .45 or a .380 that is silent. Also, in a few months I am starting an anti-Black chapter in San Francisco. I don't know about any of your racial feelings; however, I would like auto weapons for twenty people, pistols, and if you can obtain them, grenades and 15 L.A.W.s [light antitank rockets]. Can you respond to this immediately? Stephen Thompson."

The prosecutor, Jim Goodman, decided not to put the letter into evidence and it wasn't mentioned during the trial, but I released it to the media afterward to amplify Thompson's mindset before the murder.

On November 11, 1981, after a week-long trial and five and a half hours of deliberations, the jury found Stephen M. Thompson guilty of first-degree murder in the fatal shooting of Sean Donnelly and attempted murder in the wounding of Charles McKelvie. The jury acquitted Thompson of conspiracy to commit robbery.

A month later, Superior Court Judge Richard Figone, citing Stephen Thompson's "viciousness and callousness," sentenced him to thirty-eight years to life in prison—twenty-five for the murder, nine for attempted murder, two for use of a firearm in the attempted murder, and two for violating his parole on a burglary conviction.

David Lam, who was in the car with Thompson the night of the Donnelly murder, was given immunity from prosecution in exchange for his testimony. Allen Wong had several felony charges against him dismissed for his cooperation in the case.

It was a just outcome for me. As one of the "new young breed" of homicide inspectors Bob Donnelly had once disparaged, it gave me great satisfaction to know I had helped to bring a successful conclusion to the tragedy that had taken his youngest son and devastated a wonderful police family.

CHAPTER 25
HOLOCAUST SURVIVORS

In late February 1984, Chief of Inspectors George Eimil called me into his office. "Frank, do you remember the Slamovich case?" he asked me.

The name rang a bell with me but I couldn't place it. Chief Eimil reminded me that six years earlier, Miriam Slamovich had startled a burglar who had climbed through a bedroom window into her San Francisco house thinking no one was home. When he entered the kitchen and saw Miriam, she screamed. He shot her in the face. He ran out the front door, pursued by Miriam's husband, Henry. The shooter escaped in a car with two accomplices. She fought for her life for a month before she died. Her murder was tragic and heart-wrenching for her family and incomprehensible to those who knew her story.

The woman grew up as Miriam Glatt in Poland. Her grueling six-year journey during World War II from her native Polish town to the Auschwitz concentration camp and back to freedom was fraught with terror, torture, and death. Miriam and her other two sisters, Annie and Sally, miraculously survived, and all eventually settled in San Francisco.

Miriam's sister, Annie, told the saga of the family's ordeal during the war to the *San Francisco Chronicle* in 2010.

Miriam Glatt was seven in 1939 when the German army invaded Wierzbnik in central Poland. The Nazis closed schools and Jewish stores, burned synagogues, and posted curfews for Jews. Jews accused of disobedience and other minor offenses were hanged at public gallows.

When the sisters saw their parents hiding family heirlooms and valuables inside the walls of their home, they knew the worst was imminent. On October 27, 1942, Nazis marched the Jewish people of Wierzbnik at gunpoint to the train station. Families were split up, one train for a concentration camp and another for a work camp. Thanks to their mother, who pawned her jewelry to buy work papers for her daughters, the sisters were shuttled to the work train. A soldier shot Miriam's brother in the back when he refused an order. One of the four girls was also killed.

"Hang on to your sisters," the parents said to Annie as guards loaded their mother and father onto the concentration camp train. Annie, eighteen, Sally, sixteen, and Miriam, eleven, were taken to a factory called Majowka, where guards with machine guns routinely entered the sick ward and killed patients in their beds.

The girls were regularly threatened with punishments and death for the most random reasons. They avoided execution by making canvas snow covers for the cannons on Nazi tanks. Annie learned to sew while Sally and Miriam cut the fabric.

The girls never saw their father again, but one day Annie was surprised to discover their mother in the labor camp kitchen peeling potatoes. She looked wan and distraught. She told Annie she had helped another prisoner deliver a baby, only to watch as a German soldier gave the baby some type of fatal injection. It devastated Annie's mother. "A week later she died of heartbreak in my arms," Annie told the *Chronicle*. "I see that picture of mama in my eyes all the time."

After two years at the Majowka work factory, as the Russians were advancing on Hitler's forces, labor camps began closing. Workers were shipped to concentration camps. The sisters managed to stay together and were put on a train that took five days to reach Auschwitz. Once there, the guards shaved their heads and tattooed their forearms with identification numbers. They were no longer considered human, just a number.

One night, soon after their arrival, the sisters were among some two hundred prisoners who were ordered to strip and enter a gas chamber. They sat shivering on wooden benches waiting to die. But the gas never came. In the morning, they were taken out and told to cut grass at the camp. Miriam was so hungry that she ate some of it, grew ill, and was taken to a hospital. This terrified Annie because she knew the sick were being sent to the crematories.

Annie gathered twigs and weeds and fashioned a crude broom. She snuck into the hospital and found a Polish-speaking nurse. She presented the broom to her as a gift and pleaded with the nurse to look after her little sister. Days later, Annie noticed the Nazis loading patients from the hospital into trucks to take them to the gas chambers. She feared Miriam was one of those patients. She ran into the hospital to find it empty. But the nurse was still there. She opened a closet and there was Miriam hiding among the linens.

In January 1945, as the Third Reich began to collapse, the prisoners were each given a loaf of bread and a blanket and sent on death marches away from the concentration camps. "We had to march all day and night, and we didn't know where we were going," Annie said. "Many died of exhaustion." Finally, they were rescued by Russian soldiers.

Miriam migrated to Israel after the war; her sisters came to America. On a trip to the United States to visit Annie and Sally, Miriam met Henry Slamovich and fell in love. Henry was another Holocaust survivor who had been among 1,200 Jews saved by German industrialist Oskar Schindler. Despite her reluctance to leave the newly created state of Israel, Henry persuaded Miriam to marry him. Eventually, Henry and Miriam and their son, Elliot, settled into a modest home in the Outer Sunset neighborhood, close to the city zoo and Ocean Beach.

Henry became business partners with her sister Sally's husband, Harry Recht, in San Francisco, first at a market and later in a chain of laundromats and rental properties.

Monday, February 20, 1978, was a clear, sunny day in San Francisco, warm for February. Miriam, Henry, and sixteen-year-old Eliot took advantage of the unseasonable weather to go hiking on Mount Tamalpais, a state park in the Marin County hills north of the Golden Gate Bridge. When they returned to their home at 2906 Yorba Street, they opened windows in the front and back of the house to catch the afternoon breeze. After dinner, Henry went downstairs to the garage to work on his taxes. Elliot went to his bedroom to do homework.

That evening, three men were driving around the neighborhood looking for a house to burglarize. They came upon the Slamovich house and saw the open second floor back bedroom windows and no outward signs that anyone was home. One of the men got out of the car and knocked on the front door. When there was no response, he signaled the other two men, who joined him in going through the side gate. They boosted him up to reach the open rear window. The two other men returned to their getaway car and waited.

Shortly before 8:30 p.m., Miriam heard the knock on their front door. Miriam called down to Henry in the basement. "Don't answer the door," she said. "We're not expecting anybody." Minutes later, the intruder crawled through the open window into an unoccupied bedroom. He crept down the hall past Eliot's room and went into the kitchen, where he was as startled to see Miriam as she was to see him.

"Get out of here!" she shouted at him.

Without a word, the intruder, a six-foot, two-inch Black man in his twenties wearing a knit cap and a black leather coat, pulled out a blue steel automatic handgun and shot Miriam in the face. Hearing the shot, Henry ran upstairs and found the gunman standing over his wife. "Freeze, or I'll shoot you!" the intruder ordered. The gunman ran down the stairs and out the front door, with Henry in pursuit. Henry watched as the intruder climbed into a waiting car and sped away. He did not get a good look at the gunman's face and could not describe the getaway car or its occupants.

Since Miriam survived the shooting, it was not initially treated as a homicide. Inspector Tom Dickson of our General Work detail was assigned to investigate the break-in and shooting. Tom was known in the department as a hard-working, dedicated investigator. He was joined at the crime scene by Inspector Walt Ihle and Sergeant Ken Moses of the Crime Lab. These were three of the finest investigators we had. Dickson visited Miriam frequently at Kaiser Hospital in Redwood City during the month that she lived. She showed him her Holocaust tattoo and spoke of her experience during the war.

"That was my most heart-wrenching case," Dickson said in a *San Francisco Chronicle* article about the case some years later. "It was agonizing. They were a perfect family. With all she went through, why did it have to happen to this woman?"

Miriam died on March 20, with investigators no closer to solving the case.

Other than the bullet retrieved from Miriam's head, the only physical evidence they were able to come up with was a single fingerprint left on the outside glass of the Slamovichs' rear bedroom window where the intruder had climbed in. In today's world, we take nearly instant computerized fingerprint identification for granted. Back then, it had to be done manually, one print card at a time. It could often take months, years—maybe never—to match a single print.

Inspectors Ihle and Moses, who later became a sergeant, spent more than a thousand hours painstakingly trying to identify the owner of the fingerprint, comparing it with three hundred thousand prints on file, one at a time.

Over time, the investigation languished. Years went by without success. Fortunately, Ken Moses was determined and not inclined to give up on a case easily.

Ken Moses is a forensic legend. He spent twenty-six years with the SFPD from 1971 to 1997. He founded the Crime Scene Investigations Unit of the SFPD Crime Lab in 1983. After he retired, he established his own company Forensic Identification Services (FIS). FIS has worked nationwide with attorneys; local, state, and federal agencies; private companies; and military organizations on complex investigations. Ken has personally investigated seventeen thousand crime scenes and more than five hundred homicide scenes in his career. Ken knows crime scenes.

Early in the 1980s, Ken Moses and Walt Ihle were hard at work developing computer software that could match fingerprints at many times the speed of the hand-comparison method. Ken pioneered the system and advocated for department funds for the program. The computerized system for the SFPD was one of the first in the country. The SFPD launched its Automated Fingerprint Identification System (AFIS) for the first time on Tuesday, February 28, 1984.

The San Francisco Police Department never forgot about the latent print lifted from the window at the Slamovich house. It was the first one entered in the new system. Within six minutes there was a match. It was a startling development that signaled a remarkable technological change in crime fighting.

The computer identified the print as belonging to Leoncio Saulny, now twenty-three. Ironically, we found out that Saulny himself was a computer expert, working at Crocker Bank.

A matching fingerprint at a crime scene is probable cause to make an arrest, yet it doesn't automatically guarantee a conviction. Chief Eimil, a highly regarded professional and an attorney, was very aware of that fact. The print identification of Saulny was a huge start, but it was on the outside of the window glass. That fact alone would not reach the level of proof for a burglary conviction. Trespassing, maybe, but definitely not enough to sustain a murder conviction in a court of law.

A strong case takes more than that and longer to build.

Once Saulny's identification was made, but a couple of days before it was announced, Chief Eimil asked to see me. I went across the hall to his office. Eimil refreshed my memory about the Slamovich case and briefed me on her tragic childhood. He also told me about the AFIS match. I had recalled little about the Slamovich case. So many years had gone by, and I hadn't been assigned to it originally. It was not a homicide until Miriam died. By then, Tom Dickson had done all the work on the case, and because of his capabilities and knowledge of the case, he remained the case investigator.

"Frank, this is a big deal to the department to ID this guy after so long," said Eimil. "We can't mess this one up. I know you're busy, but I'm reassigning this case to you. I want you to drop what you're doing and to please look into this case and bring us a conviction."

Every officer in the police department had the highest respect for Chief Eimil. I would have gone through a brick wall for him. I told him I would get to work on the Slamovich case and the suspect Saulny right away. I studied the case file looking for supportive evidence to the fingerprint match. My initial thought was accurate; I needed more than a fingerprint. I would need a confession. That night I laid awake trying to figure out how to make an airtight case against Saulny. By morning I had a plan.

My partner Carl Klotz and I secured an arrest warrant for Saulny. We headed out of the Hall of Justice to pick him up. Waiting at the elevator, I turned to Carl and said, "The right thing to do would be to invite Tom Dickson to go with us." After all, it had been his case for six years. We walked over to the General Work detail to see Tom. He was grateful for the opportunity to be going with us. The three of us went to Crocker Bank together. I explained to the bank manager why we were there and asked him to bring Leoncio Saulny out to us. The manager went in the back office and returned with Saulny. As they approached us, Tom Dickson stepped forward and began to speak.

"Leoncio Saulny, you are under arrest for the murder of Miriam Slamovich. You have the right…"

I shot Tom a wide-eyed glare that said, *"What the hell are you doing?"* It was enough to stop him in mid-sentence. First, this was no longer his case. It was mine. Second, I had a plan to extract a confession from this suspect. It wasn't my intent to disparage Tom's investigative instincts or hurt his feelings, but I don't believe he was considering the implications of Mirandizing Saulny at that point. Miranda can be read either at the time of arrest or prior to interrogation. Once a suspect has acknowledged his Miranda rights and does not wish to make a statement, the interrogation is effectively cut off, unless or until the suspect's attorney is present. I had no intention of interrogating Saulny in the bank manager's office. I stepped past Tom and said to our suspect, "Leoncio Saulny, we have a warrant for your arrest for murder. Turn around." I cuffed him, thanked the bank manager, and we all went out to the car. Nobody talked on the drive back to the Hall of Justice. You could have heard a pin drop. When we got into the police garage, I said to Saulny, "If I were you right about now, I'd be thinking about which one of my friends gave me up." This was part of my plan. With only a fingerprint for evidence after six years, we needed a confession from Saulny. I wanted him to think that one of the other men with him on the day of the murder had snitched on him, hoping he'd think it's their word against his own.

When we all got back to the homicide detail, Tom Dickson thanked us and returned to the General Work detail. Carl and I put Saulny into an interrogation room. I retrieved the case file and put a fresh cassette into our tape recorder. When Carl and I entered the interrogation room, I told Leoncio that we would record everything we said in the room. I promised him that if he told the truth and he was innocent of the murder, I would work hard to help clear him. Then I read him his Miranda rights.

"Do you wish to talk to us now?" I asked.

"Yeah, man," he said. "I never murdered anybody."

Before continuing, I stated all the introductory information for the recording—date, time, those present, and the reason the interrogation was taking place. I began asking Saulny questions about the day of the shooting. He denied repeatedly that he had ever shot or killed anyone.

I showed him a series of photos from the Slamovich crime scene and asked if he had ever been in that area.

"No."

"Did you ever enter through this gate?"

"No."

"Look at the photo of the front of this house. Have you ever been in this yard outside these open windows?

"No."

"Did you ever work as a glazier or a carpenter?"

"No."

Finally, I told him this house was near the zoo and asked again if he'd ever been there.

"No. My father drove a city bus out by the zoo, I think, but I was never near that house."

I thanked him for his cooperation, then turned off the tape recorder and looked Saulny in the eye.

"Leoncio, you're a liar," I said. "You just lied to Inspector Klotz and me."

"No, I didn't lie!" he said, growing agitated. "I didn't murder anybody."

I showed him the fingerprint report from AFIS. "That was your fingerprint on that window," I said. "You shot and killed Miriam Slamovich. You know it. Inspector Klotz and I know it. The jury will know it. You lied to us. With the fingerprint evidence and your taped statement of denial, you will most likely be convicted of murder."

He started crying. "Please turn that thing back on," he said, pointing to the tape recorder. "I want to tell you the whole truth." I turned the recorder back on. I explained what had transpired while the recorder was off and asked Leoncio if what I said was accurate.

"Yes," he replied. "I asked you to turn the recorder back on. I want to tell you the truth." Leoncio proceeded to give us all the details about February 20, 1978. He described how they cased homes in the area, noting ones that appeared unoccupied. He told how he knocked on the door and no one answered. He talked about his friends helping him through the window and how surprised he was to see the lady in the kitchen.

"I panicked," said Saulny. "I shot her."

We had our confession. As I walked out of the interrogation room, Marge Lundquist, the homicide detail's receptionist and secretary, said to me, "Frank, that man you have in the back room, his mother is waiting for you in the foyer."

I walked out to the foyer. There were three women there, all nuns dressed in full habit. Two were white, one was Black. "Can I help you, sisters?" I asked, a bit confused. The Black nun said to me, "I'm Leoncio's mother."

"Sister, how can that be?" I replied. "I was taught by Catholic nuns. You're married to God."

"I had Leoncio before I entered the convent," she said. "My mother raised him. My son never murdered anybody. You are railroading him. I want to see and speak to him immediately."

"He just admitted to us that he committed the murder," I told her. I led her into the interrogation room where Leoncio was seated. He immediately denied everything to her. "I wouldn't hurt anybody."

After the nuns left, Carl and I took Saulny upstairs and booked him for the six-year-old murder of Miriam Slamovich. At his preliminary hearing before Superior Court Judge Joseph Desmond, the same three nuns were sitting in the first row. They were holding their Rosary beads, praying, as I took the witness stand. I had my case file and the tape recording with me. Before Assistant District Attorney Tommy Norman began to question me, Judge Desmond leaned over from his chair and asked me, "Frank, why are there three nuns sitting in the front row of my courtroom?" I explained that the nun in the middle was the defendant's mother. His eyebrows arched on his forehead. Then he told Norman to proceed.

Tommy asked me if I would play the tape on my cassette recorder for the court. I turned on the recorder and pushed "play." I was hoping the three nuns would hear how professional we were during the interrogation. Nobody was railroaded. When the recording began to play, the nuns stood up and walked out of the courtroom. They never wanted to hear the truth.

Saulny pleaded guilty and on August 1, 1985, Superior Court Judge Claude Perasso sentenced him to the maximum of seven years in prison for second-degree murder, plus two years for using a gun in the crime. =

Chief Eimil congratulated me on the way I had handled the investigation, built a solid case, and obtained the confession that concluded with the conviction. Chief Eimil looked at me and said, "Frank, there is no reward I can give you but to say thank you. However, what I can do is send you to the FBI academy in Quantico, Virginia. They have a one-week course on crime scene investigation coming up. It's not a course you need, but take the time away from the office, meet new friends, relax, and enjoy yourself. Have a great trip. It's on the department."

I stood up, reached across his desk, and shook his hand. It was truly a great relaxing week in Virginia.

With a single fingerprint and the dedication of Inspectors Tom Dickson, Ken Moses, and Walt Ihle, Miriam Slamovich's family finally had some form of closure after six long years.

CHAPTER 26
A STUNNING NEW ADMISSION

Dan White was sentenced to seven years in prison for the City Hall murders after his conviction for voluntary manslaughter in 1979. A model prisoner by all accounts, he served five years at Soledad State Prison before he was paroled in January 1984. Then-Mayor Dianne Feinstein had sent word to Dan through Police Chief Con Murphy upon his release not to come back to San Francisco because of the damage he'd caused to the city and the hurt feelings that still lingered.

The disgraced former city supervisor, now separated from his wife, Mary Anne, rented a small apartment in Los Angeles and kept a low profile, avoiding media attention for a time. But eventually word got out that Dan was in L.A. Reporter Ed Leslie from KGO-TV in San Francisco went down there to find him. Leslie stopped a jogger on the street in the area where White was reported to be and asked him about the rumor that Dan White was living in the neighborhood.

"Really? How great is that!" said the jogger.

"You're kidding, right?" said Leslie. "You're happy about it?"

"Sure! How often do you get the Dallas Cowboys quarterback living in your neighborhood?"

Danny White had been the Cowboys' starting quarterback since 1980 and had led the team to three consecutive NFC Conference Championships. Obviously, he was more famous to that jogger than the man who had killed the mayor of San Francisco.

I didn't have any contact with Dan while he was in prison, but one day in early August, seven months after he was paroled, my phone rang. When I picked up, I heard a familiar voice.

"Hi, Frank, it's Jim Sullivan." Jim Sullivan was a mutual friend of ours who had gone to St. Ignatius High School. He was Dan's police radio car partner and later became a fireman. I had a hunch it was really Dan calling. I recognized his voice, but I played along. I figured he was paranoid that someone might be listening to his calls. He didn't want to say who he really was or what he was doing.

"Jim" said he was in Los Angeles and that he had gotten tickets to the upcoming Summer Olympics. "I'd love to get together with you. Why don't you come down here for a few days? We'll go to the games together."

"Sounds great, Jim," I said. "I really want to talk to you."

I made the arrangements and flew down to L.A. I wasn't surprised to see Dan White waiting   at the airport to meet me. Looking very fit, he was dressed in jeans and a T-shirt, and wore a baseball cap and sunglasses. He didn't have a car. He said he liked to walk everywhere or take public transportation. We caught a cab downtown and stopped at a small restaurant for a bite to eat. Over the meal, Dan told me that prison had been tough on him, but he kept quiet and did his time. Because he'd been a cop, he said, other prisoners urinated and spat on him and threw feces at him to instigate a fight.

"I took it as punishment and penance for what I had done," he told me. "I never acted out, but you know I could handle myself. I prayed. I wrote letters. I did my time. I tried to be a model prisoner."

His only friend at Soledad, he said, was Sirhan Sirhan, the convicted assassin of U.S. Senator Robert Kennedy in 1968. "We talked a lot. We sort of became brothers," Dan said.

He told me that one day shortly after he arrived in L.A., he'd unintentionally run into a TV crew on the street. They were filming a damsel-in-distress type of show somewhat like the old *Candid Camera* show. A woman would pretend to be harassed or verbally abused on the street to see if anyone would come to her aid while a hidden camera recorded it. Dan said he happened upon the scenario and quickly stepped in to stop a man who appeared to be threatening harm to a woman.

"Suddenly all these people came out of hiding and began to congratulate me," Dan told me. "They demanded that I sign this waiver so they can put me on TV. I said I wasn't signing anything, and I took off. Stupid me. Here I am hiding from the world, and I get right into the middle of this thing trying to do something good."

I realized this was Dan White trying to show me that he was still basically a good person willing to defend someone who needed help. He was still trying to be the "good cop."

We went back to Dan's place. It was sparsely furnished with few amenities. He gave me the bed and he slept on the sofa. The next day, August 6, we headed out to the Los Angeles Coliseum. Dan had tickets for the track and field events. The following day, we attended boxing matches at the Los Angeles Sports Arena. Afterward, we stopped for lunch in a big parking lot that had been turned into a food venue. Over hot dogs, chips, and sodas, I finally brought up the City Hall shootings.

"I came here for one main reason," I told him. "As a homicide cop, I need to know what I missed."

"Yeah, I figured that," Dan said. "I really lost it that day. But it was going to be a lot worse."

"Worse? How?"

"I planned to take out four people. Besides Moscone and Harvey, I wanted to get Carol Ruth Silver and Willie Brown. Then I was going to kill myself."

Oh, my God! I thought. *We were right all along about the premeditation. But this?* Willie Brown was a prominent state assemblyman and a powerful figure in San Francisco politics who would later be elected mayor. As it happened, Brown had been meeting with Moscone the morning of the shootings and had left the mayor's office only minutes before White arrived. Silver was another supervisor who aligned with Milk and the liberal faction on the board.

I suddenly remembered that Dan had extra bullets in his pocket that day.

"Jesus, Dan, why? What the hell were you thinking?"

"Willie Brown was the puppeteer pulling the strings on Moscone," he replied. "And Carol Ruth was the biggest snake of all."

Dan never explained exactly what he meant about Silver, but I was gobsmacked by this revelation. Even though I believed he premeditated the killings all along, to hear him now admit it seven years later was mind-blowing. What I was having trouble registering was that he wanted to kill four people, not just two. In his view, he was deciding something he knew would make Dianne Feinstein the mayor and put the city back on the right track.

I returned to San Francisco, my mind whirling. I went to the D.A.'s office to see assistant D.A. Tommy Norman and my old homicide partner, Jack Cleary, who was by then working for the district attorney as the chief investigator, to tell them what I'd learned.

"You'd best keep that to yourself," said Norman. "The city is still recovering. There's no need to reopen this can of worms. Let the city continue to heal."

I didn't talk to anyone else about it for fourteen years. One Sunday afternoon in April 1998, I went out to Candlestick Park for a Giants game. I was watching batting practice when Mike Weiss stopped by my seat to say hello. Weiss was a local magazine writer I knew well because he had written a book about the City Hall killings called *Double Play*. We talked briefly, and then he walked away toward the field. A short time later he returned.

"I have something for you," he said. He handed me a copy of the

San Jose Mercury's Sunday magazine, *West*, from February 28. On the front cover was a full-page color photo of San Francisco Giants' first baseman Will Clark, in uniform, wearing eye black, a batting helmet, and batting gloves, a small balloon of pink bubble gum spreading out from his lips. Weiss, who had written the cover story on the Giants' outlook for the upcoming season, had gone down to the field or into the clubhouse and asked Clark to autograph the cover for me. "Dear Frank," he wrote. "Dying to meet you. Will." Clark was always one of my favorite players but I'm not sure how Weiss knew that.

Against my better judgment and out of appreciation and a sense of obligation for how hard Weiss had worked on the book and the way he presented me in it, I shared with him what Dan White had told me in Los Angeles fourteen years earlier. I made him promise never to reveal it to anyone. He did promise, but he wasn't a man of his word, or perhaps he felt it was too big a story for his promise to matter. Six months later, the October issue of *San Francisco Magazine* came out with a big cover article by Weiss about Dan White's intended targets at City Hall. Weiss had betrayed my trust. In my opinion, he broke his promise and sold me out because he was looking for a payday.

I was raised believing a man's word was golden. Big mistake on my part.

CHAPTER 27
GAS CHAMBER

In late 1984 and early 1985, during the months leading up to the Night Stalker case, Carl Klotz and I caught three new cases that proved difficult: the vicious killing of two teenage boys by the same killer a month apart—one boy had his throat slashed at Stow Lake in Golden Gate Park and another was dismembered in the caves known as the "Love Tunnels" at Land's End; the fatal beating of celebrity chef Masa Kobayashi in his Nob Hill apartment; and the home invasion and frenzied stabbing deaths of the Caldwell sisters.

We were able to capture and draw a confession from the boys' killer, a psychotic pedophile named William Melvin White Jr. He was a convicted murderer who had been paroled. We identified a prime suspect in the Kobayashi murder case but never developed sufficient evidence to make an arrest. And it took five years, but the Night Stalker, Richard Ramirez, finally helped us close the case of the Caldwell sisters by telling us he had killed them.

Things had finally begun to wind down as fall arrived and the weather turned chilly. I was on call again for the week beginning Monday, October 21. Carl was off that week, and I was paired up with Inspector Herman Clark. Herman was a dedicated homicide cop who had been my full-time partner from 1978 to 1981. Herman and I had just gotten back into our radio car after lunch when the radio squawked:

"Headquarters to 5-Henry-7."

"This is 5-Henry-7," I answered. "We are just back from 10-7M [out of service for a meal]. What've you got?"

"5-Henry-7, please respond to a report of a possible 801 at 150 Shawnee Avenue."

"10-4, headquarters," I replied. I had to think about the last time I'd been assigned to a report of a suicide. "5-Henry-7 and 5-Henry-12 responding to 150 Shawnee."

"Jeez, Herman, that address sounds familiar to me for some reason," I said as we pulled away from the curb and headed to the Excelsior District. My wife was raised about two blocks from Shawnee on Mt. Vernon Avenue, so I knew that neighborhood very well.

Herman and I had just come from our favorite restaurant, Original Joe's, on Taylor Street in the Tenderloin area downtown. Joe's was run by Marie Duggan, a lovely and energetic Italian woman married to John Duggan, a high school friend of mine. Marie's father, Ante "Tony" Rodin, founded Original Joe's in 1937. The waiters wore tuxedos, the food was tops, and the price was reasonable. Over the years, Marie and I had become the best of friends. She often referred to the large table in the back as "Inspector Falzon's booth." We regularly celebrated the breaking of a big case at Original Joe's. If we wanted to impress out-of-town detectives, we knew a meal by Marie would not disappoint. Marie was such a loving, caring woman that we often referred to her as Mother Teresa of the Tenderloin. Unfortunately, fire destroyed the original Taylor Street restaurant in 2007, but it later reopened across from Washington Square in North Beach. Today they also own Westlake Joe's, where I had dinner just prior my shootout with robber Lloyd Henry Hill in 1977.

As I've said, when you're a homicide inspector, you never know what you're walking into. This one was a total shockwave.

The moment we turned onto Shawnee I realized where we were.

The small, lime green stucco house at 150 was the home of Dan White, my longtime friend, former fellow cop, fireman, and city supervisor. And more significantly, the paroled killer of San Francisco Mayor George Moscone and Supervisor Harvey Milk.

"Oh, God, no!" I said to Herman as we pulled up.

One of my first thoughts was that I was on call the day Dan shot Moscone and Milk to death seven years before, and now I'm on call again on what looks like the last day of Dan's life. *What are those odds?* I wondered. A dozen reporters were milling about as we double-parked near the house. News organizations monitor the police department's radio traffic, and it's not unusual for reporters to get to an incident before us. Once they saw me, they surrounded the car in a group, firing questions. There were so many of them that I had trouble opening the car door.

The media had been relentless in documenting every move Dan had made since his parole. I flashed back one week earlier to a lunch I had with Susan Sward, a stalwart reporter for the *San Francisco Chronicle*. At lunch, Susan asked me, "As Dan White's good friend, do you feel justice was served, with Dan now being free and Mayor Moscone and Supervisor Harvey Milk being dead?"

"Of course not," I said. "You don't kill two people and expect there would not be severe consequences." I explained further that Dan and I were both devastated, at an early age, by the death and loss of our fathers. We often talked about being told as young boys that we were now the man of our family. To both of us, our fathers were our heroes. They had each set a high bar for their sons to follow. We both attended Catholic schools where the Ten Commandments were etched into our mind by nuns and reinforced at home by good, loving Irish mothers.

"The citizens of San Francisco could not put Dan White into a harsher prison than the prison Dan had put himself in," I said. "This moral, God-fearing man committed a sin that a priest in confession might forgive, but Dan could never forgive himself." I reminded Susan about something Dan had told me in L.A. after his parole. He had planned to save one bullet to kill himself after the murders. It was his wife, Mary Anne, who begged him not to do it when he called to tell her what he'd done and that he was about to shoot himself. Instead, she convinced him to meet her at St. Mary's Church. From there they walked to Northern Station, where he turned himself in. He obviously changed his mind about taking his own life that day, but I never discounted the possibility that he still might.

Herman and I got out of the car and walked down to the driveway of the house. I knew some of the uniformed officers who were in front of the house, and they greeted me. I ducked under the yellow tape and approached the garage.

The garage door was open. Inside the garage, the back of a 1970 yellow Buick Le Sabre was visible. I could see a garden hose duct-taped to the exhaust pipe. It snaked along the outside of the car and into the passenger compartment. The windows were rolled up and stuffed with towels. Dan had created an air-tight seal for the deadly carbon monoxide to be its most effective.

As I got closer, I saw Dan's lifeless body lying face up on the concrete floor. He was dressed in a plaid shirt, jeans, and shoes. Kneeling beside him were two Catholic nuns in full habit—tunic, starched headpiece, and scapular—gripping their Rosary beads and praying. Kneeling alongside Dan's body with them, a parish priest was administering the last rites.

I couldn't believe what I was seeing. This was a guy I considered as a kid brother, a friend, a teammate. And yes, for the past seven years, a killer. Watching the priest kneeling over Dan White in his driveway that October Monday in 1985, there was nothing I could say or do to change it. Dan had taken his own life. He had created the gas chamber from which the jury had spared him. I went upstairs into the house, where I saw Dan's younger brother, Tommy, his eyes red. When he saw me, he broke down.

"Oh, Frank, how fucking stupid is my brother to do this to me?" he bellowed. "I loved Dan. I idolized Dan." Tommy started punching the wall, crying uncontrollably, wiping the snot with the back of his hand. It turned out that Dan had called him and asked him to meet at the house, knowing Tommy would find him before Mary Ann returned from work. I was at a loss for words. I put my arm around Tommy.

"I know he loved you, too, Tommy," I said. "He was the head of the family, and I think Dan was passing the torch to you. He knew you would be the person who would step up and assume his role."

Dan had been found in the car clutching photos of Mary Ann and their kids. He left behind four notes, one to Mary Ann, one to his mother, and two for Tommy. All were taped to the car's windshield.

In one of the notes to Tommy, Dan apologized for putting him in the position to find the body, but he believed that Tommy was strong and could handle the situation. He instructed Tommy to call their mother and then call Mary Ann's parents so they could intercept her before she came home. In the second note, Dan asked his brother to look after Mary Ann and his children.

In the note to his mother, he said he was "too weary to struggle" any longer, and that it was "time to rest." He acknowledged the grief he had caused, expressed his love for all the good times in the family, and signed it, "Your loving son."

Finally, in the note to Mary Ann he expressed his love for her but said his pain was too intense and that he couldn't carry on. Remaining true to his Catholic faith, he told Mary Ann he had made an Act of Contrition, a prayer that expresses sorrow for one's sins. The one we learned at St. Elizabeth's grammar school was:

O my God, I am heartily sorry for having offended Thee, and I detest all my sins because of Thy just punishments, but most of all because they offend Thee, my God, Who art all-good and deserving of all my love. I firmly resolve, with the help of Thy grace, to sin no more and to avoid the near occasions of sin.

He ended the note to Mary Ann with, "Goodbye, my darling wife. Danny."

My heart was so heavy. This family that I knew, they don't get much better. They were all good people, all hard working, good citizens of San Francisco.

Yet I felt the same sadness for George Moscone and Harvey Milk, who were also good men and good citizens who didn't deserve to die. They were deprived of the chance to say goodbye to their loved ones, and their deaths would impact many for years to come.

This whole thing had been a devastating nightmare.

DAN WHITE SUICIDE

San Francisco Chronicle

The Largest Daily Circulation in Northern California

121st Year No. 239 ★★★★★★ TUESDAY, OCTOBER 22, 1985 777-1111 25 CENTS

Former Supervisor Dan White

Hose Hooked to Car Exhaust

S.F. Mayor's Killer
Dies in His Garage

Brother Finds Body, 3 Notes

By Susan Sward
and Mark Z. Barabak

Dan White, the convicted killer of Mayor George R. Moscone and Supervisor Harvey Milk, committed suicide yesterday in the garage of his Excelsior District home.

The 39-year-old former supervisor used a garden hose to funnel carbon monoxide from the exhaust pipe of a 1970 yellow Buick Le Sabre into the car's passenger compartment, police said.

White's brother, Tom, went to the lime-green, stucco home at 150 Shawnee Avenue shortly before 2 p.m. and found White's body — dressed in jeans, shoes and a plaid shirt.

White, a former policeman and fireman, had used towels to make sure the car windows were tightly shut. He left behind three notes — to his brother, mother and wife — all apologizing for the trouble his death would cause them.

Police Captain Michael Lennon paraphrased White's note to his brother, which was taped to the car's windshield, as saying something to the effect of: "Dear Tom, Sorry you have to find me this way. I'm sorry for all the pain and trouble I've caused. Dan."

Contents of the other notes were not disclosed by Police Chief Con Murphy, who announced White's death to a cluster of reporters gathered in front of the home.

The chief said Tom White told him that his brother "seemed despondent lately, but no one expected him to kill himself." Murphy said White had told Tom to meet a friend of the family at the house at 1:30 — thereby assuring Tom would find him.

Time of death was put at between 8 a.m. and 1:52 p.m. yesterday. Police said White's wife, Mary Ann, left home about 6:50 a.m., and White must have driven the Buick into the garage — which has space for only one car — after she left.

Paramedics, summoned to the scene, tried without success to revive White after pulling him out of the car and stretching him out on the garage floor.

At 3:15 p.m. White's body, laid out on a gurney beneath a white sheet, was wheeled out of his home

Page 4 Col. 4

By Tom Levy
Dan White's body was put into an ambulance by coroner's deputies E. L. Bigbee (left) and David Zimmerman

The Paths Cross Again For White and Falzon

By Mark Z. Barabak

Dan White and Frank Falzon, two men whose lives intertwined as if scripted in a tragic play, were together again for yesterday's final act.

They were chums as fellow officers on San Francisco's police force, and Falzon happened to be the homicide inspector on duty Nov. 27, 1978, when White shot and killed Mayor George Moscone and Supervisor Harvey Milk.

Until he reached City Hall, Falzon did not know the killer was White — someone he considered almost like a kid brother.

At the Northern Police Station, Falzon took White's tearful confession within hours of the slayings, and he testified at White's trial.

Critics blasted Falzon after White was convicted of voluntary manslaughter, calling it a classic example of a cop protecting one of his own. Still stung by the criticism even years later, Falzon angrily denied that he ever went easy on White.

"Dan was a friend of mine, but he got no breaks from me," Falzon once said. "In fact, after I took his statement, all I could think was, 'This guy just admitted two murders — he's going to the death box.'"

Again yesterday, Falzon was the inspector on duty when another urgent call came, this time from White's younger brother, Tom, reporting Dan White's suicide.

Falzon went to the Excelsior District to inspect the scene and talk to witnesses, then turned the case over to two other detectives for follow-up work. Falzon later spoke to reporters.

"The tragedies of Nov. 27, 1978, affected many people's lives," he said, his tone measured and demeanor calm.

"Now hopefully the final chapter in San Francisco's most notorious murders has been put to rest with Dan White taking his own life.

"Prior to November 27, White always tried to do the right thing. But the day when he crossed that line by taking human lives was something he could not live with.

"I feel grief now for the family of the victim as I did for the families of the victims in 1978."

EPILOGUE

In September of 1989 I marked my twenty-fifth anniversary in the police department. I seldom thought about retirement, but I knew that the time was nearing for me to make the life-changing decision to end my police career. I could envision the day in the not-too-distant future that I would turn in my star and my gun and retire as a San Francisco Homicide Inspector, a job I aspired to, achieved, and had cherished.

My decision was made easier by the last case I would work in homicide. It started like any other, with a call from the Operations Center informing me of a 187 behind a grocery store in the Sunnydale Projects area. Carl and I responded around 1:00 a.m. to the scene where a young Black man lay dead with his head blown off by a shotgun blast.

As the uniformed officers filled us in on the details, for some reason I became fixated on the dead boy. They say in homicide work that your crime scene tells you a story. This was one of those cases. Here on the ground in front of me was yet another dead young Black man. I had been to similar crime scenes throughout my career. The young man was wearing a heavy gold chain around his neck, a white T-shirt, and designer Levi's jeans. He had on a very expensive 49ers football jacket with embossed lettering. On his feet were Air Jordan tennis shoes over white socks. This expensive attire no doubt was way beyond the victim's means to afford.

The patrol officers told us that the young man was driving his car when several men in a pickup truck began to chase him. There were men in the cab and others in the bed of the truck, one man with the shotgun.

During the chase, the victim smashed his car into the chain link fence surrounding the Sunnydale Playground. He jumped out of his car and ran across the ball field trying to escape his pursuers on foot.

He ended up trapped in a dead-end alley behind the grocery store. The suspects soon found their prey and killed him.

Carl and I immediately surmised his gang or a rival gang had their drug money ripped off and our victim paid the price of this crime with his life.

After we left the crime scene, Carl and I went to the victim's address. He lived with his mother in the projects, a government subsidized housing for low-income families. We knocked on the door and were invited inside by the victim's mother. She had been asleep and was awakened by us. She was dressed in an old worn nightgown with holes. On her feet were slippers, also worn with holes. When she opened the door, I thought this could be my mother except for the color of her skin. She was a nice lady.

When we told her that her son had been murdered, she began to cry. She said her son was mixed up with the wrong people and she had feared for his safety. As she talked, I noticed two cockroaches, one fat and one skinny, climbing up the wall toward the ceiling and I found myself wondering which would win that race, the fat one or the skinny one.

That was it. I had hit a wall. I never wanted to see another young Black man killed. I told Carl I was done; I was leaving the Homicide Unit. Carl tried to talk me out of it, but my mind was made up. That morning I walked into the lieutenant's office and told Lt. Jerry McCarthy that I was retiring.

Jerry quickly reminded me I was a year and half from qualifying for my police pension. I didn't care, I told him, "Money won't change my mind, Jerry, I'm done."

The lieutenant had me sit down. Over the next half hour, Jerry convinced me to transfer to the Special Investigations Unit (formerly the Intelligence Bureau). I had never requested a transfer from homicide so my name was not on any waiting list for pending openings in any unit, particularly one as coveted as the Bureau of Special Services.

When I questioned Jerry about this oversight he said, "There's an exception where if you jump someone on any given list, they can challenge your appointment by proving they are more deserving. I guarantee you, Frank, no one will challenge you."

I stayed after all, working my last two years out of the Bureau of Special Services, handling Chinatown gang-related murder cases. I needed this change; it was the best move I could have made. The pace was slower, the men in the unit were comparable to homicide, all good hardworking cops, and the cases were more about organized crime killings.

On my fiftieth birthday, February 22, 1992, I quietly walked out the back door, down the staircase to the garage, got in my own car, and drove home for the last time.

I wasn't expecting a retirement party, but I was thrilled when I heard friends were putting together an event in my honor. Herb Caen, the *San Francisco Chronicle*'s Pulitzer Prize-winning man-about-town columnist, mentioned this in the newspaper on April 14. "There'll be a retirement party May 8 at the Irish Cultural Center for Frank Falzon, the legendary S.F.P.D. homicide inspector who was on the Zodiac, Zebra, SLA, and Moscone/Milk cases … Falzon, who quit the force on his 50th birthday after 28 years, says, 'In the old days, a good cop could aspire to be chief someday, like Cahill and Nelder. Now you have to be a social worker or a politician, so it's time to get out.'"

On the evening of May 8, 1992, my retirement dinner was held at the Irish Cultural Center's main dining room. The room was packed with more than four hundred people in attendance.

Early on the morning of the event, I received a call from District Attorney Investigator Mike Koppel, one of the principal organizers of this dinner. He advised me that the current Chief of Police Richard Hongisto had bought a ticket to the dinner and wished to be seated with me at the head table.

Over the years, whenever an event like this took place, politicians and city leaders would come out of the woodwork, buy a ticket, and request to be seated at the head table with the honoree. Their request was always granted, and the honoree would feel important because he was surrounded by the city's high-ranking officials.

I had worked the Potrero 4 car with Hongisto in our early days on the police force. I told Koppel I was honored the chief would be in attendance, but he would not be seated at the head table with me. The only people I wanted at the head table was my family. They were the real important people in my life, the ones who endured the ups and downs of a homicide inspector's often turbulent life.

Besides, I had a distain for most city officials and politicians, knowing they were the very ones who would use the police to quell a disturbance only to turn their backs on the police when complaints were filed. The police were used, abused, and left feeling like a piñata for doing their job protecting the citizens of the city they served. I feel these people are hypocrites, and I wanted no part of contributing to their need for recognition.

Late in the day, on May 8, I learned that a large demonstration was planned in San Francisco that night to protest the verdict in the Rodney King trial in Los Angeles. All uniformed officers had their days off cancelled and were required to be in riot gear for this expected huge protest.

I was disappointed because I had worked so closely with the uniformed officers and knew most as friends who played in the police softball league. Many were major contributors to whatever success I had as a homicide inspector. While we celebrated at my retirement dinner, my uniformed friends, including Chief Hongisto, were arresting 320 demonstrators for various infractions during the Rodney King protest.

Despite that, the dinner was a huge success. The only ones at the head table were my immediate family, per my wishes. Many awards were presented by various speakers from City Hall, the SFPD, the FBI, and others. Among them was Deputy District Attorney John Rowland.

John took the podium and honored me with a Champion of the People plaque, an award previously given only to attorneys. It read, "In recognition of his dedication and outstanding service to the citizens of the City and County of San Francisco. Presented by Arlo Smith and the staff of the District Attorney's Office." I was the first police officer to be so honored. I was so touched because I believe that is exactly what a good cop is, a champion of the people.

I knew my turn to speak was drawing near. I had not prepared a speech. I wanted my words to be straight from my heart. When I walked up to the podium and looked out at the audience, I was humbled, not a characteristic word many would use to describe me. I was humbled and proud because all those individuals who had shared my police career were giving of their time to be there to honor me.

I started by saying that growing up in a poor family, having lost my dad at an early age, all I wanted was to become a rich and famous baseball player. I didn't make it to the big leagues, but I was somewhat famous in San Francisco, and looking out at that audience, I told them they made me feel like the richest man in the world. They were the good police officers, men and women, whom I respected, friends I loved, and I was so very appreciative to see them all there.

Career hopes change as you age. I was proud to have them honoring me. My career took me in a different direction.

Inspector lived S.F. history

Novato man helped solve some of City's most notorious homicides

by MARY CONNELL
Staff Writer

ADVANCE PHOTO BY ALAN DEP
Novatan Frank Falzon has lived in Novato for 22 years, but before retiring he earned his living by investigating San Francisco homicides.

Frank Falzon still has rugged boyish looks, like an altar boy who'd gone on to play pro ball.

At 55, he's been retired from the San Francisco Police Department for five years, but he's the first to admit that the department will always be a part of his life.

So is Novato, where he and his family have lived since 1975.

S.F.P.D AWARDS AND COMMENDATIONS

Police Officer of the Year – 1978
Gold Medal of Valor – 1977
Meritorious Conduct Awards – 1966 (2), 1967 (2), 1968 (2), 1975, 1976, 1985
Police Commission Commendation – 1972

Veterans of Foreign Wars, 91st Division
Policeman's Award for Heroism – 1978

San Francisco Police Officers Association
Sports Hall of Fame – 2005

ACKNOWLEDGEMENTS

Like a murder to be solved, a book needs a team of skilled and dedicated people behind the effort to succeed. No single detective or author can do it alone. In my case, I was extraordinarily lucky to have such a team for both endeavors.

After I retired, I always planned on writing a book about my police career. For a variety of reasons, it never happened. Until now. During the pandemic and lockdown, the opportunity became a reality with a phone call from an old friend, former *San Francisco Chronicle* crime reporter Duffy Jennings. Our paths had crossed often at crime scenes and murder trials back in the seventies. Duffy had the innate understanding of San Francisco during that period, of police work, and of storytelling. I had the cases, now I had a top-notch writer, and the book flowed from there. I extend my enduring thanks and gratitude to Duffy and to his wife, Bonnie Becker, for her encouragement and counsel from start to finish. Both helped to make this dream come true for me, my family, and my friends.

Thanks especially to my two sons, Dan and Dave, for their contributions. Dan, formerly of the SFPD and a retired FBI agent, proofread the early chapters and provided his wise advice and feedback all along the way. Dave, currently an acting captain with the SFPD, suggested our book's title and stepped up to write an elegant and insightful foreword. He provided valuable background information and counsel throughout.

I am indebted as well to my daughter, Kerri Baetkey, for her constant support, critiques, and love throughout the duration of writing the book.

I extend my own meritorious commendations to my former partners in the Homicide Detail, Inspectors Jack Cleary, Ed Erdelatz, and

Herman Clark, along with dynamic Assistant District Attorney James Lassart. All gave us their valuable time and attention by reading chapters, verifying details, and agreeing to be included in the manuscript. They are four of the finest men I've known. Any success I had in my career would not have been possible without my dear late colleague, Inspector Carl Klotz, a superb partner on the job who became my closest friend and golf buddy in retirement. Whenever we needed extra help on major investigations, we turned to another skilled and meticulous homicide inspector, the late Mike Mullane, who unselfishly stepped in to form the three amigos.

Much gratitude is owed to my longtime dear friends and teachers, including Judy Schredl, Dave Favro, John Giovanola, George Johnson, and Julie Ortiz, for their diligent proofreading and valuable input that helped to make this book as authentic as possible.

I could not have been as thorough and accurate about the Night Stalker case without the aid of retired police Lieutenant James Spillane, who pulled several boxes of evidence on the case and provided copies that increased the accuracy of the first four chapters.

Retired Glendale Police Detective Sergeant Jon Perkins deserves a salute for his input on the Night Stalker case in his jurisdiction and his uncanny recall of the details and circumstances around the manhunt for Richard Ramirez in Los Angeles. The same salute goes out to retired SFPD Crime Lab Specialist Larry Dubour for his input and insight during the Ramirez case.

Nor would this book have been possible without the support and guidance of my Wednesday morning breakfast club of retired police officers, including Rich Shippy, Mike Puccinelli, Gary Marble, Armond Pelissetti, Ed Kenney, John Morotto, Vic Macia, and Mike Koppel. They listened, they laughed, and they shored up my memories when necessary to support me over the entire year that I was working on the book.

Thank you as well to the late SFPD Chiefs Alfred J. Nelder and

Donald M. Scott and former Deputy Chief Charles Barca for throwing their support behind the inaugural 1965 San Francisco Police Department Softball League that continues to the present day, and to all the fine officers who have participated over the years.

Many thanks to *San Francisco Chronicle* reporter Kevin Fagan for his genuine encouragement and assistance throughout the latter years of my career and during the writing of our book; to San Francisco author Joel Selvin for his experienced advice; to Jim Bloom and Art Agnos for their flattering comments about my career; to Katie Vandergriff, Alexandra Lapointe, and the team at Palmetto Publishing for a professional and efficient design and production process; and to Kristin Delaplane and Joanne Asala for their keen-eyed proofreading skills.

All S.F. Chronicle articles are from San Francisco Chronicle, www.sfchronicle.com, © 1975, 1977, 1979, 1985, Hearst Newspapers. All rights reserved. Used under license.

I'd be remiss in not mentioning my nephew, Greg Friley, for his support and assistance, and my darling granddaughter, Caroline Baetkey, for creating my web page, frankfalzon.com. Caroline also designed the original cover for our book. Thank you both so much.

In closing, I send my heartfelt thanks to my wife Donna, who was there from the beginning and was constantly encouraging me to write a book. Her support and love throughout our sixty-one years of marriage made everything I did possible.

I'm a lucky man. I'm now 80 years old. I have a great wife, fine children, terrific grandchildren, a good nephew, and outstanding police partners who were all contributors to my success.

Donna, at 79 you are just as beautiful as you were on the day we met in 1957.
Thank you for taking this lifelong journey with me.

The next generation, our nine beautiful grandchildren in 2006

Back row, L-R: Frankie Falzon, Kevin Ashburn, Dave Ashburn

Middle row, L-R: Bridget Falzon, Christina Falzon,
Stephanie Falzon, Catherine Falzon, Caroline Baetkey

Front: Matthew Baetkey

ABOUT THE AUTHORS

Frank Falzon was a highly decorated and accomplished homicide inspector who investigated more than three hundred murders and other cases during his twenty-eight-year career with the San Francisco Police Department, twenty-two of them in the homicide detail.

He played the key role in breaking the notorious Night Stalker case, investigated his childhood friend and former fellow cop Dan White for the murders of San Francisco Mayor George Moscone and Supervisor Harvey Milk, and participated in the Zodiac and Zebra serial murder investigations and other high-profile cases.

Falzon was a recipient of the San Francisco Police Department's highest honor, the Gold Medal of Valor, after he survived a face-to-face street corner shootout with an armed robber while off duty. He also earned a Gold Medal Medallion as the city's Bravest Police Officer and numerous other commendations and was the department's 1978 Police Officer of the Year.

Falzon was a principal figure in the hit 2021 Netflix series, *Night Stalker: The Hunt for a Serial Killer,* and was interviewed about his role in the case on the Michael Smerconish program on Sirius XM, which has 25 million subscribers. Falzon has been depicted in movies, plays, and video games, and has been featured internationally in numerous documentaries, radio and TV interviews, magazine articles, and books.

He has appeared in *The Most Dangerous Animal of All* mini-series on FX, as the homicide expert in the True Crime Network's *I, Detective* and *World's Most Evil Killer* series, CBS' *48 Hours,* and some two dozen documentaries on the San Francisco City Hall murders. He is a sought-after speaker and instructor.

Born in San Francisco, Falzon has an AS degree in criminology from City College of San Francisco. He and his wife, Donna, live in Novato, California. They have four grown children, including two who followed their father's path into law enforcement, and nine grandchildren.

Duffy Jennings is an author and former prize-winning reporter for the *San Francisco Chronicle* in the tumultuous 1970s. His coverage included the City Hall murders of Mayor George Moscone and Supervisor Harvey Milk, the Patty Hearst kidnapping, and the Zodiac and Zebra serial killings. Actor Adam Goldberg portrayed Duffy in the 2007 film, *Zodiac*.

The newspaper submitted Jennings's reporting on the murder trial of the City Hall killer, former supervisor Dan White, for Pulitzer Prize consideration. All told, Jennings's byline appeared on more than five hundred articles for the *Chronicle*.

After his newspaper career, Jennings served as vice president of public relations for the San Francisco Giants baseball club for twelve years. He oversaw media relations, publications, business communications, community relations, and alumni relations. Following the Giants, Jennings ran his own public relations company for more than twenty years. He also launched and published *Los Gatos Magazine*.

Jennings is the author of *Reporter's Note Book: A San Francisco Chronicle Journalist's Diary of the Shocking Seventies*, published in 2019 by Grizzly Peak Press. Jennings's essay, "Paper Boy," appears in the anthology, *The End of the Golden Gate: Writers on Loving (and Sometimes Leaving) San Francisco*, from Chronicle Prism in 2021. He has also written for *Rolling Stone, San Francisco Magazine, Los Gatos Magazine,* and online publications.

A San Francisco native, Jennings holds a BA in Journalism from San Francisco State University. He and his wife, Bonnie Becker, live in Danville, California. Duffy has two grown children, a stepdaughter, and two step-grandsons.

Lightning Source UK Ltd.
Milton Keynes UK
UKHW020053231222
414339UK00014B/1518